Choreographing From Within

Developing the Habit of Inquiry as an Artist

Diana F. Green, MFA

Photos by *Julian*

Human Kinetics

Library of Congress Cataloging-in-Publication Data

Green, Diana F., 1950.
  Choreographing from within : developing the habit of inquiry as an artist / Diana F. Green.
    p. cm.
  Includes bibliographical references and index.
  ISBN-13: 978-0-7360-7619-7 (soft cover)
  ISBN-10: 0-7360-7619-0 (soft cover)
  1. Creative ability--Study and teaching. I. Title.
  LB1590.5.G74 2010
  370.15'7--dc22

                  2009041089

ISBN-10: 0-7360-7619-0 (print)
ISBN-13: 978-0-7360-7619-7 (print)

The Web addresses cited in this text were current as of December 2009, unless otherwise noted.

Acquisitions Editor: Judy Patterson Wright, PhD
Developmental Editor: Ragen E. Sanner
Assistant Editor: Anne Rumery
Copyeditor: Jan Feeney
Indexer: Andrea Hepner
Permission Manager: Dalene Reeder
Graphic Designer: Nancy Rasmus
Graphic Artists: Patrick Sandberg and Kathleen Boudreau-Fuoss
Cover Designer: Keith Blomberg
Photographer (cover and interior): Julian Green, unless otherwise noted
Art Manager: Kelly Hendren
Associate Art Manager: Alan L. Wilborn
Illustrator: Tammy Page
Printer: Sheridan Books

The cover photo of Adria Ferrali of New Dance Drama was taken by Julian Green. Adria is shown perfo
choreography, *Notte*.

Printed in the United States of America   10 9 8 7 6 5 4 3 2 1

The paper in this book is certified under a sustainable forestry program.

Human Kinetics
Web site: www.HumanKinetics.com

United States: Human Kinetics
P.O. Box 5076
Champaign, IL 61825-5076
800-747-4457
e-mail: humank@hkusa.com

Canada: Human Kinetics
475 Devonshire Road Unit 100
Windsor, ON N8Y 2L5
800-465-7301 (in Canada only)
e-mail: info@hkcanada.com

Europe: Human Kinetics
107 Bradford Road
Stanningley
Leeds LS28 6AT, United Kingdom
+44 (0) 113 255 5665
e-mail: hk@hkeurope.com

Australia: Human Kinetics
57A Price Avenue
Lower Mitcham, South Australia 5062
08 8372 0999
e-mail: info@hkaustralia.com

New Zealand: Human Kinetics
P.O. Box 80
Torrens Park, South Australia 5062
0800 222 062
e-mail: info@hknewzealand.com

To all my students,
who have inspired me with their artistry and passion,
and to Christopher and Mariana Green.

CONTENTS

It is often said that you cannot teach choreography. One must have talent and an artistic ability in order to become a creative artist. I tend to disagree. I think the artist is in every one of us, but it is driven out by fear, cultural identity, social requisites, and—yes, dare I say it?—dance technique classes. When we train to be dancers, we spend hours and days and years perfecting our ability to duplicate with utmost accuracy the dances and techniques created and demonstrated by others. We learn the fine art of self-critique in search of that perfection. Often a dancer becomes so skilled at imitation and self-critique that creation becomes terrifying, if not impossible. What it will take for you to become a proficient choreographer is an extraordinary amount of courage and a good dose of faith in yourself. You must break away from lessons learned and boldly explore and experiment without thought to immediate self-evaluation, because self-evaluation before or during exploration will stop creativity at the onset.

This is a college-level text for choreography and dance composition courses. However, it may also function in a rigorous high school dance program and become a resource for choreographers at any stage in their development. With scrutiny to details that apply, a K-12 classroom teacher may find this text useful in understanding basic dance concepts to be used as tools for **arts integration,** a process of learning that combines equal and significant instruction simultaneously in arts and non-arts subjects.

The text covers any and all dance techniques because creativity is the same, whatever vocabulary is used. Often the instruction for creating dance is left to modern dance teachers, which has left a void in the quality, sophistication, and understanding of creativity in the formula-based techniques such as classical ballet and jazz. Choreographers in these more formal techniques develop the habit of arranging

A man should learn to detect and watch that gleam of light which flashes across his mind from within, more than the luster of the firmament of bards and sages. Yet he dismisses without notice his thought, because it is his. In every work of genius we recognize our own rejected thoughts; they come back to us with a certain alienated majesty. Great works of art have no more affecting lesson for us than this. They teach us to abide by our spontaneous impression.

Ralph Waldo Emerson in his essay "Self-Reliance," first published in 1841.

the steps, as in classroom exercises, without realizing that elements of craft apply to their work. But it is never okay to string classical ballet steps together without logic and intent, nor should the dance competition artist depend only on flashy tricks. Good choreography will always rise to the top. It is my hope that students and teachers in these techniques will use this book just as often as modern dance students and teachers.

Art and Craft of Creativity

There are various schools of thought about how to approach students with the art and craft of creating dances. One approach is to teach the rules of fundamental design and form and require the students to use carefully planned formulas. The other school of thought maintains that these rules are too limiting and stultify creativity. In fact, some believe that if these rules are taught at all, students will be unable to break the barriers. I am a student of both schools of thought. The rules of craft may become a framework on which timid choreographers find footing until having gained the confidence and maturity to strike out on their own. However, following the rules rigidly, without thought to intent and logic, may create artificiality. Learning to defy the rules for the sake of intent and logic is an important process. Rules are broken only after they have been practiced and their effects on the work are understood. Ignorance of the rules and all the opportunities they present may be even more limiting than the rules themselves.

My approach to choreography alternates between anarchy and form, using craft with a continual eye on ways to rebel. My belief is that whatever the talent of the individual, every student has the ability to create spontaneously and to become a fine craftsman of movement. The most important task remains to find the unique artist within the self. A choreography class or text simply offers pathways to be selected by the developing choreographer. It is my goal to provide you with as many pathways as possible so that your choices are difficult, but the result belongs to you and not to your teachers. In this way, every student is provided with the tools for creating great works of art. A few of you may use these skills to forge a career in choreography. You will soon learn that perhaps a little talent but mostly determination and luck are the prerequisites for success. If you enroll in a choreography class as a requirement, or just for fun, these skills will nurture and sustain your creativity and your ability to explore the arts and life itself.

Inquiry-Based Learning

Traditional education has focused on the memorization of facts and knowledge. Dance teachers also have taught classes by imparting knowledge from previous teachers, handing down theory and practice that may be hundreds of years old. Students have not often been encouraged to question or discover their own pathways even as choreographers, but they have been given the vocabulary, technique, and formulas with which to arrange their dances. Current trends in education are recognizing the need to prepare students for a changing world, to help them adapt by encouraging habits of mind that question and find new relevance. Inquiry means to question. It is the most natural form of learning, the most engaging, and the most rewarding for the student. It places the student at the center of the learning. The teacher becomes the mentor, guiding the student toward a focal point and allowing for multiple pathways chosen by the student. It requires teachers and students to admit that neither of them have all the answers, that answers are boundless and infinite, and that answers change as variables change. For this reason it is important to continually ask questions, particularly after solutions are found. Inquiry is the habit of mind of the true artist, who is always searching for a greater truth. This book is not a cookbook with a smorgasbord of recipes guaranteeing success. It is more like *Beard's Book on Bread*, offering a thorough understanding of the medium itself, providing a few examples, and leaving the rest up to the reader to create in his or her own unique style.

Organization

Part I of the text deals with process. This process encourages you to discover the dance within you through questioning (chapter 1) and to always create movement with intent (chapter 2). It will be important to understand these approaches before beginning the in-depth study that follows.

Part II introduces you to the elements of movement as they are used in choreography. The sequence of these elements (chapters 3, 4, 5, and 6) will elicit variety and spontaneity from you as a new choreographer at an early stage in your explorations. I have found that approaching intent and energy of movement before exploring space encourages a full and courageous commitment to creating movement, which is later supported by the study of design and musicality. I see quality as an element of movement created by a combination of energy, space, and time; therefore it is included last in part II. As you study these elements of movement in separate categories, note that none of these elements exists in isolation. However, your focus may or may not settle on one or the other for particular effect. And since the human brain likes to compartmentalize in order to understand, you will learn to analyze and separate these elements before you begin to synthesize.

In part III, you will begin a synthesis of the elements of movement through the exploration of music and sound as they relate to choreography (chapter 7). Although you may think that it is easier to create movement with some music as inspiration, you will discover that creating a sophisticated relationship of music and sound is not a simple process. That is why you will explore the elements of movement in silence before adding a layer of sound. In the rest of part III you will discover the importance of transitions in your work (chapter 8), learn to use formulas to manipulate movement (chapter 9), play with various numbers of dancers (chapter 10), and explore how props add interest to your choreography (chapter 11). You will need to combine the elements of energy, space, and time while exploring these choreographic techniques.

Part IV introduces methods for refining and forming your work. You will have completed your explorations of the key concepts in parts I to III and at this point will be ready to formalize your presentation of these concepts in a production for the stage. The discussion of style in chapter 12 will help you understand cultural differences and support you in developing and recognizing your unique style as a mature artist. The chapter on form (chapter 13) will help you define the boundaries you have already begun to set in your work. You will learn to evaluate your choices, discover how they affect form, and discover how form will affect the intent of your work. Finally, in the appendix is a discussion of the arrangement of works in a full-length production or dance concert. The rules for creating this arrangement should be the same as the rules for creating a single choreographic work, but I find that choreographers often forget to acknowledge the power this arrangement may have on the overall impact of the entire experience for the audience. And manipulating the audience's experience is the ultimate goal of the choreographer.

Within each chapter of the text, a systematic approach is used to actively support your discoveries of each key choreographic concept. These discoveries will be led by the format shown in preface table.1.

Preface Table.1

	Description	Procedure
Exploration	The study of each key choreographic concept begins with an exploration.	Unless indicated, each exploration is intended to be completed in one movement session.
Essential question	The essential question frames an understanding that is essential to the key concept.	To frame the exploration, answer the question before the warm-up and again after the improvisations. Record your responses in your journal.
Warm-up	The warm-up has three purposes: raise body temperature, focus concentration, and introduce the key concept.	Perform these exercises individually without watching others. Begin to focus on your kinesthetic sense.
Improvisations	Improvisations provide an in-depth exploration of the key concept.	Perform these exercises in groups to allow for some observation.
Reflective questions	These questions focus your discoveries from the movement explorations.	Respond to these questions and discuss them with your peers. Record your responses in your journal.
Discussion of key concept	This discussion is a description of generally recognized theories about the key concept.	Read this after completing the exploration of the key concept and before you create your movement studies.
Movement studies	A movement study tests your discoveries of the key concept by requiring you to apply those discoveries in the solution of a movement problem.	Create your movement studies independently and share them with your peers.
Assessment	Assessment measures your understanding of the key concept.	You may wish to explore alternative methods of measuring your understanding.
Class critique	Class critique is a discussion between choreographers, peers, and mentor that includes an analysis and evaluation of the work.	Every movement study should undergo a critique. Record key points from the critique in your journal.

~ continued

Preface Table. 1 ~*continued*

	Description	Procedure
Rubric	Rubric is an instrument used in measuring success according to particular criteria.	Use rubrics as a guide to class critiques, as a written assessment in your journal, and to accompany your work in your portfolio.
Documentation	Documentation is a record of your work. This text requests video recordings of your work.	Documentation is an effective assessment tool if it is accompanied by an evaluation instrument, such as a rubric or a formal critical analysis.
Drawing conclusions	Drawing conclusions is the final act of inquiry. Discoveries are summarized, knowledge is assessed, and opinion is formed, often spawning additional questions that lead to new inquiry.	Generally a conclusion is requested at the end of an in-depth study of a key concept or at the end of a chapter.
Breaking the rules	This is a movement study that goes against all that you have learned. It is a final test of the key concept and may open new ideas and concepts for you to explore.	Create these movement studies as they appear in the text.
Critical thinking essay	This is a formal written essay that follows the critical thinking model explained in chapter 1.	A critical thinking essay is suggested at the end of each chapter. Include these essays in your portfolio.

This format will change slightly in part IV, at which point in the text you will bring together previously explored fundamental concepts to create a whole work. This application of concepts takes conscious thought and planning, rather than improvisation. Therefore, in these last two chapters, you will begin this format at the Discussion section and practice the applications through the Movement Studies section.

Developing a Habit of Inquiry as an Artist

Having conversations about dance, questioning what you see, and listening to others converse about dance may be the most important catalyst to your development as a choreographer. These conversations will develop your eye and expand the opportunities for your own creations. All choreography students should talk about dance, whether they are new to the field with little knowledge of dance vocabulary or veterans with a great deal of experience. Dance is created for a general audience, so every viewpoint is valid. Your point of view will expand: The more you see, the more you converse about what you see, and the more you explore creating dance for yourself. The more you converse, the more you will develop your vocabulary for describing what you experience.

To maximize a point of view, you must not be a passive viewer. Passive viewers sit back and watch, waiting for an impact (or not). They finish by saying, "I liked that," or "I didn't like that." Creating a dance that is well liked by an audience may not be the goal of the choreographer. Dance is a complex form of communication that often goes beyond entertainment. Dance may be about expressing the human condition. Active viewers will ask themselves why they like or dislike something they have seen. Yet, because dance is an art form that uses nonverbal language, the why may be elusive at first. So, in search of the why, refrain from making an immediate judgment about a dance. Instead, your task in learning to choreograph is to describe what you see, listen to or read descriptions related by others, and then try to make sense out of those descriptions. To describe, you must analyze what you see. To begin to make sense of what you see, you must reflect on the meaning of the movement or the choreographer's intent, relate it to your life experience, and evaluate it for its effectiveness on you as an audience.

The inquiry-based approach will require a lot of conversation about the dance you see. Beginning choreographers may not have practiced serious discussions about dance. Having material to converse about is the first problem to solve on this road to discovery. Even before your class begins to create, there is much to see. Television provides opportunities to view dance in commercials and on popular dance competition shows. Track public television listings and arts channels for dance performances. Search the Internet for particular choreographers, companies, and classic pieces of choreography. And always keep informed of live dance performances that take place in your area. You will gain from watching all dance, regardless of its quality or source. Eugene Loring (1910-1982), American choreographer and one of the three founding choreographers of the American Ballet Theatre, told his choreography students that he made it a point to see as much dance as possible in order to gather material for his work. "You will learn much, or even more, from what you consider to be bad dance than what you will learn from what you consider to be good dance." Later, he mentioned that when he began to create his own work, he refused all invitations to dance concerts and ballets. At that point, he did not want to be tempted into territory that was not his own. As a professional choreographer, before beginning to choreograph, Loring would enter what might be considered the research phase, gathering as much material as possible to be used in his work. Once the work entered the creative phase, the research came to a halt and the artist searched for his own unique voice. You, as a student of choreography, should consider yourself in the research phase of your development as an artist and gather all you can.

Before you go any further in this text, begin your inquiry immediately. Find some dance to view and begin conversing about it with others. Ask questions. Listen to the questions of others and try to respond. Develop a habit of inquiry. Develop the habit of an artist.

ACKNOWLEDGMENTS

I know that my approach to teaching choreography is a collection of thoughts from many personal experiences, workshops, conferences, books, teachers, and colleagues. It is tough to separate which ideas are truly mine and which ideas have been borrowed from others. But then who can say that anyone's approach to choreography is totally original?

I began my training as most dancers from my era: with the traditional Doris Humphrey text *The Art of Making Dances*. Martha Hill Davies gave me my first shot of confidence as a choreographer at a National Association of Regional Ballet Craft of Choreography Conference. Eugene Loring, who originally terrified me, mostly because of my own insecurities, became my trusted mentor and friend. His example as a true craftsman and choreographic genius nurtured me during my four years at the University of California at Irvine which extended through the generosity of his residencies with my youth company for several years after my graduation. As luck would have it, because of my ability to read dance notation scores, I was assigned to Antony Tudor as a rehearsal assistant during my two years of graduate work at Irvine. Tudor recognized my desire and perhaps some talent as an instructor and director and made it his mission to train me in the intricacies of teaching classical ballet and creating dances. He is responsible for tearing me away from my relentless acknowledgment of music structure.

I attended numerous craft of choreography conferences held by the National Association of Regional Ballet, where my work was torn to shreds, requiring me to start anew and gain strength with each rebuilding. Students from the Montgomery Ballet in Silver Spring, Maryland, became my inspiration for the first 15 years of my teaching and choreographing. Later, in my move to higher education, my colleagues at Hamilton College, Elaine Heekin and Bruce Walcyzk, opened my eyes to the opportunities of postmodernism. Tim Wilson at the University of South Florida introduced me to methods of teaching contact improvisation during a Southeast Regional Festival of the American College Dance Festival.

My students at Huntingdon College in Montgomery, Alabama, honed my skills as a provider of instruction in choreography. To them I owe my deepest gratitude for trusting me, giving of themselves, delivering their creativity, blossoming in their craft, and urging me to write. In those classes I used *The Intimate Act of Choreography* by Blom and Chaplin, which I found to be the closest approach to my own philosophies. Eventually I began teaching out of pieces of this text in draft form.

Special thanks to Judy Wright, acquisitions editor at Human Kinetics, who encouraged me to forge ahead and complete this text, even as I remained unsure whether the schedule in my new career would allow it. In preparation for the completion for this text, I was honored to receive advice from Patty Phillips, Vincas Greene, and particularly Maida Withers.

In the last stages of my work, I must acknowledge the tireless and patient efforts of Ragen E. Sanner, developmental editor at Human Kinetics. I am also greatly appreciative of the generous gifts of time and images from dancers of Montgomery Ballet, Melissa Ann Beck, Sabrina Davini, Whitney DuBose, Adria Ferrali, Thomas Johansen, Meredith Bernal Peden, Aimee Rials, and Kaiser A. Wagstaff. Many thanks also go to Randy Foster, Cathy Wright, the Alabama State Council on the Arts, Janette Wright, and Baldwin Arts and Academic Middle School.

Finally, a huge acknowledgment goes to my husband, fellow dancer, teacher, and friend, Julian Green. Without his suggestion, insistence, and beautiful photography, this book would not exist.

Part 1

Starting the Process

Chapter 1

Discovering the Dance

To choreograph

from within means the capturing of one's innate ability to create movement in a very personal and unique way. **Choreography,** very simply, is the arrangement of movement to express an idea or concept. But the art of choreography is far more complex and defies boundaries provided in definitions. It involves searching within your soul for truths that may be expressed only through movement. It involves the process of discovering movement that provides a window into your soul. No one can tell you what exists within your soul or how to express those innermost secrets through movement. That ability for discovery already exists within you. Once you connect to that ability and create a movement that belongs to you, no matter how small, because it expresses who you are, then you are a choreographer. Before that you are simply an arranger of movement. The craft of choreography teaches you effective ways to arrange movement. This text provides you with an exploration of craft through a process of discovery designed to help you connect to the choreographer that already exists within you.

As a student in the learning process, you may initially feel most comfortable with "Tell me." When you are told what to do, it keeps you from having to solve problems and make your own decisions. You may mistakenly believe that if you follow someone else, rather than make your own decisions, you are less likely to make a mistake. But without experiencing what you are told and practicing a method, you will quickly forget what has not been applied. And without problem solving and exploring choices, learning becomes narrow and limited to the experience of the person delivering the knowledge and your ability to interpret that knowledge correctly. This is particularly true when translating words, in the telling, to movement as the interpretation of that knowledge.

Most dance classes involve "show me." Teachers demonstrate and you repeat the movement,

Tell me
and I forget.
Show me
and I remember.
Involve me
and I understand.
Ancient Chinese Proverb

therefore experiencing what you are shown. You become involved immediately in the experience, developing a deep kinesthetic understanding of what is being taught. So the teaching of dance automatically progresses to the third and most effective level of learning in this proverb, "Involve me and I understand."

However, in the learning of the choreographic process, it is important to go a step further. Rather than repeat a process that is demonstrated to you by a teacher, or create what is described to you in words from a text, you must be involved in the creative process itself. You, as the learner, must be involved in the discovery of the **concepts** you will use as tools of this trade. There will be no right or wrong decisions to be made but only choices that work better for you and your audiences. You must learn to evaluate those choices to find what works best for you as a choreographer. In this way you will discover the dance within you; that is completely yours and is not a copy of any other dancer or teacher.

This text gives you enough structure, or telling, in the instruction to allow for a degree of comfort, but at the same time it will require you to discover, solve problems, and make individual choices before any telling takes place. This is the **inquiry-based approach**. It begins with exploration and without detailed explanations of rules to follow. This process allows you the freedom to find your own way. Later you are offered generally accepted rules that you may either conform to or break away from, depending on your unique approach as a choreographer.

Inquiry, Science, and Dance

Inquiry is an established approach to discovery for the field of science. Scientists search for a truth often just beyond reach. Theories are established and tested and inquiry begins again in order to get closer to the truth. When one discovery is made, it is always possible to explore further without stopping at a right or wrong answer. Science advances by these new discoveries. Artists also create in search of an expression of truth. Both art and science involve a form of discovery that leads to a deep understanding, or truth, that remains elusive enough to encourage more discoveries and greater truths. It is the mystery of this truth that engages us and holds us to our task.

The scientific method includes explore (collect data), describe (analyze data), question (hypothesize), explain (conclude or develop theory), test (experiment), communicate (publish theories), and retest established theories. Compare this method to the inquiry-based approach to choreography in this text (see table 1.1).

> *The fairest thing we can experience is the mysterious. It is the fundamental emotion which stands at the cradle of true art and true science.*
>
> *Albert Einstein*

Exploration

The study of each choreographic concept in this text begins with exploration. I encourage you to read and perform each chapter in sequence in order to gain the maximum benefit of this inquiry-based approach. This is not a text in which you should read an assignment the night before and then try the exercises the following day. The movement exercises and questions that accompany them will help you discover the knowledge for yourself before you are given the accepted rules for the craft of choreography in the discussion of key concept.

 ## Essential Question

Each exploration begins and ends with an **essential question**, which provides the focus for the exploration. (An essential question frames an understanding that is essential to the learning of a particular concept or idea.) The icon shown in the margin will appear with each essential question. This question begins the inquiry and points toward an understanding of the key choreographic concept being explored without providing the answer. To test your current knowledge or your instincts about the concept, you may wish to attempt to answer this question before you begin the movement activities. Record your first answers in your journal and compare them to the answers you formulate at the end of your study of each concept. If you feel you cannot answer the question at the beginning, simply keep it in mind as you progress through the lesson. You should ask the question again at the end of each in-depth study of the choreographic concept. Essential questions frame your exploration, so it is important to revisit the question at the end.

Warm-Up

Each warm-up exercise has three objectives. The first objective is to raise the body temperature gradually and prepare you for more intense movement. Second, the warm-up should bring your concentration into focus, exclude outside noise, and leave the mind completely free to follow a **kinesthetic response** to the exercises given. During the warm-up you must work toward an **internal focus** that excludes worries, frustrations, and everyday business that may follow you into the dance studio. And finally, each warm-up provides an introduction to the particular concept to be explored.

Improvisations

After the warm-up, specific movement **improvisations** are suggested. They provide an in-depth exploration of the concept. It is recommended that

Table 1.1   Comparison of Inquiry-Based Approach and Scientific Method

Inquiry-based approach to choreography	Scientific method
Exploration: essential question, warm-up, improvisations, and reflective questions	Explore (collect data), question (hypothesize)
Discussion of key concept, journal writing	Describe (analyze data)
Movement studies	Test (experiment)
Assessment: class critique, rubric, documentation	Describe (analyze data)
Drawing conclusions: breaking the rules, critical thinking essays	Explain (conclude or develop theory), retest established theories, publish theories

you break into groups for these exercises to allow for observation. Dance is experienced both kinesthetically and through observation. Sometimes what you experience kinesthetically is not the same as what you experience while observing dance. The best example of this is a dancer spinning. A dancer who is spinning very fast feels a strong **centrifugal force** kinesthetically and may choose this as a way to show strength in choreography. However, the audience may perceive spinning as calm and soothing, making this an inappropriate choice for conveying strength. Dancers also have their own unique ways of moving, often controlled by body type and personality. What one person perceives as extremely fast movement kinesthetically may be observed by an audience as moderately fast. You need to get constant feedback from an observer during the discovery process. Remember that the purpose of improvisation and feedback is to provide a simple discovery process with no right or wrong solutions. You may discover new opportunities for movement choices by watching your classmates, which is a valuable skill to develop. A group working together on one concept will provide many choices and solutions. The discussion following improvisation will be rich with information about slight variations in effect. Do not look for evaluation during improvisations. This will hinder the process.

Here are some notes to the instructor about warm-ups and improvisations:

- Warm-ups and improvisations are written as dialogue. They are meant as instructions given to the dancer, who then responds to the instruction. As part of a class, the instruction would normally be given by the teacher. As homework or independent study, dancers may take turns giving instruction to each other and watching the results, ideally sharing reflections at the end.

- Warm-ups are intended as exercises to be performed together as a class and are done without an audience. Improvisations should, whenever possible, be performed while part of the class watches to allow students to both feel and see the concepts being explored.

- Whoever directs the warm-ups and improvisations suggested in this text should read instructions slowly. Pause after each instruction to allow the dancers to assimilate and react to and explore each new idea. Watch the dancers to guide your timing of each instruction. If there is confusion, you may need to repeat an

Dancers use the word *inquiry* to create a group sculpture.

instruction or perhaps reword something. If you are not getting enough variation of movement, it often helps to direct the dancers to change body parts and spatial elements. As a **director,** I look for opposites. If something is not working, I ask the dancers to try it the opposite way.

- To culminate each warm-up and improvisation, use the following instruction: "Find a **logical** conclusion to your exploration and find a stillness that you can hold until everyone is finished." This allows the dancers to complete a movement thought without being interrupted in the middle of a particular exploration, and the entire class can finish together. It also reinforces the need for (and allows the dancers to practice) a careful ending to every creation. Note that every creation should have its own beginning, middle, and end without being constrained by outside stimulus, whether the creation is spontaneous as in an improvisation or planned as in a movement study.

Reflective Questions

This text makes suggestions for reflective questions during the exploration process. **Reflective questions** are open ended, with no right or wrong answers, often leading to more questions. They are designed to elicit class discussions with descriptions and explanations of your discoveries. Every response to a reflective question should be honored as valid because each response made by you and your group will indicate how far you have come in your understanding of the concept, which may be monitored and used as a guide in the progression of your training. Reflective questioning will indicate whether you are ready to move on to movement studies or whether you need further exploration of the concept. You and those you are working with should use this process to form your own questions, as well. The person who develops the ability to form questions understands with more depth than the person who seeks only to provide explanations.

Reflective questions may be approached after each exploration as they are placed in the text. Or an instructor may wish to wait until all the movement explorations (both warm-up and improvisa-

tions) have been completed in order to avoid disrupting the flow of discoveries. But it is important for instructors to find a time in each movement session for students to share answers to these questions in a class discussion. As a student, you should develop a habit of recording your answers and any additional questions in your journal after these discussions. You will find it useful to reflect on your discoveries as you progress in this learning process, and the material you collect will be useful in developing your critical thinking essays.

Discussion of Key Concept

The discussion of the key concept after each exploration provides a description of generally recognized theories about each concept and rules for indulging in the craft of choreography. I use the word *indulge* because it is easy to rely on the rules for choreography to create works without much thought about **intent**, or why the work is being created. Works created without regard for intent may wander aimlessly, building step upon step and missing the opportunity to engage the audience. However, **craft** is a powerful tool; when mastered, it will be a structure you can always rely on, especially when you base that structure on the intent of your work. The key is to focus on how these concepts affect the intent of your work and to use them accordingly.

The theories offered are a combination of generally accepted rules tempered with a good deal of author experience. You may find that the discussion clarifies some ideas for you that you experienced in the movement exercises. Or you may find that it opens doors to further questioning. Whatever the result, after reading the discussion of key concept, you should compare your discoveries made during the movement explorations with the theories offered in the discussion. Make some decisions about what you know to be true from your own experience as it relates to this discussion. Formulate some of your own ideas about the key concept and record those ideas as personal discoveries in your journal.

The choreography journal is an important aspect of the choreography class. You should write in the journal daily and in depth after each choreography class. Then, take time to read your journal at least once a week. Erica Jong (author of eight novels, including *Fear of Flying*) once said that in order to understand life, you must live it backward. The same can be said for the creative process. A choreography journal helps you understand the creative process by reminding you of past discoveries as you progress. Choreographers do experience writer's block. When you get stuck in the creative process, you will find many ideas recorded in your journal, which you may wish to use. This journal will continually provide source material for critical thinking. Your choreography journal should be a collection of impressions, ideas, and revelations from you and from conversations with your classmates and faculty.

Movement Studies

You will be asked to test your new understanding of a concept by solving a **movement problem** in one or more movement studies. You solve the problem by creating a dance that fits within the assigned parameters while seeking to apply what you have discovered about the concept you are working on. **Movement studies** are complete works and must have a beginning, middle, and end. They may be very short, perhaps only about eight counts, or much longer, although rarely as long as three minutes. The length is determined by how long it takes to make a complete statement within the

parameters provided. As you progress, you will be asked to develop your ideas, and your studies will become longer.

A good way to create a movement study is to begin with improvisation and eventually set movement that may be remembered and repeated. It should be practiced so that it may be performed easily without having to stop and remember a sequence. Sometimes students will plan movement in their heads and wait until the showing to perform it. This is not recommended, particularly for a beginning choreographer. Only after a great deal of practice will you be able to imagine all the possibilities at your disposal. This is because you will usually imagine only movement that you have previously experienced, whereas if you improvise, you will discover new movement and increase your vocabulary. It is also helpful to develop a kinesthetic sense and understanding of the movement you have selected. Without exploring the movement physically, a kinesthetic understanding is not available to you.

Do not be tempted to perform an improvisation for your movement study. What makes a movement study different from improvisation is that the movement is set and the performance is practiced. The practice you undertake in preparation for showing should enable you to perform accurately, with commitment, and with consistent timing and good technique. If you are unable to perform a

Keep a choreography journal to record your discoveries.

work consistently while you are practicing, you or your choreographer should consider changing your choreography to something you are able to perform repeatedly and consistently. This rule extends to group work. If you are choreographing for a group, you must make sure each dancer is able to perform the work repeatedly and consistently. If the dancers cannot master the movement in a short time, change your choreography. You should never refer to a dancer's mistakes as an excuse for the lack of success in your choreography. The ultimate responsibility for the success of the dance lies with the choreographer. Here is a wonderful quote I often say: "He who cannot dance blames it on the floor." I would like to add this: "He who cannot choreograph blames it on the dancer."

Here is a note about preparing movement studies and assignments: Creating movement through improvisation is the best way to ensure that the movements you are creating have intent. (See chapter 2, Creating With Intent.) A beginning choreography student must recognize this and take the time to get into the studio and move when creating for the first time. Many students like to be planners: They refuse to get up and try movement themselves, instead working it out in their heads or writing it down on paper. They will use this method even in short classroom studies when only a few minutes are assigned to complete a study. When asked to work it out themselves by doing it, they will only mark the movement, refusing to dance full out. They feel safe by not moving in front of their peers, who incidentally are paying no attention to them because they are too busy working things out for themselves. Or they find it easier to do their assignments in the dorm room rather than arrange the studio time necessary for completing an assignment. These students are wasting valuable time. They have not tried the movement before the class presentation and have no idea whether the movement has logical intent. Sometimes they are lucky, but more often the work lacks the necessary intent. It certainly does not show the student's best ability, nor does it allow the student to explore new territory. Usually this student will use these excuses upon critique: "It worked in my dorm room, but it just didn't work here," or "I know what I meant it to be, but I just can't perform it in front of everybody."

To be successful, students of choreography must put aside worries and inhibitions and jump into each lesson with full and firm **commitment**. This is what I mean when I discuss courage in the preface. There will always be those students who are more shy and reluctant; when they evaluate themselves against other students who seem to be courageous and bold, they withdraw further with the firm knowledge that they will never measure up. I understand those students, because I began my own training in choreography with inhibitions. But all students should realize that they have something unique and valuable within themselves to offer the art form, and tapping into that will benefit not only the art form and the class in which they participate but also their own self-discovery and esteem. There is nothing more satisfying than hearing from peers that your own personal creation, however small and insignificant, was understood and appreciated.

Assessment

Assessment is a means by which you determine whether a goal has been met. The goal to be assessed in this text is an understanding of the key concepts presented. Ongoing assessment is imperative for growth and should be undertaken by you as the student choreographer, your peers as observers of your work, your teacher who undoubtedly is responsible for your grades, and your audiences. The inquiry-based approach includes **embedded assessment**. During your exploration of each key concept, you are continually checking your kinesthetic sense to see if you understand the instructions given. You are looking around at others to check their understanding and you are making decisions about your own choices based on these assessments. Your teacher or mentor is also using **observation** to evaluate the progress of the class in order to inform choices about the length of an improvisation and whether to repeat or modify the improvisation. The reflective questions will indicate the depth of your understanding, and your movement study will indicate your ability to apply that understanding.

Daily assessments of this nature are imperative to the progress of your study. Movement studies, on the other hand, require more formal assessment. Class **critique** is the most common form of assessment and provides immediate feedback to the student choreographer. The class critique will include evaluation by your peers. **Rubrics** may be used in evaluating movement studies according to identified criteria. These rubrics are an assessment tool and may be designed by the teacher or the student. If the rubric indicates that the criteria have been met, then a student may assume the assessment of his or her work has been a positive one. **Documentation** is another tool that may be used in assessing students' learning and evaluating class progress, teaching effectiveness, and institutional effectiveness. Remember that documentation is only a record. It must be accompanied by an evaluation in order to be effective as an assessment tool.

It is appropriate here to discuss the difference between assessment and evaluation. Assessment is a determination of whether a goal has been met. Evaluation is a value judgment based on particular criteria. A teacher will evaluate the progress of a class; students will evaluate their own work and that of others to form an opinion of whether the work is valid and appropriate for a particular intent. Assessment in this text is reserved for a determination of whether a student has understood a key concept and is able to apply it in the creation of a dance.

Class Critique

Peer critique guided by a mentor is the most effective way to evaluate your movement studies. After each showing, take a minute or two to write your observations in your journal before volunteering a response. This will enable you to remember your thoughts during the critique process, at which time you should enter the responses of others as well. Responding to the movement studies is the first step toward assessment, and you should document assessments in order to understand your progress.

The class process for evaluating dance may vary according to the teacher, but all choreography classes involve time for your peers' and mentor's critique. Several approaches for critiquing dance work well, but the most important thing to remember about this process is just that: It is a process, not an end in itself. A critique of your work in class given by your peers or your teacher is not an evaluation of your ability as a choreographer but simply the impressions of a group of people, both experienced and inexperienced, about the work you created for that particular showing. Rather than focus on the success or failure of your work, you should collect

impressions, ideas, and suggestions so that eventually you are able to make informed judgments as you create new work. You will not always agree with what is said. The best environment to work in is one where everyone is allowed to agree and disagree. Your teacher will expect your opinion to be supported by explanations that are constructive. Every viewpoint, regardless of the source, is valid and should be recorded in your journal.

The class critique is a difficult process to establish as a constructive tool. Yet providing a safe environment, where everyone is willing to take a risk, is essential to the creative process. So how is it possible to establish a risk-free environment and to allow for conversation about the works created in order to provide new choices for every student to grow as a choreographer? Obviously, the critique must be constructive. The first rule of being constructive is to never label something as good or bad or even wrong. There is no absolute right or wrong in creating dance. Everyone will have an opinion of what is a better choice for a particular intent. Opinions are not absolute, even when they come from experience. I have often noted that a student's opinion that is not jaded by experience has more validity than a professional opinion. Listen to all opinions.

Although you are evaluating each other's work, overt value judgments are not constructive. Avoid saying things like "This was the best!" You must realize that even though you are being positive and you may be very excited about the success of a fellow student, this kind of statement dismisses the critiques of the rest of the class and devalues all of the other work shown. You have set this student up for failure in the future if he or she cannot maintain an expected level of success. You have also just cut off all conversation, because no one else will want to disagree with you. You may communicate your excitement for your fellow student's success in a much more meaningful way by describing the movement, explaining your interpretation, and giving your reasons for why the movement choices seemed appropriate to you. This helps your fellow student understand why the work is successful in your eyes, but it leaves the field open for alternative opinions.

Sometimes you may want to admit to misunderstanding a concept and to making the "wrong" choice for the assignment. I prefer the word *inappropriate* to *wrong* even in self-critique. You should also refrain from labeling what you deem as inappropriate choices made by other students. It is better to question the choreographer about why the choice was made, stating that you, as an audience member, were confused. Usually the student choreographer will realize that some intent was not clear once it is questioned. The focus should remain on descriptions, individual interpretations, and suggestions for new choices. You and your classmates should be left to form your own conclusions about your work. At the same time, you should remain open to the opinions of others, particularly when considering the intent of your work, how it is interpreted by the audience, and whether there are other choices to consider. Artist colonies were developed in order to allow artists to show work and receive feedback from peer artists. Your class may be a fermenting ground, much like an artist colony, if everyone works to create a safe, active community of learners.

The simplest approach to class critique, and the quickest when time is limited, is to answer the questions, "What part worked the best for you?" and "What would you change?" Sometimes if you are inexperienced and not accustomed to describing movement, you can easily relate your favorite part. This is also a good exercise for finding something valuable in every work, regardless of how successful the choreographer has been in creating an effect or illustrating an assigned concept. Beginning with what is most valued will foster confidence in the choreographer and encourage open dialogue and the ability to listen to suggestions for improvement or change.

An extension of this approach is for the person who makes the suggestion to take over as choreographer of the piece being critiqued. This person gives instruction to the dancers and makes some suggested changes, and the work is shown again. This can be repeated with several students making changes to the choreography with discussion after each showing about how the change affects the impact of the work. This method actively engages everyone and provides additional practice in creating movement for the entire class. Sometimes it is easier to manipulate movement created by others than to come up with ideas of your own, so this will help everyone to gain confidence in creating alternative movement choices.

Class critique should be nonthreatening and constructive.

Critical Thinking Model

A more thorough approach to critique, and one that may be used for class critique, journal writing, and essay writing, is well worth the extra time it takes to accomplish. This model has a four-step process: analysis, reflection, integration, and evaluation. You should take each step in order. Analysis, reflection, and integration may blend to a certain extent, but you must never attempt evaluation before you've exhausted the other three steps.

Analysis

The first thing you must do when beginning to talk about what you have just seen is to describe what you have seen as precisely as possible and as objectively as possible. This is called the **analysis**. The sophistication of this analysis will increase with training, but even the beginning student who has been a nondancer can communicate to others what has been seen. Here are some examples of descriptions that might be given by a beginning student:

- It began very slowly, became very frantic, and then died down to a stillness at the end.
- The dancer's arms were very stiff and rigid while his head was very loose and relaxed.
- The dancers seemed to wander around the stage without knowing where they were going.

All of these comments are completely objective and do not make any judgments about right or wrong. Later, if there were a specific assignment given, some analyses may relate whether or not the work contained the required elements, but there is still no evaluation of the work itself.

Reflection

Not to be confused with reflective questions, the second part of the critique should be a discussion of what the audience perceived as the intent of the work. What was the choreographer trying to communicate? Here it is difficult not to get into a discussion with the choreographer, but it is better if the choreographer remains quiet and listens to the reactions of the audience without comment. The intent may have been as abstract as creating a particular picture or quality for the audience. It may have been more expressive, communicating a mood or feeling to the audience. Or it may

have actually communicated a **narrative**, which could be literally understood and interpreted. It is possible that the intent was not clear, and this should be communicated at this point. Reflection includes a discussion of why the choreographer made particular choices in movement and how those choices affect the audience. Here are some examples of reflections that might be the result of viewing the same movement studies referred to in the previous analysis:

- This dancer seemed to be grappling with some internal struggle, which exhausted her in the end.
- He looked a little like a circus clown, but I think there might have been something deeper in meaning. I just wasn't sure. Maybe we were supposed to just enjoy the contrast of movement.
- This dance looked like a group of people in the aftermath of a bombing, almost like no one was aware that the rest of them were even there.

Notice that these responses remain open to additional interpretation without cutting off conversation. Using verbs such as *seemed* and *looked like* make it evident that the responses are from a personal perspective and allow for additional perspectives to be addressed.

Integration

Integration is a process of finding relationships between choreographic material and all other experience. Each person views a dance according to his or her own experience. Focusing on those relationships is a necessary process in developing an understanding of the individual interpretations of a work. Many surprises will surface for the choreographer during the reflection process, and the integration process will help the choreographer and the viewers in their understanding of these reflections. Following are examples of the process of integration for the previous three reflections:

- The slow movement at the beginning seemed very controlled, which reminded me of how I feel when I am trying to hide my own anger.
- I have never seen anyone move like that, except maybe once when I went to the

circus. It made me feel uncomfortable, because it seemed so unnatural.

- These people reminded me of the characters in many science fiction films I have seen, where everything on earth is destroyed and no one has a place to go.

As you progress in your studies of choreographic elements, you will be able to use this process of integration to compare new material with past assignments or performances you have seen. Relating new work to previously seen choreography is a valuable tool. This might be a discussion of how the work was similar to or different from the past work created by the same student. Or you might discuss how this work reminded you of something else you have seen performed. This integration will include discussion of dance **elements** using dance vocabulary learned in the **course**. At first this process is difficult, because beginning students have little experience to compare the process to and are limited in the vocabulary of dance elements. This part of the critique will increase in potential and scope as the class progresses.

Evaluation

The last part of the critique should be the **evaluation**. Now you are free to decide whether the work was a success and why. But you must use your analysis, your reflection, and your integration to support your evaluation. I encourage students to use the words *that worked for me* or *this part did not work for me* rather than *I liked that* or *I didn't like that*. Every critique is subjective; one person might like something, but another will despise it. Realize that the success of a piece does not always rely on people's liking it. And success for the choreographer is obtained through honest critiques from peers, not glowing, emotional support from friends. This part of the critique is also the time for you as the choreographer to speak up and communicate what you were trying to do. This allows for discussion and suggestions. Here are evaluation examples that might follow the previous analyses, reflections, and integrations:

- I was completely spellbound by this piece. The controlled energy at the beginning made me anticipate the frantic section. Then the dancer moved with such incredible energy that it exhausted me to watch. I wanted to collapse with her.

- I think this piece was very clever and I was amazed that the dancer could accomplish the contrast in movement. It is not the kind of choreography I like to watch, and I would have to know more about the piece before I decide if it works for me.

- This movement was effective in getting the mood across, but I found it a common theme, and would have liked something a little more surprising and unusual.

Notice in these evaluations that they begin with something positive in every case. You and your classmates should strive to find a balance between positive comments and constructive suggestions for all the work shown in your class.

If you use this critical thinking model in class to evaluate the work you see, you should also keep a record of all the comments in your journal and list them under each of the four steps so you begin to understand the process. If you are thorough in this record keeping, you will have plenty of material to use in formal essays.

Rubrics

Rubrics function as an assessment tool and help you evaluate the success of your work. Examples of rubrics are shown in tables 1.2 and 1.3 on page 14, but the most effective rubrics are designed by students after the explorations have taken place and the assignment has been given. Student-designed rubrics are accomplished by asking, "What do you think the best solution to this movement problem would look like?" After you have several ideas and criteria written down, select the most important criterion that you would like to evaluate. The more you evaluate, the longer it takes, so if you want to do a quick evaluation, pick one or two criteria. If you want to be more comprehensive, choose criteria that include knowledge and application of the key concept being studied, the development of new and unique **movement vocabulary**, the creation of logical movement sequences that may be performed well, and the presence of intent throughout the performance. (Intent is discussed in chapter 2.) I recommend a two- or four-point rubric rather than the typical three- to five-point rubric. An even number of options requires the evaluator to decide if what he or she is evaluating is closer to accomplishing the criteria or closer to not accomplishing the criteria. It is too easy to

Table 1.2 Sample Rubric for Exploring Movement With Intent

Criteria	Strong evidence (2 points)	Little or no evidence (1 point)
Visible movement intent		*There were two or three times when the outside force was clear, but the force from inside was never clear and the dancer seemed uncomfortable with the presentation.*
Clear beginning, middle, and end	*There was good focus at the beginning and it was obvious when the piece ended.*	
Consistent performances		*The two performances were quite different. The dancer had not learned the choreography and was improvising.*

Total score: 4 (maximum 6 points)

Table 1.3 Sample Rubric for Symmetry and Asymmetry

Criteria	Strong evidence (4 points)	Some evidence (3 points)	Little evidence (2 points)	No evidence (1 point)
Clear use of symmetry and asymmetry		*A few of the symmetrical shapes were not well executed and became asymmetrical.*		
Balance of stage space			*The only balance of stage space existed in the symmetrical shapes and one asymmetrical shape.*	
Clear movement intent				*All intent was lost. The focus was only on design.*
Beginning, middle, and end		*The beginning and ending were solid but the middle was choppy.*		

Total: 9 (maximum 16 points)

place something in the middle and evaluate it as average rather than give careful thought to whether it meets the criteria.

Documentation

Documentation is a means of assessment that includes recorded information that may be evaluated. Keeping a daily **journal** is a simple process of record keeping. An evaluation of this journal may include an assessment of your understanding of the key concepts. **Recording your work** on video is a tool for documenting your work during class, in rehearsal, and during performance. The increased accessibility to digital cameras and computers that play back and preserve video clips allows you to easily maintain a digital **portfolio** of your work. I recommend securing a small camera, such as a Flip Video (available from Pure Digital Technologies), which will not only record video clips but also allow you to edit your clips and isolate single photos from the video recording. In order for these recordings of your work to function as assessment tools, they must be evaluated. This text includes suggestions for recording comments, rubrics, and in-depth critical analyses along with your video clips to ensure the usefulness of the documentation.

A note on evaluation: Evaluation provides a strong tool for change and growth. As long as the evaluation is positive and constructive, the door will remain open for growth. Destructive evaluation will hinder any progress. Most of us have experienced some form of destructive criticism. As we mature, we learn to filter that criticism and analyze its value according to the experience and intent of the deliverer. In the 50-plus years I have spent in the field of dance, the most destructive evaluations I have witnessed have come from the individual dancer to herself or himself. It may begin with a peer or mentor, but usually the self delivers the worst critique. It can be vicious: "It knows where to strike, where it hurts" (Nin, 1974, p. 107). It is extremely important to negate this destructive tendency of the self if you wish to grow as a dancer and choreographer or even as a human being. As you embark on the road to creativity, you must provide a positive environment for yourself and allow for risk, adventure, and absolute fun. A playful attitude will take you further than any regulations you place on your goals.

Drawing Conclusions

After an in-depth study of key concepts, you will be asked to process the information, understanding, and knowledge you have gained by breaking

Videotape your work regularly to maintain a comprehensive portfolio.

the rules you have learned and writing critical thinking essays. These activities will help you draw conclusions concerning the key concepts you have studied. The ability to draw your own conclusions is the final process in the inquiry-based approach.

Breaking the Rules

Creating movement studies that break the rules you have discovered will further test your discoveries about the key concepts, giving you opportunities to explore alternative possibilities. Sometimes you are given examples of broken rules that have been successful for well-known choreographers, providing evidence that going beyond what is obvious or accepted practice may also be an appropriate solution. Once you have tried breaking the rules, you may choose to use them or break them, deciding whether craft or anarchy best suits the intent of your work. You may or may not discover new ways to create your chosen intent, but it is important that you establish a practice of pushing those boundaries in order to draw your own conclusions and create your own style. The ultimate goal of this text is to support you in developing that style through discovery.

Critical Thinking Essays

A portfolio, journal entries, and ideas amassing in your mind will provide a collection of data that you may analyze and choose to use as you choreograph; but a **synthesis** of this information along with a comprehensive evaluation must take place in order for you to fully understand these choreographic tools. Each chapter includes an assignment of an essay that asks you to follow the critical thinking model described in the Class Critique section. By following this model, you will be able to draw conclusions based on solid reasoning rather than opinion alone. It is easy to make value judgments as you discuss dance, but if you always require yourself to back up every value judgment with analysis, reflection, and integration, your

opinion in the evaluation will be valid. The critical thinking essays will become additional evidence to be used in assessing your understanding of the key concepts and how they apply to the choreographic process. You must understand something in order to communicate it well. That which you can explain becomes acquired knowledge that may be measured.

These papers should be approached with as much academic rigor as you would approach any other writing assignment in courses outside of dance. It is not appropriate to be informal in your writing just because you are an artist. Do not use names of your fellow students or complain about personal problems. Stick to the choreographic concepts in your discussion. Your papers should have a structure that includes an introduction, a body of discussion, and a conclusion.

Summary

The goal of this text is to support you in discovering the dance within you rather than acquiring the dance from some outside source. To accomplish this, you must take ownership of your learning. You will need to be active in each phase of the learning by jumping into improvisations, contributing profoundly to reflective questions, engaging and thoughtfully questioning the reading assignments, honing your creative skills during movement studies, objectively evaluating your progress and contributing to the objective evaluation of the progress of your peers, and communicating your thoughts and ideas with scholarship. All of this requires an above-average engagement in the process. Remember that you have much to learn from others and they have much to learn from you. Working creatively with your peers may be one of the most rewarding experiences you will encounter. Take advantage of this structured time together and enjoy the rich and diverse accumulation of ideas that will surface among you. But always keep an eye out for who you are and what dance exists within you. Only you can find it.

Chapter 2

Creating With Intent

Initial Inquiries

> Never let the fire go out, no matter
> how dimly it burns.
> *Advice given to a dancer by Eugene Loring.*

In your choreography, how do you make sure that your dancers engage the audience? • How do you make sure that their fire never goes out? • How do you make sure that your dancers perform with conviction and that they are genuine and not superficial? • Is this something that simply must be taught to the dancers as they learn to dance? Or is it something that can be instilled by a director? Or is it possible to build this into the choreography itself?

To move on stage, or to be still with a fire that never goes out, is to dance with intent. This chapter includes an extended exploration of intent. You may wish to spend at least two sessions performing the warm-ups and improvisations recommended here. Keep the essential question in mind as you perform these explorations. Engaging in conversations using the reflective questions to focus those conversations will guide you toward an understanding of intent that may be compared to the discussion of the key concept and used in creating your movement study. Show your movement study to your peers and evaluate each other in class critique. A rubric is provided as a guide, but you may wish to create your own. This movement study will provide you with your first opportunity to document your work in a portfolio. Remember that you are not expected to show work that is ready for the stage. Label this work as your first, and include comments about the work. In this way, you will be able to learn from a collection of your work. After evaluating the need for creating with intent, you will be asked to create without intent and decide if this works for you. You may wish to document this study as well and compare it with your first movement study. Finally, organize your thoughts about intent in a formal critical thinking essay. If you use the model for critical thinking provided in chapter 1 for your class critique, you will find it easier to organize your critical thinking essay.

Essential Question

Why is it important for dancers and choreographers to create movement with intent?

Warm-Up

1. Lie on the floor on your back in a constructive rest position (a concept used in the Alexander Technique: knees bent and leaning in toward each other with feet flat on the floor so that no muscular effort is necessary to remain still; see figure 2.1). Close your eyes and focus your attention on your breathing for about 20 seconds. Next, as you inhale, imagine a movement of your arm above you moving toward the ceiling; as you exhale, imagine the release of that arm so that it drops gently toward the floor. Imagine this several times until you have a picture in your mind of how long it will take to lift your arm, how it will coordinate with your breathing, how it will feel when you withdraw all your energy, how quickly it will fall, and where it will land. Finally, continue to focus on the breathing and the image you have acquired, and actually perform the movement with your arm. Try it several times until it feels comfortable and logical. Repeat this with the other arm, remembering to visualize the movement first.

2. Build on the first warm-up by adding body parts—individually at first, and eventually with full-body movement (i.e., right leg, left leg, head, upper body rising to a sitting position, full body rising to your feet and returning to the floor). The timing no longer needs to be coordinated with your breathing. You should explore ways to move while rising (keeping the eyes closed). Visualize each movement before actually doing it. Always return to a relaxed position lying on the floor.

REFLECTIVE QUESTION How does visualizing a movement before it is performed affect the performance of that movement?

Figure 2.1 The constructive rest position.

Improvisations

1. Perform the following sequence: Sit on the floor. Stand and reach for the ceiling. Balance on one leg. Fall back to the floor. Return to a sitting position. Do it one more time.

2. Now, sitting on the floor with your eyes closed, imagine yourself performing this sequence. Think about timing; the shape your body will make; the feeling it will have as it reaches, balances, and falls; how you will fall safely; what position you will be in when you fall; and how you will return to your sitting position. When will you use the most energy, and how will you release it? How will you string the movements together so they look like they belong together as one long movement? How will you begin? Which muscles will you use first? How will you end? Perform the sequence again as you imagined it, paying particular attention to the beginning, the transitions from one movement to the next, and the end. Take as much time as you need to perform the entire sequence. Practice as many times as necessary to get it the way you imagined it. If you cannot perform it the way you imagined it, sit down and visualize again, making adjustments to accommodate the challenge. Then, in your own time, return to the performance of the sequence. Finish at the end of a sequence and wait for the others to finish.

   REFLECTIVE QUESTIONS How did the performance of the movement sequence change? • What was different about the sequence when you first performed it and when you did your final performance? • Which performance of the sequence was your best performance, and why?

3. Walk around the room, finding your own pathway. Do not follow anyone else. Try to fill the space in the room. Be aware of the people around you, and leave plenty of room between you and the other dancers. As you walk, imagine that a person every so often gives you a shove, and react to that shove by showing it with movement in your body. Keep exploring various ways of doing this while you continue walking around the room. The person may be coming from different directions. The person may shove different body parts. Sometimes the shove is sharp and quick. Other times it is a slow pressing action. Continue to develop this improvisation by allowing any outside force to act on your body. Allow your reactions to develop further and longer, using movement through space that is both high and low. Whenever you lose your focus, return to walking and start again. Find a conclusion to your movement and become still.

   REFLECTIVE QUESTIONS How did the external forces affect your movement choices? • Which of your reactions seemed most natural? • What reactions did you observe that were most effective to you as an audience?

4. For this improvisation, begin by standing in place. Do not travel. You may shift your weight out to one foot, but it must return to the same spot. You may go to the floor to find another means of support, but stay in your own space. Begin to explore all the space around you with your arms in slow motion. You may follow this movement with your torso and change your means of support, but the focus is movement of your arms exploring all the space around you—under, over, behind, in front, above, below, through. As you are moving, I will give you instructions that may change the way you are moving. But keep exploring the space. First, you are feeling a sharp pain in the right side of your rib cage. Focus on how this pain changes the way you are moving. Now it is gone. Begin to move normally again. Now your lungs are expanding with air until your whole chest cavity is filled with air like a balloon. Focus on the changes this makes to your movement. Now, something is squeezing the air out in short, sharp bursts. Repeat the last two—filling with air, and squeezing it out in short sharp bursts. Now there is a motor inside of you beginning to vibrate. The vibrations get bigger and stronger, and

then they dissipate. Explore how that same impulse inside you changes the way you are moving. It may be in any part of the body you choose, even your shoulder or a foot. Find a conclusion to your movement, and become still.

REFLECTIVE QUESTIONS How did these internal impulses affect your movement? • How was this internal focus on motivation for movement different from the previous external motivation? • What were the differences you noted as you watched others?

5. Origination of movement: Make a still shape with your body. Any shape you like. Imagine in your mind how the shape looks. Focus on how the shape feels. Where is the energy in this shape? Can you find a place in your body that has the most energy? What does that energy feel like? Is it strong? Is it weak? Where does it want to move? When I say go, use that energy to move yourself to a new shape. Go! Repeat with the new shape. Continue this exercise, moving into new levels and new spaces in the room. Continue the exploration until you are comfortable finding a place of origin for each movement. Come to a logical conclusion and wait for the rest of the class to finish.

6. Finding intent in technique: Create a short movement phrase from a classroom technique. Use something you might perform in ballet, modern, jazz, flamenco, anything at all. Make sure it is a movement sequence that you would use to learn technique and remember a sequence. You may choose a combination that you recently practiced in a technique class. It should be approximately 8 counts long or the equivalent. Make sure you have a beginning position and an ending position. Practice it a few times to make sure you remember it. Now, go back to the first position and focus (as in the previous improvisation) on the energy. Where is it? What part of the body will carry you into the first movement? What will the energy be like? When I say go, allow that energy to propel you into the first movement of the combination. Go! Did it work? Was it logical? Did you find the correct energy to use? If you were not happy with what you discovered, go back and try it again. After finding a logical intent for the first movement, continue to the next movement. What new shape is your body in now? How does it feel? Use this same process until you complete the entire combination. Then go back and perform the entire combination with this newly discovered intent.

7. Finding new directions: Repeat both of the previous improvisations, except after discovering the energy and the way it seems to want to move, go in the exact opposite way with your movement. In other words, if it feels like the energy should move you forward, try going backward. If the energy seems to want to lift you up, try having it pull you down into a fall. If you're supposed to turn to the right, find the energy to turn you to the left. If the energy seems strong, allow it to dissipate as it moves you gently into the next shape. All of these explorations will continue to have intent, but they will be more surprising and take you in directions away from the obvious.

REFLECTIVE QUESTIONS How was each of these performances unique? • Which ones worked the best for you? Why? • How might you use this process to improve your technique as a dancer? • How might you use this process as a choreographer?

Discussion of Key Concept

In my many years of teaching, I have discovered that the most difficult thing to get across to a student, as a performer or a choreographer, is that every movement must have intent. The intent may be abstract or literal, but it must be visible. The dancer must have a connection to the work, and the choreographer must provide that connection for the dancer. As early as 1760, Jean George Noverre was expounding his disdain for choreographers who treated **scene d'action** by following formulas with little thought to purpose or content. (Scene d'action is a scene in a piece of narrative choreography that moves the plot or story line forward.) A maître de ballet, devoid of intelligence and good taste, will treat this portion of the dance mechanically, and deprive it of its effect, because he will not feel the spirit of it (Noverre 1975, p. 13).

Feeling the spirit is perhaps the most critical lesson to learn. Therefore, I approach intent at the very beginning of the process. But an effective mentor will keep an eye on a student's intent through every part of every lesson, because students often sway from the logic of a piece as they become enmeshed in new ideas and formulas.

Dance is a visual and kinesthetic art form, but it goes far beyond the science of sight and body sense. It is difficult to describe the mystery in the method of communication that is accomplished through dance. We have all witnessed two types of dancers on stage: dancers who reach their audience, and those who do not (see figure 2.2). The novice dancer, who is trying to accomplish difficult steps just recently learned, rarely reaches an audience, because the act of remembering the steps and performing them accurately overtakes the intent of the movement. There is no focus on why the movement is being performed. This dancer is not ready for the stage. However, the novice dancer who becomes imbued with the spirit of the movement during an improvisation may reach an audience without having to spend years in training. And with proper guidance and choreography, that dancer may be ready for the stage immediately.

It is all a matter of allowing the body to move in a logical and natural way without hindering it with excess thought. The moment the dancer begins to think rather than feel, the intent of the movement is lost. The brain instructs the individual muscles what to do, but it is a slow

Figure 2.2 (*a*) The dancer on the left lacks intent in her performance, while (*b*) the dancers on the right show intent in the performance.

process. A student of kinesiology knows that to speed the process, motor patterns are formed after many repetitions of practice, allowing a dancer to perform complex movements and combinations with only a simple signal from the brain. This is the science behind the statement "practice makes perfect." The muscles respond in set patterns without the need to think. They move naturally. Performance is not a time to train motor patterns. Motor patterns are set in the technique class, where dancers learn through countless repetitions how to perform something efficiently and with a particular style. During a performance, your goal should be to move as naturally as possible with the motor patterns that are already set in your body. The motivation, or intent, behind the movement is of ultimate importance in a performance.

Intent for movement may come from one of two places: from within the body or from without. Philosopher Susanne Langer (1953), a mid-20th-century American philosopher who focused on the understanding of art, tells us that dance began as a requirement of the gods. People's gestures were controlled by outside forces, mysterious forces elicited by the gods. Dancers either were moved by the gods after being possessed, or they moved for the gods in order to seek favor. Langer maintains that all dance stems from this primal beginning and that, although we no longer dance for or because of the gods, there is a virtual realm of power that controls the **gestures**, or our movement as dancers. This power is the intent I search for in dancers and choreographers. Another train of thought is more common and follows the idea that movement must come from within. It must begin in the soul, that spiritual place that we all have but cannot necessarily define. We say an excellent dancer performs with heart and soul as a metaphor to indicate this internal presence. The inspiration and force for movement have come from within. There is intent.

Improvisation is the best method by which a dancer may come in touch with the intent of a movement, because it requires the dancer to react immediately without thinking. This immediate response is acquired when the body reacts by using movement patterns already set in the performer. Each performer will respond according to those set patterns, but the intent will govern the selection of the particular movement patterns chosen out of the billions of options. Improvisation is not a time to learn new movement patterns, as we do in technique classes. It is a time to explore and discover new ways to use movement patterns already set. That is why it is easy for the beginning dancer to improvise alongside the advanced dancer. Everyone has billions of movement patterns to choose from, regardless of how those patterns were trained. And each person is unique. The beginner should never look around at this time and feel inferior. The beginner must realize that the advanced dancer may also be without a comfort zone. Improvisation may be very difficult for trained dancers who are accustomed to teachers and choreographers telling them what movements to accomplish. These dancers are used to thinking and processing the required movements according to steps, lines, combinations, and sequences. They are apt to become uncomfortable when the specific instructions are taken away, and only the intent remains. So regardless of the starting point, everyone must approach improvisation in a new way—without thinking and with feeling.

Students who are new to the art of dance will be more comfortable in the nonstructured format of improvisation. They realize that they can simply move in their own natural patterns, focusing on the intent described for the specific exercise. They would much rather improvise than try to accomplish the complex movements that are easy for the trained dancer. So it is never a surprise to me that theater majors often take to improvisation much more readily than dance majors.

Movement intent is not entirely the responsibility of the dancer. In fact, the majority of the responsibility remains with the choreographer. It is the choreographer's job to make sure the dancers understand the intent of the movement and are comfortable performing it (see figure 2.3 on page 24). If the intent does not come across, it is necessary to change or clarify the movement. Too often I have heard this excuse: "Well, I meant for that to happen, but my dancers just didn't do it the way I wanted them to." It is easy to blame the dancers, when really the choreographer has not clearly discovered the *intent* behind the movement choices.

This is not always the case, because there have often been times when it was obvious that the movement intent existed for the choreographer, but the dancer could not accomplish it. But the choreographer needs to recognize the moment when the movement must be adapted to suit the body of the dancer, and not struggle to adapt a dancer to fit the movement. Dancers are the choreographer's medium. It is necessary for choreographers to work with the medium they have, develop it perhaps, but not expect it to change, especially in the short period usually allowed for rehearsal.

Movement Study

Create a movement sequence that explores virtual forces from without and from within. This will be your intent. You may put the forces in any order you like, but make sure you have a good representation of each and make sure your audience sees the intent in your work. Use improvisations 3 and 4 from this chapter as a guide. Be sure your work has a beginning, a middle, and an end; and make sure that you are able to perform it clearly. Know your work so that you will be able to perform it at least twice without variation for viewing.

Figure 2.3 Strong intent.

Assessment

Use these assessment tools in evaluating your progress toward understanding intent as a key concept in choreography.

Class Critique

Identify movement that is motivated by an outside force. Do the same for movement that comes from within. Identify any moments in the movement study that are not clear about where the motivation from the movement is coming from. Discuss the effect of these forces.

Rubric

Select "strong evidence" or "little or no evidence" for each criterion and support your selection with a description in the space provided. For a broader range, create a four-point rubric: strong evidence, some evidence, little evidence, and no evidence. The maximum score for the four-point rubric is 12 points. Examples of a completed rubric can be seen on page 14 in chapter 1.

Rubric for Exploring Movement With Intent

Criteria	Strong evidence (2 points)	Little or no evidence (1 point)
Visible movement intent		
Clear beginning, middle, and end		
Consistent performances		

Total score: 4 (maximum 6 points)

Documentation

Videotape your movement study. On your computer, create a digital portfolio for your work. Save this video along with a copy of a completed rubric for the work and comments from class critique. Add your own personal comments. Make sure you save the rubric and comments in the same folder as the video clip, or label them clearly so you will know which evaluations coincide with each video clip.

Drawing Conclusions

Breaking the Rules

In this exercise, you will create *without* intent. Create five separate shapes and learn them well so that you may repeat them. Try to pick shapes that have a variety about them, such as some supported low on the floor, some high, some large, some small, some strong, and some weak. Assign each shape a number. Memorize the number for each shape. Get with a partner now, and have the partner call out numbers from 1 to 5 in random order. Perform each shape as your partner calls out the numbers. Do not make any attempt to focus on your transitions. Simply get to your shapes when they are called.

REFLECTIVE QUESTIONS   After both of you have performed for each other in this way, discuss how it felt and how it looked. Did it work? Why? Why not? • When might it be appropriate to use this process in your choreography? • What personal discoveries have you made concerning movement intent?

Drawing Conclusions

Critical Thinking Essay

Refer to the critical thinking model in chapter 1 (page 12) when writing critical thinking essays.

Visit the dance library and view any sample of choreography on video or DVD. Watch for the intent in the movement. Evaluate the work according to its intent and write an essay about your observations. The essay should include a definition of intent and descriptions of the choreography that either illustrate your definition or lack the characteristics described in your definition. Here is an outline to help you get started:

    I. Introduction: Definition of intent

   II. Discussion

      A. Analysis: Describe the work, including indications of movement intent.

      B. Reflection: Describe what you believe to be the purpose of the choreographer in creating this work.

      C. Integration: Relate what you see in the work to the explorations you have completed in class and to other works you have viewed or performed in the past.

  III. Conclusion (evaluation): Draw some conclusions about the work concerning movement intent, using your analysis, reflection, and integration to support your evaluation.

Part II

Discovering the Basics

Chapter 3

Creating With Energy

Initial Inquiries

How does energy affect intent? • How do we perceive energy when we view dance? • Are we able to perceive all the energy it takes to create a movement? • When we say a dancer looks effortless, is the dancer really taking it easy? Or does it take more energy to create the illusion of being effortless? • Why do some techniques look stronger than others? • Why do some dancers look softer and lighter than others?

A keen sense of the use of **energy** and how it creates effects on stage is an important skill to have as a choreographer. In this chapter you will explore energy in two ways. You will explore the amount of energy you may use at any given time (dynamics), and you will explore how that energy may be controlled (**flow**, which is a movement term first identified and used in dance by Rudolf von Laban as he and his colleagues began to analyze movement in Germany at the beginning of the 20th century). Each of these concepts is approached separately. The exploration on dynamics will take at least two sessions to perform before progressing to the movement studies. Remember to repeat the essential question at the end of the explorations and record your answers in your journal. Each exploration is followed by a discussion of the key concept and multiple movement studies. If you have time, you may complete all the movement studies. If time is limited, you may want to choose the one most appropriate for you and your group. Or perhaps you would like to use different movement studies for different members of your group. Continue to collect a record of your work in a digital portfolio. Draw your conclusions about the use of energy by "breaking the rules" and writing your critical thinking essay.

 **Essential Question**

Why do variations in the amount of energy used by a dancer affect choreographic intent?

Warm-Up

1. Begin in a standing position, with the feet apart in a small parallel second position with your knees slightly relaxed. I recommend facing anywhere in the room that is away from a mirror. Begin shifting your weight side to side between your feet, setting up a gentle rocking motion. Focus on how this rocking motion feels in your body, allowing your joints to release in your ankles, knees, and hips. Now allow the arms to swing side to side with the shifting of the weight. Continue to allow the rest of the body to release and react to the gentle swaying motion by releasing the spine. Your head should gently swing from one side, dropping lightly forward en route to the other side. The entire body will be engaged in this swaying motion now. Gradually begin to increase the size of your pendulum, eventually creating a full-body swing from side to side, with arms and fingers inscribing a large arc through space. Progress to the point where, after a reach to one side, the knees bend and the torso releases forward, the fingertips dragging along the floor in the middle of the swing. As you shift your weight to the opposite side, lift your torso up and reach to the other side. Allow the opposite foot to lift off the floor while you reach to the other side with your arms at the end of the swing. Repeat and maintain this large swinging action while you focus on the kinesthetic feel of the energy in the swing. Now, gradually allow the size of your swing to get smaller, returning to its original size. Progress to a simple weight shift in the legs alone, and eventually stop all movement, keeping a stillness and waiting for the rest of the group to complete the movement.

   REFLECTIVE QUESTIONS   How does your use of energy vary when performing a swing? • When do you use the most energy? • When do you use the least energy?

2. This is another swing, but rather than side to side, you will use the space directly in front of you and behind you. Again, stand in a parallel second position, but this time raise both arms high above your head. Swing the arms down and in front of you; drop your arms and torso forward while bending your knees. Scrape your fingertips on the floor with your head down while you allow the arms to continue the direction of the swing down and back until they are behind your feet. Gently stretch the knees until almost straight but still released at the end of the downward swing. Keep your back curved. Change the direction of the swing, bringing your arms back through the same arc, bending your knees at the bottom of the swing, and lifting your body back to a standing position with the arms raised over your head. Again, keep a forward curve in your spine until the very end of the upward swing. Repeat this swing continuously about 10 times, or until you are well warmed up. To protect your back, make sure your abdominal muscles are fully engaged. Remember to keep your joints loose and to focus on the kinesthetic feel of the movement itself. Ask yourself where the energy in this movement is and how much energy you are using and how it changed throughout.

   REFLECTIVE QUESTIONS   What kind of energy do you feel kinesthetically in a swing? • What is the difference between the energy you use to create movement and the energy you feel kinesthetically from the movement you create?

Improvisations

Note: Because of the large number of improvisations listed here, you may wish to divide your exploration of dynamics into two separate sessions. Improvisations 1 to 7 give a complete exploration for one session. Improvisations 8 to 11 could also stand alone and will provide a logical progression without a separate warm-up.

1. Work with a partner. Begin at one side of the room. Stand facing your partner and hold hands. You should have your back to the other side of the room, in the typical line of travel across the studio floor, as your partner faces you. Back up across the floor, trying to take your partner with you. Gradually pull your partner with your hands (see figure 3.1a). Your partner resists, trying to stay in place. Both of you should bend your knees to gain stability and take care of each other. It is not a game to win or lose, but an opportunity to feel the energy needed to perform this action. Eventually, you and your partner are to find a way to get to the other side of the room. This may mean that your partner will have to give in a little to allow you to travel. This will seem like tug-of-war. (Safety hint: Make sure the pulling action is gradual and constant to allow your partner to react. Do not try to surprise your partner by pulling the arms quickly. You must be responsible for your own safety and the safety of your partner.) Repeat this improvisation, changing places with your partner. Allow your partner to do the pulling while you resist.

Figure 3.1 (a) Pulling a partner across the floor and (b) pretending to pull a partner across the floor.

2. The next improvisation is the same as the previous, but this time you will perform the action with an imaginary partner. You will go across the floor, pretending to pull someone, showing in your movement that it is difficult to get that person to come with you (see figure 3.1b). Take as much time to get across the floor as you did with a real partner. Show all the variations of movement and energy, or create new variations with this imaginary partner. Make it visibly obvious when you are "winning" the tug-of-war and when your "partner" gets the advantage. Repeat this by changing roles as you did before. Return across the floor pretending to be pulled by a partner. Again, focus on the amount of energy you are using and how that energy changes throughout the improvisation.

3. Again, work with a partner. Your partner should be passive while you are active. Come to the center of the dance space and spread out away from the rest of the group, but stay close to your partner. Take your partner's hand in your own and gently guide your partner's hand in an exploration of space. Your partner should allow your guidance by reacting to your touch immediately, staying passive, but following your lead. You should be in control but maintain a gentle approach. You may lead your partner in a turn or in a change of support, such as sitting on the floor or jumping, but do not travel around the room. Help your partner explore all the space around the body—high, low, forward, back, side, over, under, and through—as you move around your partner. Your partner should follow your lead with movement of the torso, head, knees, and even feet as well as the hand and arm. Once your partner becomes comfortable with your lead, you may try going faster and slower and actually begin to travel, watching out for other travel patterns in the group. Continue to keep your guidance gentle and light. Repeat this improvisation, changing places with your partner. You become passive and allow your partner to lead you through space.

4. Repeat the previous improvisation by yourself. First be active, leading an imaginary person gently through space. After exploring this for a while, change to being passive, allowing an imaginary person to lead you through space. Eventually try this imaginary leading and following by initiating the movement from other body parts, such as leading with your foot or following with your hip.

    REFLECTIVE QUESTIONS How would you describe the energy created in each of these improvisations? • How did the energy change when you changed roles? • What effect was created by the use of imaginary dancers? • What was the most interesting movement you saw? Why?

5. This improvisation may be accomplished by as few as two dancers, but it works well as a group activity with the group standing in a circle facing into the center. One person begins by pretending to have a ball. That person tosses the ball to someone else in the circle. The person who is intended to catch the imaginary ball must react immediately. This is a simple pantomime exercise. However, your focus should be on reacting in a way that is consistent with the way the imaginary ball is thrown. In other words, if the ball is thrown toward you fast and hard, you must react quickly and catch a ball that has a strong impact. If the ball is tossed high and slowly, your reaction must change. It will take longer for the ball to reach you and it will be light. It is important to remain aware of the way the ball changes hands each time. Everyone should explore different ways to throw and react to an imaginary ball. You may even want to change the size and weight of the ball as you handle it. How will this affect your movement as you catch the ball? Allow your entire body to become involved. Continue until everyone has had an opportunity to explore sending and receiving the ball.

6. This improvisation is a preparation for the next improvisation. You will need to understand how to move as if an imaginary ball of energy is inside your body. This ball can

move from any place inside your body to another place, but it may not leave your body jumping from one body part to another. Imagine there is a ball of energy in your right hand. Take time to feel the energy in your hand. What kind of energy is it? Make it travel in your hand, up and down your fingers, into your palm, into your thumb, and back to your palm and then to your wrist. Allow your hand to react to this energy by moving a little through space. Next, allow the ball of energy to move up your arm into your elbow. Explore the energy there, moving your elbow around a little before the ball continues up the arm farther to your shoulder. Explore how it feels to have that energy in your shoulder, and allow that energy to move you through space. Remember that you are leading with energy in your shoulder. Now allow the ball of energy to move across your shoulders and down your left arm in order to reach the other hand. Explore what it feels like to move this imaginary ball of energy throughout your body and changing body parts, but never losing sight of where in your body the ball of energy is. Remember, it may not leave your body to get to another body part. It must make pathways through, and your movement should make the traveling of that ball of energy visible to anyone watching you. Begin with light energy, because that will be the easiest, and then gradually increase the energy until it is very strong. Alternate back and forth, and allow yourself to use as much of the performance space as you need. Another variation is to use music to suggest energy for this imaginary ball that is moving through your body. Choose music with variations in dynamics (i.e., loud and soft), or change music often during the improvisation.

7. Like improvisation 5, this improvisation requires throwing and receiving. However, the object being thrown is no longer a passive imaginary ball, but the active imaginary ball of energy you created inside your body in the previous improvisation. One person in the group begins by exploring movement created by an imaginary ball of energy in the body. It must be evident to all watching exactly how much energy this ball has. After moving long enough to establish a particular amount of energy, this dancer will require that ball of energy to leave the body by propelling it with some body part and directing it to another dancer in the room (see figure 3.2). The person receiving the ball of energy must react by receiving a ball with the precise amount of energy that was established by the dancer sending it. It may enter the body through any body part that seems in line with the trajectory sent by the original dancer. The new dancer then begins to explore movement created by this imaginary ball of energy, first with the same amount of energy that was sent. Gradually this dancer must change the energy and establish a different amount of energy that is evident to all who are watching. Once a new amount of energy is well established, this dancer will send the ball through a body part to another dancer. Again, that dancer must receive the energy in precisely the same way as it was sent. This takes a great deal of concentration and careful observation. You should not rush the exploration of the energy before sending it on to the next dancer. You must be very clear with your movement and give everyone else time to recognize what you have established. You are encouraged to explore many gradations of energy, from very strong to very weak and everything in between. It is often difficult to explore and establish extremes in amounts of energy. You will begin to note your own movement preference. Some people are more comfortable moving with a lot of energy, some are comfortable using very little, and some are midrange dancers. It is important to push yourself beyond your comfort zone. Take the time to do this.

REFLECTIVE QUESTIONS How did the variations in energy change the movement you were able to create? • What kinds of energy did you observe? • When was the movement most interesting? • How might you use this movement as you choreograph?

8. This improvisation requires music. Select music that has variations in dynamics (loud and soft) within a short selection. (See the Variations in Dynamics section in Music Resources.) You will also need a large sheet of newsprint and a thick crayon (dark or

Figure 3.2 Throwing a ball of energy.

bright color that will show up on the paper). Begin by sitting on the floor with your eyes closed, crayon in hand, and newsprint on the floor in front of you. Feel the edges of the paper so you know approximately where it is, reducing the risk of drawing on the floor when your eyes are closed. Place the tip of the crayon on the page. As the music begins, allow the tip of the crayon to move across the page to the music. Keep your eyes closed. Keep the crayon on the paper. Do this several times with several pieces of music. You need to listen to only about a two-minute segment from each piece of music. As you change music, change the color of your crayon. When you are finished, observe the drawing you have created on your paper. How does your drawing relate to the music? How does your drawing relate to other drawings by the group? (Note that crayon marks can be removed with Scotch-Brite, soap, and water.)

9. Repeat improvisation 8 while standing with an imaginary crayon in your hand. Instead of drawing on a flat piece of paper, draw with your imaginary crayon on all of the three-dimensional space around you. You may stay in place or travel around the room. Open your eyes to make sure you do not run into any other dancers. Begin drawing with your dominant hand. Then draw with both hands. Try drawing with other body parts: hip, nose, ear, knee, foot, and so on. (Improvisations 8 and 9 are adapted from lessons taught by the late Eugene Loring, who used these explorations in his choreography classes at the University of California at Irvine.)

10. Again, improvising to the music, instead of drawing with an imaginary crayon, simply allow your body to move with the energy suggested by the music. Explore small movement with only one body part, and explore large movements with the whole body. Also explore all the space in the studio (high, low, forward, back, up, down, diagonal), taking care not to disturb the space that is being used by someone else. You may also wish

to change your means of support. You begin standing, but you do not have to remain standing. You may want to go back to the ball of energy exercise and imagine the ball of energy inside your body is being controlled by the music. But you are not restricted to one ball of energy. There may be many points of energy inside and outside your body as you dance. Have someone fade the music at the end so as not to abruptly end your improvisation.

REFLECTIVE QUESTIONS How did the music affect the energy you used in your movement in all three improvisations? • What did you observe as you were watching others, and how did the use of energy change from drawing on paper to drawing in space to freely improvising to the music?

11. I call this improvisation "Be the Conductor." As the conductor, you stand in front of a group of dancers as if you are about to lead a dance exercise. Everyone else is facing you, but try not to have anyone facing the mirror. Imagine that you are conducting music. The group must be the "instruments" and perform the music you are conducting with the energy you suggest in your arm, or both arms, or even your whole body. These dancers do not pantomime the playing of literal instruments but react by performing movement that has the amount of energy suggested by you as the conductor. Hopefully everyone has observed a conductor in at least one musical performance. If not, I recommend watching the Disney movie *Fantasia* (the original 1950s version with Leopold Stokowski as conductor) to see how much movement the conductor may use to gain the energy he wants from his musicians. If you know anything about conducting, you know that the conductor sets the time signature. We forgo that necessity in this exercise. Using your right arm, simply begin to move it through space with energy, focusing on the dancers in front of you. Play with extremes in energy, both strong and light. Other elements may creep in, such as timing (fast and slow) and space (high and low), but these are not your focus. You may want to try splitting the group in front of you as conductors do with the different instruments in the orchestra. Using eye contact and direction with your arm, you may have one side of the room moving with a lot of energy while the other side moves with very little energy. You might even bring out a soloist. But everything must be done with gestures—no speaking. Make sure you have a beginning, middle, and end to the "music" you are conducting. Take turns so that everyone has a chance to conduct.

REFLECTIVE QUESTIONS What were your challenges in conveying the energy you wanted performed by the dancers you were conducting? • How might you use this knowledge to help you as a director and choreographer of dance?

Discussion of Key Concept

One way that dance communicates is through a device called kinesthetic response. The simplest example of kinesthetic response is the tapping of a foot to music. When people hear music with a strong beat, it is virtually impossible for them to remain still. Another somewhat more complicated example is that of a spectator becoming involved in an extremely close-scoring and intense athletic event. The spectator comes away from the event not only with a sore throat from yelling but also with pure physical exhaustion. This occurs because the spectator has been performing with the athlete, sending impulses to parallel muscle groups in his own body, in order to "assist" the athlete in reaching the desired goal. When a dancer performs with clear intent, the audience members actually experience impulses to their own muscle groups parallel to those being used by the dancer. When we observe energy, we feel it. In this way, communication occurs through parallel body sensations directly, without having to pass through the brain. Our brains react by interpreting these feelings of energy in our muscles into meaning. This means of communication in a dancer is useful information for a choreographer to have and illustrates the necessity for establishing clear degrees of energy within the dance.

Energy is perceived by the audience through sight. There is some delay in the time it takes to perceive energy and to react to it. For this reason, performance must be exaggerated and time must be expanded. This does not preclude the ability to stab the audience with a surprise that occurs instantaneously. But the space in time surrounding the surprise must be expanded. The surprise must be given time to register. And the stab must have the energy of a lightning bolt in order to take effect.

In music, the term *dynamics* indicates the loudness and softness of a musical note or phrase. To create the loud and soft moments in music, the musician must use either more or less energy to create the sound. **Dynamics** in movement refers to the amount of energy used to produce a particular movement or stillness. It might be translated as the amount of muscle power necessary to create or sustain a particular movement or position. We would consider something that requires a great deal of muscle power to be high in dynamics, or *strong*, whereas something that required little muscle power to be low in dynamics, or *light*. The irony here, however, is that since dance is interpreted through sight, often what may seem extremely high in dynamics to the performer may be read as a lower dynamic by the observer. I repeat my example of a turn here. To the performer, the sensation of energy in a turn is extreme, especially if it is a fast turn, because the dancer feels the powerful centrifugal force that results from the turn. However, the observer perceives a flowing movement through space and reads it as midrange in dynamics (see figure 3.3). So, whereas a good method for discovering extremes in dynamics is through the use of improvisation, the choreographer must also take a step back and observe, somewhat detached, to discover the dynamics that have been created.

The most common fault of a novice choreographer is to work constantly within a midrange of dynamics. It takes courage to release extreme amounts of energy. It also takes courage to allow energy to seep out until there is almost nothing left. Dancers and choreographers worry that they are not doing enough for the audience. Comfort lies in that midrange where commitment is minimal. It is important to gather the courage to find the extremes. The extremes are where you will find variation in movement and intent and where you will develop the ability to phrase your movement by forming a beginning, middle, and end that make a statement to your audience.

Figure 3.3 Turning feels strong but looks soft.

Numerous explorations through improvisation with continuous peer feedback can be beneficial yet somewhat frustrating at times. If you are new to improvisation, you may perceive your own movement to be extreme, whereas your peers may discover that your attempts are falling short of the mark. Your peers know the extremes are lacking, but as novices themselves, they lack the expertise to communicate to you just what is lacking or how to improve. This is the point where critiques tend to become mediocre. Peer observers are unwilling to say something is not strong enough when they cannot explain *how* to make it stronger. Also, students who know each other well and see each other working within their own capabilities on a daily basis tend to believe that the dancers are working within their limitations and are reluctant to expect more or to criticize each other for what is deemed natural for a particular dancer.

This process is complicated by the fact that each dancer has a realm of comfort in dynamics. If your personal style of movement typically falls within a low range of dynamics, you will have incredible difficulty approaching an extremely high dynamic. Your peers may observe your movement as just a little above a low dynamic, whereas you will feel as if you are performing with your maximum energy. If you are a dancer who likes to exude incredible amounts of energy every time you move, you may have great difficulty performing extremely light movements that are low in dynamics. You will feel like your movements are very light when you are really working in a midrange.

It is important to recognize that discovering extremes in dynamics and developing an ability to use them logically in movement patterns may take much longer for some than for others. Taking the time necessary to ensure a good understanding of the use of dynamics at an early stage will enhance your work. You should also be aware of the use of dynamics continually as you progress beyond this chapter to explore additional elements of craft.

Movement Studies

1. Create a very short movement phrase that is extremely high in dynamics. Repeat the same movement with extremely low dynamics. Do the movement 20 times, going from extremely high dynamics to extremely low dynamics, never performing the same amount of energy twice. Rehearse this until you can perform it consistently as one unified dance.

2. Students often confuse high dynamics with fast movement and low dynamics with slow movement. *Strong* is not synonymous with *fast*, and *light* is not synonymous with *slow*. Dynamics and speed are not necessarily connected. For example, a fast run does not have to be high in dynamics, even though it usually is. You may wish to explore the quality created by fast runs that are low in dynamics. A slow walk may be executed with extreme tension, or it may have a lethargic weakness about it. Both of these walks may take an identical amount of time but involve very different dynamics. Create a movement study that includes all three of the following images in your movement. Or you may create your own images that involve unlikely combinations of speed and dynamics. Perform them in any order. Make sure your sequence is unified, and establish a beginning, middle, and end to your work. Here are the suggested images and dynamics:

   • You are trying with great difficulty to push a heavy object across the floor. Go beyond the literal and explore various ways of pushing the object with many different body parts. Allow for some variation in success so that the timing varies within the piece. (Slow and strong.)

   • You are trying to flick off spiders that are crawling all over you. Again, consider exploring many body parts. (Fast and midrange.)

   • You are a dust particle on top of a boiling pot of water. (Fast and light.)

Assessment

Use these assessment tools in evaluating your progress toward understanding dynamics as a key concept in choreography.

Class Critique

- Identify the dynamics in each piece.
- Discuss the variations and how they affect the choreography.
- Talk about the challenges of performing slight variations in energy and why you would want to be able to do this.
- Identify the effects created by mixing different speeds with different amounts of energy. Any surprises?

Rubric

You may wish to design your own rubric after you have explored many variations in dynamics. Ask yourself what evidence you expect to see in your work if you have a good understanding of the use of dynamics in choreography, and develop your own criteria for evaluation. Following is a rubric for the second movement study.

Rubric for Dynamics

Criteria	Strong evidence (2 points)	Little or no evidence (1 point)
Clear variations in the amount of energy used		
Distinct separation of dynamics and speed		
Unified work with obvious beginning, middle, and end		
Total: (maximum 6 points)		

Documentation

Have someone videotape your movement studies. Add these video clips to your digital portfolio. Make sure you include a completed rubric or comments that evaluate your work. Include your own comments as well as those made by others. Label your work with a date to make sure you understand where this work exists in your progress as a choreographer.

 Essential Question

How is effort perceived in dance?

Warm-Up

1. Begin standing with eyes closed, or with an internal focus. (*Internal focus* here is used to indicate complete concentration on the kinesthetic or internal sense of the movement, and no focus at all on how the movement looks, or how others are moving. There is also no expectation for planning movement. You should simply allow the movement to happen according to movement cues.) Concentrate on your right arm. Engage all the muscles in your right arm without moving it. Imagine that you are trying to move, but something is restricting your movement, not allowing your arm to move more than a very small amount. Work as hard as you can, creating as much tension in your arm as possible. Use the muscles in your shoulder, elbow, wrist, hand, and fingers. Do this until you can no longer sustain the strength in your muscles, and then release. Next, allow the same arm to move freely through space. Release all the joints in your hand, fingers, wrist, elbow, and shoulder. Explore various amounts of energy, but allow the joints to remain free and loose. They should no longer be restricted in any way. Repeat both extremes with the other arm.

2. Again, while standing in place, lunge out on your right leg. While standing in that lunge, use every muscle in that right leg, again without moving it. Focus on where the muscles are and make sure they are all activated. Concentrate on the hip, the knee, the ankle, the foot, and even the toes. Imagine that you are trying to move them but something is keeping you from moving them. Create as much tension as possible without releasing your joints. Next, push off from the floor with your right foot and begin swinging your right leg freely through space, allowing all the joints to release. Release your hip, knee, ankle, foot, and toes. Explore different amounts of energy, but allow the joints to remain free and loose. They should no longer be restricted in any way. Repeat both extremes with the other leg.

3. Explore the previously described extremes with all the joints in your body at once. Activate all your muscles, but restrict your joints from any movement. Concentrate on all the areas in your body to make sure all muscles are engaged, and create a tension in all your joints. Now release all your joints and allow your body to move freely through space. Again, explore many degrees of energy while concentrating on allowing complete freedom in all your joints.

REFLECTIVE QUESTIONS How do restricting movement in the joints and allowing the joints to move freely affect the way energy is used by a dancer?

Improvisations

1. Begin standing. Explore ways to move in one dynamic or constant amount of energy. Make sure you are using a dynamic that you are able to sustain for some time. Do not change the amount of energy you are using, but you may change the body part involved. You may move only a finger or your elbow, or you may use the entire body. Explore different ways to move using only your determined amount of energy, and focus on how it feels to change that energy from a small body part to full-body movement. Make sure you have established how much energy you are using, and try not to change. Now, without changing the amount of energy you are using, find a stillness or a very restricted movement that continues to use the same amount of energy you had established. Again, you may change body parts that expend the energy, but do not move without restriction.

Alternate back and forth from moving freely to moving with restriction to not moving at all, keeping the energy constant at all times. Finally, release everything and come to a logical stillness that uses no energy at all. You will be lying on the floor in some position, because in order not to expend any energy at all, your muscles will not be able to hold you up. Repeat this improvisation with several different dynamics, exploring the kinesthetic sense of movement with varying amounts of energy that is both free and restricted.

2. In the previous improvisation, you explored energy that created movement freely and energy that was restricted so that no movement, or very little movement, was possible. These are two extremes. Many variations are possible between these two extremes. For this improvisation, begin by establishing a particular dynamic with free full-body movement. After you have established that free dynamic, begin to gradually restrict the movement in your joints so that very slowly you come to a stillness, keeping the amount of energy you are using constant. Then begin to free your joints gradually so that eventually you are again moving freely through space. One more time, restrict your movement gradually until you come to a restricted stillness, then release and wait until everyone in the group is still.

REFLECTIVE QUESTIONS   How does restricting your movement change the way it feels to use a particular amount of energy? • How does changing the amount of restriction you impose on movement change the way the energy looks and feels? • What effects may be created by varying this control in a dance?

3. Isolating body parts: From a standing position, reach your right arm straight forward, and hold it in that position without moving your elbow, wrist, or fingers. Now begin moving the left shoulder, circling it, lifting it, dropping it, and generally exploring the looseness of that joint while continuing to hold the right arm in place out in front of you. Continue moving the left shoulder freely while adding movement with the left arm and the left side of the torso. Allow the joints you are moving to be very loose while holding the right arm rigid. Now add movement in the neck, hips, and legs along with the whole torso. You may travel through space and change your facing direction, even change your means of support, but the right arm must remain rigid, reaching out in front of you. Explore many ways of moving, allowing all your joints to be free except those in your right arm, which must remain restricted. Hold its position in relation to the rest of your body. Now find a logical stillness to complete the improvisation, releasing everything, including your arm. Repeat this improvisation with the left arm extended out to the side. Continue this exploration with different body parts remaining rigid while the rest of the body moves freely.

4. In this improvisation, the isolated body part remains loose while the rest of the body alternates between free and controlled. Find a space in the room that is your own; stay in that space and begin to explore the space around you with only your right arm. Allow only the arm to move freely, and explore the space that is high, low, over, under, around, through, near your body, and far away. Focus on the amount of energy you are using in that arm and continue to move it freely as you allow your torso to react to what your arm is doing. Allow the rest of your body to follow the arm. This may mean that the arm will move you through space in the room, so you may travel. You may change dynamics and your means of support. Your arm may take you into a jump or require you to fall to the floor, slide, and spin. Explore many ways that the body may follow and react to the movements of the arm. Now, gradually return to moving only the arm while keeping the rest of your body restricted and unable to follow the arm. Try to do some of the same movements that you did with the arm when you were allowing the body to follow. Notice the difference in the how the arm feels as it repeats the same movements now that the body is restricted. Repeat this improvisation with your left arm. Then repeat with different body parts, such as the head, hip, rib cage, and leg.

5. Continuing to focus on an isolated body part. Repeat the previous improvisation, but use restricted movement in the isolated body part. In other words, you will move the right arm with a lot of energy but restrain the movement, or control that energy so that the arm has difficulty moving through space. Progress to allowing the rest of the body to follow the arm freely. Focus on creating a restricted intent in the body part, followed freely by the rest of the body. Return to restricting the body so that it remains still in relation to the isolated body part. Find a logical stillness that releases everything to complete the exploration. Repeat the improvisation, isolating other body parts. This is the most difficult of the isolation improvisations, because it requires moving with two separate intents simultaneously. Take your time exploring it, and return to it on another day if you become frustrated trying it the first time.

REFLECTIVE QUESTIONS What intent is created when one body part is continuously restricted in its movement? How is that different from the intent created by allowing an isolated body part to move freely in relation to the rest of the body being restricted? • What happens when the different parts of the body move in contrast to the rest of the body? Why is this difficult to perform?

6. Explore a classroom exercise: In whatever technique you choose, create a complete plié exercise using at least four positions of the feet (first, second, third, fourth, and fifth). Make sure you choreograph arms as well for the pliés, and add any transitions you like between the positions. Be creative. Next, perform the entire exercise with the highest dynamic possible, but restrict your movement so that your performance is very slow and controlled. Be sure to use every possible muscle to perform the exercise. After resting a little, repeat the exercise, this time with the same amount of energy, but allow that energy to be free to move you through space quickly. It will take much less time, and you will not be quite as tired at the end. But be sure you still use a lot of energy. Repeat the exercise a third time using very little energy, but control it. Again, it will take a long time to complete, but since you are using very little energy, you will not get tired. Complete the fourth repetition with very little energy, but allow the energy to move through your body freely, with no restrictions in your joints or the size of your movements. The fifth (last) repetition should be executed the way you know it should be executed according to the technique you are using. Different techniques require a different use of energy. Try to develop a new awareness of that energy, how much you are using, and how much you are restricting it, now that you are performing it "correctly."

REFLECTIVE QUESTIONS How does training in a particular technique affect your ability to use variations in energy? • Why is it important to understand variations in the use of energy in order to perform selected dance techniques?

Discussion of Key Concept

To qualify the effort it takes to accomplish a particular movement, or stillness, not only is it necessary to analyze the amount of energy being used by the dancer, but you also must analyze how restricted the movement is. Movement that is restricted shows up as tension that is unleashed. Unrestricted movement shows up as effortless, even if a lot of energy is being expended. Rudolf von Laban labeled this control of energy as *flow* in his system of effort shapes. Movement that flows easily is free, and movement that may not flow easily but is restricted is bound.

Scientifically, and very simply, your muscles are capable of only two actions: contracting and releasing. A contraction places force on a joint and usually causes the joint to move. The number of muscle fibers you recruit for one action determines the amount of force exerted on your joints. If you decide you want to use less force, you may lessen the number of muscle fibers recruited, which will slow the action of the joint, but the joint will still move easily. It is possible to recruit new muscle fibers on the opposite side of the joint to counteract the original force, which may also slow or even stop the movement, but the effort required to move will increase rather than decrease. This increase in effort causes a restriction in the joint. Any force on a joint that does not have an opposing force, such as opposing muscles or gravity working against it, will be free, and movement from that joint will flow easily. Any force on a joint that is accompanied by an opposing force will be bound. Movement from that joint will be restricted. These two terms are useful in their simplicity, because they can be employed as cues while directing movement (see figure 3.4). Here are examples: "Alternate between bound and free as you complete the movement phrase." "Bind the movement in the torso while moving the legs and arms freely through space."

Movement patterns in the body are set by habit, training, and even state of mind. Allowing a joint to move freely may go against habitual patterns and can be difficult in times of stress when the body seems to hold muscle tension, or contraction. That is why you often hear in a dance class, "Release! Allow the movement to flow freely!" Often dancers must recruit more muscles than necessary in order to move a joint that is being held in position by muscle tension. This requires extreme effort when very little effort should have been necessary. This is the reason for the many **somatic approaches** to movement that focus on the release of muscles around a joint during a joint action. However, this discussion deals with the longevity of a dancer's career and correct technique. There are times in choreography when extreme tension and bound movements are desirable for creating a specific effect.

Restricting the movement possible in a joint by adding more muscle action creates more effort and tension in the dancer. Releasing that tension is like a breath of fresh air both to the dancer and to the audience. Actors use this process when creating the emotional qualities of a character. How much tension you hold in your body and where it is held can be translated into a state of mind. A choreographer can create variations in moods with great efficiency by paying attention to subtle variations and gradations of energy flow.

Figure 3.4 Bound movement (downstage dancer) against free movement (upstage dancers).

Movement Studies

Movement studies are most beneficial to you when you are not dancing in your own work. This allows you to observe the results of your work as you create rather than having to rely on the feel of the movement alone. Placing yourself as the audience will give you the perspective you need in making choices about audience impact. However, creating a solo for yourself may allow you to gain a greater understanding of the kinesthetic impact of your work. It may even be that you are able to create a very successful solo for yourself that no one else could perform quite as well because only you understand the depth from which the movement originates. The choice of whether you choose to dance in your own work becomes a delicate balance between self indulgence and personal artistry. I require my students to stand outside their work and create it on others because it develops their communication and observation skills and allows them to evaluate their own work from the audience's point of view. But there are times when it is necessary for the choreographer to dance, either due to lack of dancers or for a need to insure maximum performance quality.

1. Create a duet of opposition. Choreograph for two dancers: When one dancer is working with bound energy, the other must work with free energy. Play around with ways to connect your two dancers. You may simply create playful abstract movement, or you may find that some literal intent materializes out of your improvisation. Each dancer may change from bound to free, but when one dancer changes, the other must react by changing as well. The two dancers must never be the same, even during stillness. Make sure there is a beginning, a middle, and an end to your work. Although you will begin to set this study through improvisation, make sure you select the best choices to show for the complete dance, and make sure your dancers are able to repeat it exactly the same way numerous times.

2. Create a solo that explores very gradual changes between bound energy and free energy. Also explore the use of isolated body parts as well as full-body movement. Be sure you have a beginning, middle, and end so that the solo looks like a complete dance.

3. Establish and practice a movement phrase in any dance technique you like. It may be a combination you learned in class, or you may create your own. Make sure the phrase has a clear beginning, middle, and end, and perform these sections distinctly. Now play around with the flow of energy in the phrase. Add tension in places that were moving freely, and add free-flowing movement in places that were bound. Create a new phrase with these alterations and perform it after the original phrase. Finally, play around with the original phrase once more by improvising changes in the body parts that are bound or free. (For example, a grand battement in ballet is usually performed with a bound torso and a free leg. Try performing it with a bound leg and a free torso.) Create another new phrase that includes these variations and perform it following the second phrase. Complete your movement study by either repeating the original version of the movement phrase or, if you are feeling adventurous, including a fourth variation that changes both movements and body parts together. Your performance will include four movement phrases. Make your transitions from one phrase to the next logical so that all four phrases look like they belong together as one dance.

Assessment

Use these assessment tools in evaluating your progress toward understanding energy flow as a key concept in choreography.

- Identify moments in the works that are bound and free. Note the gradations of energy flow, including extremes and contrast, and discuss how these affect the works. Ask if there are any moments when "the fire goes out." If this happens, can you make suggestions for fixing the problem? Or is it a problem?

- Discuss what happens to a technical movement phrase when the energy flow within it is manipulated. How does it affect the style of the work? What creates unity in each of these movement studies? Which pieces look most like a complete dance? Why?

Rubric

Following is a sample rubric that you may use in evaluating the third movement study for energy flow. Try filling in evaluator comments for yourself and for your peers, or create your own criteria according to what you believe to be important in the understanding of energy flow.

Rubric for Energy Flow

Criteria	Strong evidence (2 pointes)	Little or no evidence (1 point)
Clear contrast between bound and free		
Clear variations in energy flow among different body parts		
Clear beginning, middle, and end		
Total: (maximum 6 points)		

Documentation

Record your work on video and date the entry in your portfolio. Add narration to the video that explains your process. Evaluate the effectiveness of that process by including a rubric and a record of peer or mentor critique.

Drawing Conclusions

Breaking the Rules

Variations in the use of energy can often make or break a piece of choreography. However, the use of energy and the comfort level of using and viewing these variations vary dramatically according to the cultures involved in creating them. Eastern cultures have far more patience than Western cultures and are willing to wait for subtle changes of energy in a performance, whereas most Western cultures grow impatient without constant change to generate interest. Interpretations of what is performed will also vary according to the culture and experience of the viewer. Try these movement studies without variation in energy. (If it is available to you, I recommend viewing the video *Butoh: Body on the Edge*

~ continued

of Crisis, directed and produced by Michael Blackwood. This is a Japanese modern dance form. But beware that there is some nudity. If this video is not available to you, there are numerous samples of butoh available to you as video clips on YouTube.)

1. Create a work composed of high energy that is bound to the point of barely moving during the entire piece. Maintain a high dynamic that is bound throughout without change.

2. Create another work that is free and very light. Again, maintain the established dynamic and flow of energy throughout the entire piece.

REFLECTIVE QUESTIONS What effect is created by keeping a constant dynamic and flow of energy in an entire dance? Is it logical, and does it work for you? • How does a constant use of energy affect the beginning, middle, and end of the piece? • When might it be appropriate to use a process of maintaining constant dynamics and flow of energy?

Drawing Conclusions

Critical Thinking Essay

Discuss your personal progress on the use of energy in your movement studies, and relate it to the use of energy in the movement studies created by your peers or other dance or choreography you have experienced. Your essay should include definitions of dynamics and energy flow. You may wish to include a narrative of your process from the explorations through the movement studies, highlighting key moments of learning. Use the critical thinking model from chapter 1 for your essay. Here is a sample outline for your essay to help get you started:

I. Introduction. Define energy, differentiating between dynamics and energy flow. Make a statement about the importance of these choreographic concepts.

II. Discussion
   A. Analysis. Include a narrative of your learning process, focusing on key moments.
   B. Reflection. Why did you make the choices you made in relation to the assignments you were working on, such as improvisations and movement studies?
   C. Integration. How were these choices similar, or how did they take you in new directions from your previous experience? How did these choices relate to others in your group?

III. Conclusion. Evaluate your progress in understanding the use of energy in your work. Make sure your evaluation is supported by your previous analysis, reflection, and integration.

Chapter 4

Creating in Space

Initial Inquiries

How can dance be related to a painting or architecture? • What are the elements that are common to a visual art form and a kinesthetic one? • Is it possible or even preferable to create spatial designs in dance? Or should dance simply focus on movement and energy, allowing spatial design to happen naturally and without planning? • How do you keep dance from being static when the focus is on shapes and architectural forms? • Is it possible to create meaning by arranging the space on a stage? • Is it possible to mistakenly create the wrong meaning when focusing on design rather than intent?

Space is the most complex

element of movement to explore. Because dance exists in three-dimensional space, and with time that space is continually changing, there is much to consider. You will begin with a focus on things close at hand: how to find variations in size of body shapes and movement, how to change movement from one body part to another, and how to dance in high, middle, and low levels. Then you will explore your place in the performance space and how it relates to the space around you. You will explore body shapes created by dancers both on their own and in relation to other dancers and objects. You will learn many forms of symmetry and how they may be used to create balance and variation and how asymmetry may add to dynamics. And you will explore the use of negative space and direction. The combination of each of these key concepts attempts to define the infinite possibilities you may discover within the limitless confines of three-dimensional space. In the end, you may discover that you want to define space in more ways than are offered here. Be sure to record your discoveries to be used in creating your own unique style of choreography.

 *Essential Question*

Why is the intent of movement affected by variations in the use of size, body parts, and levels in space?

Warm-Up

1. Start lying on the floor in any comfortable position you like. Take a few moments to find an internal focus. Try to feel each joint relaxing and dropping to the floor. If any part of your body feels uncomfortable, shift your weight until you have found a position where you can relax. Very gently pull yourself into a tight fetal position. Make your body as small as you possibly can. As soon as you get there, begin to open up and stretch yourself out so that your hands and feet are as far away from each other as possible. Curl up again into a small tight ball, and again stretch out to be as large as possible. Continue alternating between very small and very large, remaining on the floor. Explore various ways to curl up and stretch out. Find a place you would like to end your exploration, and be still until everyone has completed the exploration.

2. Begin in a standing position. Keeping your weight supported on at least one foot, curl your body into as small a position as you can. Then stretch it out into a very large position, with your arms and legs spread very far away from each other. Curl back into another very small shape. Continue alternating between large and small, but remain standing for the entire exploration.

3. Repeat the previous exercises, but this time you may change from being on the floor to standing, to kneeling, or whatever you wish. Explore various ways of making very small shapes and very large shapes. Also begin to explore various ways of getting from one to the other, sometimes fast, sometimes slow, sometimes sharp, sometimes calm and smooth.

   REFLECTIVE QUESTIONS   How would you describe the difference between the feeling of a shape that is small and tight and one that is large, open, and stretched out? What feeling do you get when you go from one to the other?

Improvisations

1. Create a very small movement with your right index finger. Repeat it over and over. Analyze the movement. Is it bending and stretching? Wagging? Circling? Now take that same movement and do it using your left arm. Because you are using a larger portion of the body, the movement will become bigger. You may need to take more time to complete the same movement. Continue this movement over and over, thinking about how the movement is the same as when you were doing it with just your finger and how it is different. Now transfer this same movement to a movement that uses the entire body. Make sure you hold on to the essence of the original movement you were doing with your finger. Find a way to repeat the movement involving the entire body. Once you have figured out one solution, can you find another way to transfer the movement to whole-body movement? Keep exploring different ways to do this. Which one seems the closest to the original movement?

2. Do this improvisation with a partner. First you create a very small movement that you can repeat over and over and show it to your partner. Your partner should learn the movement and perform it with you for a while until you are both performing it with the same accuracy. Then your partner will take that movement and transfer it to a different body part. You learn the new movement from your partner and then transfer it to

another body part. Keep doing this, passing the movement back and forth to each other and changing the part of the body that performs the movement. Allow the movement to change in size and timing according to the size of the body part used.

REFLECTIVE QUESTIONS What changes do you have to make to transfer a movement from one body part to another? What part of the movement can remain the same?

3. Walk around the room using a normal-size step that feels comfortable to you. Notice the size of your steps and how they relate to the other dancers' steps. Now increase the size of your steps. Make them very big—so big that you almost have to jump to take the step forward, as if you are trying to step across something very wide, such as a puddle, or a patch of mud. Notice what happens to the rest of your body as you attempt these extremely large steps. Now switch to very tiny steps. Continue taking your steps at the same speed, but make the steps very small. Then try them very fast, then very slow. Notice what happens to the rest of your body as you take these very small steps.

4. Repeat the previous exploration with a repetitive movement from a particular technique. You may choose any movement that is performed in repetition, such as piqué turns from classical ballet, three step turns from jazz, waltz clog in tap, or a suspend-and-fall sequence from modern dance. Explore many kinds of repetitious movement, either those that travel across the floor or those that stay in place. Create your own repetitious movement and explore ways to change the size of the movement. Note the effect of the changes.

REFLECTIVE QUESTIONS How does size affect a simple movement, such as walking? How might you use this to create intent?

5. Sitting on the floor, explore movement that stays on the floor in a low level. Explore all the space around you with your arms, head, torso, legs, and other body parts. Keep moving on the floor, finding different ways to support your weight by sitting and lying down. Find ways to travel through space without leaving the floor. Find ways to turn, slide, extend, roll, fall, and so on. Next, explore movement at a high level while standing, reaching, or jumping. Again, explore all the space around you. Make your movements as high as possible. Although your movements must be supported from the floor, focus on the movement that takes place far away from your support, in the air. Consider changing your means of support, but keep your focus on movement at the high level. Travel through space trying to fill the space above you. Finally, explore movement that takes place in the space between this low space, which is close to the floor, and this high space, which is as far above your means of support as possible. Think of having to perform in a space that has a low ceiling, requiring you to duck or kneel. Explore all the space around you in this middle range. Again, explore different ways to support you and find ways to travel.

6. Explore contrast: Create movement with a partner that uses various levels. If your partner is dancing on the floor, you must be either high or in the middle space. Try not to plan. Be playful. Find ways to surprise each other by changing quickly and chasing each other from one level to the next. Put on some lively music and explore moving very close together and very far apart, keeping an eye on your levels, always contrasting with the level of your partner.

REFLECTIVE QUESTIONS How does the level of movement in space affect its intent visually? Kinesthetically? • How are relationships between dancers affected by the use of levels?

Discussion of Key Concept

Because dance uses the body as an instrument, and because it is impossible to dance without the body, the elements of size, body part, and level are inseparable from every movement exploration. Rather than treat these elements of space separately, this text uses these elements to provide possible variations in many movement explorations. Levels in space and variations in body parts were introduced in chapter 2 during improvisations. However, their effect has not been discussed. And since the effect is spatial, a discussion of that effect belongs in the category of spatial elements. Definitions only are provided here, but you will find a focus on them in every spatial exploration that follows.

- **Size**—Size may refer to the shape of the entire body or a movement being performed. Again, size is relative. A shape may be as small as possible and as large as possible. Size may expand in all three dimensions, up and down, side to side, and forward and back. A movement, such as a step, may be very small or very large or somewhere in between. Very large movements can be seen easily by an audience, whereas very small movements require focus in order not to be missed. Exploring shapes and movements in all sizes rather than what seems normal or typical to the dancer will broaden the scope of movement choices available in the creation of a dance.

- **Body parts**—Isolated body parts are used continuously in dance. Dancers in every dance discipline practice and perfect the use of individual body parts as well as full-body movement. Some techniques isolate individual body parts more frequently than others. Hindu dancers' and Balinese dancers' eyes and hands are choreographed with incredible detail, whereas classical ballet dancers must focus on isolating the legs and arms from the torso, with little movement for the eyes, hands, and feet other than to extend a straight or curved line. Transferring movement from one body part to another creates automatic movement variation, because each body part moves according to its unique structure and mobility. Entire dances may be constructed with one movement only, changing from one body part to another, or combining body parts, because this provides numerous possibilities.

- **Levels**—Low level, middle level, and high level are relative terms that provide a description for the space the body occupies during a dance in relation to the surface supporting the dancer, such as the floor or ground. Low is the closest to the floor, or supporting surface. For the able-bodied dancer in the studio or on the stage, this involves movement or positions that occur on the floor, usually with some means of support other than the feet, such as sitting or lying down. A person dancing in a wheelchair might not be able to get this low but can create a lowness to his or her movements or positions within the wheelchair. Each dancer must find his or her lowest level of movement for this category. High, as relative to low and the supporting surface, is movement that occurs as far away from the supporting surface as possible. Obviously, the body must remain supported, except for possible short bursts of time in the air during jumps. So a high level is usually performed with support on the feet, with movement occurring through the space above. This does not preclude an acrobat from dancing upside down with support on the hands and with the feet stretched upward. This would also be considered working in a high level. Relative to these two extremes is the middle level. It should be considered as halfway between low and high. Support might be on the feet in a rather deep plié, on the knees, or on the elbows; the majority of the movement occurs in this in-between space, neither high nor low. To this I like to add artificially high, which refers to the use of props, scenery, or a partner to raise the level of the dancer even higher than the dancer might accomplish alone. Working in this level requires a degree of safety precautions. Exploring movement in all levels provides variation and depth to choreography (see figure 4.1 on page 52).

Figure 4.1 Contrasting levels provide interest in choreography.

Variations in size, body parts, and level provide opportunities for contrast and design in your choreography (see figure 4.2). Whoever directs movement improvisations should take the opportunity often to suggest exploring changing size, transferring movement or focus to a new body part, or moving in a different level spatially. If you are directing others in improvisations, noticing a lack of variation in these areas will allow you to suggest more interesting explorations and help other students as they become caught in their own clichés.

Movement Studies

1. Create a movement study that uses only one small movement that changes from one body part to another. Begin with the simple movement, repeating it a few times and then allowing it to change size, level, and timing according to how it changes to different parts of the body. Keep your transitions smooth and create a beginning, middle, and end.

2. Create a duet that includes the use of levels to designate a relationship between the two dancers. The two dancers may never be in the same

Figure 4.2 Focus on the hand (body part) while contrasting levels and size.

level at the same time. Create a sequence of events for these dancers that is supported by your use of levels. For example, one sequence might be argument, followed by reconciliation, followed by leadership.

3. Create a sequence of steps using a classroom technique that travels across the floor. Repeat the sequence varying the size, level, and body part creating the movement. See how many variations of the original movement sequence that you can create. Create a movement study with a beginning, middle, and end that includes the original movement phrase and variations created by levels, size, and changing body parts.

Assessment

Use these assessment tools in evaluating your progress toward understanding size, body parts, and level as key spatial concepts in choreography.

Class Critique

- Identify variations that occur in size, the use of body part, and the use of levels. Reflect on any emotional content or narrative that may surface using these variations.

- Note variations in overall design that occur in the works. How do these variations create interesting design visually? How does this relate to the combinations you have performed in class? Are some designs more interesting than others?

- What should you think about as you create these designs in order to create the most interest in your choreography?

Rubric

Following is a sample rubric that you may use in evaluating the third movement study for size, body parts, and levels. Try filling in evaluator comments for yourself and for your peers, or create your own criteria according to what you believe to be important in the understanding of these key spatial concepts.

Rubric for Size, Body Parts, and Levels in Space

Criteria	Strong evidence (2 points)	Little or no evidence (1 point)
Clear variations in size		
Clear transformation of movement from one body part to another		
Clear variations in level		
Total: (maximum 6 points)		

Documentation

Partner with someone else and videotape that person's work. Identify all the variations of size, body part, and level that you see in your partner's work and label it on the video by adding narrative or labeling stopped frames as slides. Exchange videos with your partner after you have identified these spatial variations so that each of you has your own work that you may add to your portfolio. Indicate with your work any areas that were intended to show variation that your partner did not identify. Comment on how you might have made these variations stronger or more evident. Or if you think it was okay that these variations went unnoticed, comment on why.

Performance Space

 Essential Question

How does a dancer's place in the performance space affect the intent of choreography?

Warm-Up

1. Assume a constructive rest position on the floor with your eyes closed. Lie on your back with your knees bent, feet flat on the floor, and knees leaning in toward each other and resting together so that no muscular effort is necessary to remain still. Fold your arms across your chest (see figure 2.1 on page 19). Quietly focus on your breathing. As you inhale, feel as though all your joints are filling with air; as you exhale, feel the joints release toward the floor. Continue this breathing as you search with your mind's eye to joints that need releasing. Focus on the full range of joints, starting at the neck (pause to allow one breathing sequence for each new joint named), thoracic spine, lumbar spine, sacrum, hip joints, knees, ankles, feet, toes, shoulder blades, shoulders, elbows, wrists, hands, and fingers. Shift position as you inhale or exhale to facilitate joint release if necessary. Now, still with your eyes closed, focus your concentration on the space around you. Without leaving the position of lying on your back, begin to explore the space above you with your arms, legs, head, and shoulders. How far away from the floor can you reach without allowing your back to leave the floor? Now shift your weight to one side and continue to explore the space around you, leaving your side anchored to the floor. Then shift to the other side. Finally, roll to a prone position and try to explore the space beside and behind you without lifting your hips off the floor. You have been exploring movement that takes place in your personal space.

2. Stand with your legs slightly apart and open your eyes using an internal focus. With the knees slightly bent, begin shifting your weight back and forth between your two feet. As you do this, begin to develop a sense of place, where you are in the room, where your center is, and how you are establishing your balance in that space. Although you may shift your weight back and forth, maintain that space in the room and do not move away from it. Remain anchored to that one spot by at least one body part at all times. Leaving your left foot anchored, explore ways to shift out to your right foot, and then return. Add upper-body movement and arms to this step out and return. Use this extra movement to explore additional space around you. Try stepping in many directions. You may change your facing direction and turn as long as your left foot remains anchored to the same spot on the floor. Repeat with the other foot, anchoring the right foot in place. Explore anchoring various body parts to your spot in place. Sit on the floor and place your left hand on the floor. Explore ways that the rest of the body may stretch out into new space without letting the hand leave its anchor. You may turn around the hand, but the hand must not leave its spot. Continue to explore anchoring various body parts, and create various kinds of movement in and out from the anchor point. Vary your energy and control. Progress toward changing the anchor point to different body parts as you move so that it is not always the same part that remains in place, but make sure the anchor point stays in the same spot on the floor. You may change levels, the size of your movement, and the body parts that are moving. Stay true to the intent of moving only from one spot, never traveling. Find a logical conclusion to your exploration and finish in a standing position. You have been working in what we call self-space.

3. Begin walking around the room. Be aware of the people around you. Do not allow yourself to touch anyone else in the room as you travel, and do not follow anyone else around the room. Create your own pathways. If you feel there are spaces in the room not being used, try to fill up those spaces with your pathways, but do not touch any of

the boundaries in the room, such as walls, barres, and mirrors. Make sure you maintain space between the boundaries in the room and the other dancers in the room, and pay attention to the new spaces that are being created between dancers and between dancers and boundaries. Begin to explore ways to pass through those spaces. Now, paying attention only to the spaces being created by dancers, try to decrease the amount of space between all the dancers without actually touching each other. You must continue your walking. Be very aware of what is happening around you so that you can adjust your pathways to the movement of others. Take initiative in finding new directions. You do not always have to walk forward, but be careful not to run into anyone if you decide to move backward or sideways. You must watch where you are going. Gradually decrease the space again, allowing yourself to brush lightly against other dancers, but keep your movement along pathways flowing through the space. Now gradually begin to open up the spaces. Increase the distance between you and the other dancers. Find the farthest possible distance in this particular performance space, and continue to create pathways through the space. Remember to look at the distance between you and others from all directions. Now, as a group, decide on a time to stop walking, and everyone should stop at the same time. You have been moving in general space.

REFLECTIVE QUESTIONS   Using these explorations, how would you describe personal space, self-space, and general space? How are they similar? How are they different?

Improvisations

1. In this improvisation, you will work in both general space and self-space, alternating between the two. Begin by walking, as you were doing in the previous warm-up. Again, be aware of everyone around you and create spaces and walk through spaces created by others. Whenever you feel like it, you may stop in one of those spaces that you have been walking through and explore movement in self-space. Remember that once you transition to working in self-space, you must remain anchored to one spot. You may change levels and means of support. You may sit, lie down, spin, or jump, but you must remain in one spot. Never take more than one step away from an anchor point. When you choose to walk and when you choose to explore movement in one spot are up to you. However, you should pay attention to the entire group and the energy and space being used and try to use as much variety as possible in the improvisation. Begin by spreading out around the room. Everyone should begin by walking. After exploring this improvisation for a few minutes, the entire group should come to a logical conclusion and stop all at the same time. Not everyone has to be standing or walking at the end. You must be very aware of each other at all times in order for this to work.

   REFLECTIVE QUESTIONS   In this particular improvisation, how did the feel of the movement in self-space differ from the feel of the movement in general space? • What are some of the differences in intent that you noted while watching the other dancers?

2. Stand very close to a partner. You should be close enough so that you can easily touch or embrace each other, but you are not to touch each other at all. Decide on an anchor point in order to work in self-space. Explore ways to work in self-space from this position without actually touching each other. Begin moving very slowly so that you can anticipate your partner's movements and react in order to get out of the way or provide space for your partner to move through. Explore ways to move over, under, around, and through your partner without leaving your own self-space. You may change facing directions, levels, the size of your movements, and the body parts you are moving. You may also change the body part that remains anchored to the floor. Use movements that you discovered in the second warm-up to add variation to your choices. Change partners and

repeat the improvisation. You may adapt this improvisation to include three dancers by having the dancers stand in a very tight triangle to begin.

REFLECTIVE QUESTIONS   What challenges did you face as you tried to work within self-space as it overlapped with the personal space of your partner? • How does it feel to have someone working within your personal space?

3. Repeat the first improvisation with a slight variation. This time, when you choose to work in self-space, get very close to someone else, making sure that person notices you, as you begin your self-space movement. This will cue that dancer to stop and also work in self-space as in the second improvisation. You might want to actually get in another dancer's pathway to force that dancer to stop and notice you. Or you could begin walking side by side with another dancer, or follow or lead another dancer to signal an intent to work together and then both of you begin dancing in self-space at the same time. When someone comes up to you and begins working in self-space, you must follow that lead and change to self-space. In this way you will be creating duets moving in self-space while others are walking through general space. Again, pay attention to the entire group to create as much variation as possible for the improvisation as a whole. Find a logical conclusion for the entire group and end the improvisation.

REFLECTIVE QUESTION   How did the intent in this improvisation differ from the intent in the first improvisation?

4. Repeat this improvisation one more time, only this time instead of working in self-space close to someone else, make eye contact with someone very far away from you, and you will both begin working in self-space at the same time. You will choose to end your self-space exploration and begin walking again at the same time. This is much more difficult because you have to make sure you are both aware of your intent to move in self-space before you begin, and the person must be as far away from you as possible in the room. You must not talk and plan while you are close to each other. This should be a spontaneous improvisation. Remain focused on each other as you explore your self-space so that you know when to begin walking again. The choice should be mutual.

REFLECTIVE QUESTION   How did the intent of the duets in this improvisation differ from those in the previous improvisation?

5. Stand at one side of the room with a partner. Begin moving in self-space together as in the previous improvisations. Pay attention to each other's movements and adjust your movements accordingly. After you get a flow of movement established, begin traveling slowly across the floor, staying very close together. Do this by shifting your anchor point in the new direction and wait for your partner to catch up. Then shift again. The same person may lead all the way across or you may change, whichever seems most natural according to the improvisation you have established. The improvisation is finished when you reach the other side of the performance space. Take your time to explore possibilities.

6. Repeat the previous improvisation, but increase the space between you and your partner. It will become more important to focus on your partner and react accordingly since you are farther apart. It should be a duet, however, so your movements need to show the intent of working together. Try doing it once across the room with one person leading, and then explore ways to alternate the lead. Use your partner's movements to give you ideas for your own movement by choosing to react to or answer your partner's movement. If your partner is moving at a high level, you might decide to cower at a low level. Or if your partner runs past you, you might want to spin to try to maintain a focus. You

might mirror high energy or contrast it. Again, try to think of ways to provide maximum variation in your movement with consideration to logical intent. The variations will help you to develop new movement vocabulary for yourself. Explore increasing the space between you even more until you are actually moving around the room rather than across it in order to allow you to stay a maximum distance apart.

REFLECTIVE QUESTIONS How did the intent of the duets change as each of you began to travel in general space? • How did the intent change as the space between you and the other dancer increased?

Discussion of Key Concept

Terms that define a dancer's place on the stage or in the performance area are generally arbitrary. There are really only two possibilities. Either a dancer remains in one spot or the dancer travels through the performance space. The space that exists around the dancer and how that space is defined by other dancers, props, and set pieces make it advantageous to consider more than two concepts within this discussion of stage space. As you consider designing the space of your dance, you must consider not only the space defined by the dancer but also the relationships the dancer creates in that space. And since dancers are people with emotions, you should consider the psychological aspect of these relationships as well as the design.

Personal Space

All of us have thought about our own personal space and how we exist in a bubble, which is that space around us that we do not like others to intrude on. There is much discussion about how large that space is and how our comfort with others entering our space differs depending on experience, personality, and culture. **Personal space** may be defined as the space reaching outward from the center of the body that may be reached by the extremities as the dancer travels. You carry your personal space with you wherever you go. Rudolf von Laban called this space your kinesphere, or the sphere in which your body moves. Expanding this personal space or shrinking it may contribute to the intent of your work. For example, a dancer who moves with bent arms and legs, a slouched torso, and a sinking head will have created a very small personal space and will have a very different expression than a dancer who moves with arms and legs stretching out as far as possible and head reaching high, expanding personal space.

Self-Space

The difference between personal space and **self-space** is that you take your personal space with you when you travel, but you are working in self-space only when you do not travel. Self-space is anchored to one spot in the performance space. Another common term for movement that occurs in self-space is axial movement, or movement that occurs around the center axis of your body. Self-space rather than axial movement is used in this text because there are an infinite number of possibilities for movement in self-space, whereas axial movement is often defined as a limited list of movements. Dancing in self-space may seem restricting to the dancer, especially if the movements have a great deal of energy. Or it may simply seem as if the dancer is comfortable, and traveling to a new space is simply unnecessary. Contrasting between movement that travels and movement that stays in place provides variation in choreography and can be used effectively in solo work.

General Space

Movement that travels through the performance space and is not anchored to one spot is considered movement in general space. **General space** is shared by all the performers and may be manipulated by numbers of dancers, props, and environment or set design. General space may be vast if the space is large and a solo dancer is using it. Or it may seem crowded with increased numbers of dancers. It may seem full of energy if a lot of dancers are moving through general space, or it may seem static if a soloist moving in general space is being contrasted with a group of dancers using only self-space. It is more difficult for one dancer to create energy in general space than it is for multiple dancers. However, we have all seen those performers who seem to electrify the space around them. Note that it takes more effort for one dancer to create energy in general space than it does for many working together in general space.

Relationships

George Balanchine (1904-1983), founder and artistic director of the New York City Ballet, once explained that he need not consider stories in his choreography, because the art form of dance, because of its use of the human body, creates stories for us. Often it is the relationships that develop in the choreography that enhance these stories. Relationships should be considered not only with other dancers but with the environment in which each dancer performs. Relationships may be enhanced by lighting effects as well, which you should research and explore when you begin to produce your work for the stage. As a beginning choreographer, you may be reluctant to place dancers extremely close together, as was required in the previous improvisations. However, some of the most interesting relationships develop when dancers are required to adjust and react to one another in this tight space. It can be extremely intimate but it can also be combative, depending on the movement that is created and its intent. These duets may progress to actual physical contact, and contact improvisation, which is discussed in chapter 10. As relationships develop, additional space is created that could not occur with a single dancer because of the connecting lines and shapes. This should be considered by the choreographer even when the distance between dancers or a dancer and a set piece or prop is great. For now, the focus should be on the intent created by distances either far or near. Near may include beside, in front, in back, over, under, above, below, around, and through. When dancers are far apart, it is more difficult to envision relationships, but there are any number of reasons for creating space between a relationship; the obvious reason is to symbolize distance that is even greater either physically or conceptually. Traditionally, a close relationship will depict intimacy, and a far relationship will depict distance and isolation.

Split Focus

A choreographic trick may be used in regard to placing distance between dancers (see figure 4.3). On a **proscenium** stage, people viewing from the orchestra section will find it virtually impossible to watch dancers at opposite sides of the stage at the same time. If two dancers are placed far apart on the stage, the audience has to make a choice about which dancer to watch or

Figure 4.3 Split focus requires the audience to choose which group to watch.

will have to keep looking back and forth. We call this a **split focus**. If you want your audience to be able to see all the action at once, then you must move your dancers together. However, split focus may be very effective if you have two or more dancers who have difficulty moving in unison with precision but you want to create the effect derived from unison movement. Or you may have dancers working together who are not matched in their ability to perform a technique, and you might want to disguise that. If it is impossible for the audience to watch them all at the same time, the audience may be fooled into thinking they are moving at the same time or with the same level of technique using split focus. Or you may simply be interested in the effect created that causes the audience to continually roam the stage with their eyes to see what is going on. This can give the illusion of chaos if everyone is doing something different. It is important to also realize that if you have a particular movement that you want the audience to see, split focus will take the attention away from your intended focal point. So you must give your audience more time to shift to that intended focal point, or you must greatly increase the dynamics at the focal point using energy, sound, or lighting to draw all eyes back to that area of the stage or performance space (see figure 4.4).

Movement Studies

1. Create a group dance with five or more dancers that explores the effects created by the use of general space as opposed to the use of self-space. Play with the contrast to create your intent. Keep it short. You may use the previous improvisations to help you create the movement, but make choices about which movements to save and use to be the most effective for your finished work.

2. Create a duet that explores the two extremes in relationships: very near and very far away. After creating the work, step back and watch it, making a decision about what the meaning of the relationship is that you have developed. Tweak it to emphasize the narrative that has developed, and prepare it for viewing. Be careful not to overdo the narrative. Focus on the relationships and allow the narrative to come from the movement rather than create the movement to fit a narrative.

Assessment

Use these assessment tools in evaluating your progress toward understanding the use of performance space as a key concept in choreography.

Figure 4.4 The group on stage left (right side of the picture) is strong enough to draw the audience's eyes away from stage right.

Class Critique

- What is your favorite part of the work you are critiquing? Why did it work for you? What happened in the use of the stage space that created this effect?
- What suggestions do you have concerning the use of stage space in the work? Try a few alternative choices by suggesting changes in only the use of stage space (not the movement) in the work (ask someone traveling to stay in self-space, or place two dancers very close together who were far apart). Discuss what happened as these changes were made.

Rubric

Following is a sample rubric that you may use in evaluating the second movement study for performance space. Try filling in evaluator comments for yourself and for your peers, or create your own criteria according to what you believe to be important in the understanding of performance space.

Rubric for Performance Space

Criteria	Strong evidence (2 points)	Little or no evidence (1 point)
Contrasting use of self-space and general space		
Narrative supported by the use of near and far		
Total: (maximum 4 points)		

Documentation

Videotape your work. Make sure you place the camera in a location that will encompass the entire performance space so that you will be able to see how the space is used. Do not move the camera while you are taping. Use a tripod. Include comments and a completed rubric with each work you record, and add it to your portfolio. You may wish to include comments on intent and energy as well.

Drawing Conclusions

Breaking the Rules

1. Manipulate personal space. Instead of using personal space in a traditional way, which would be to overlap personal space to depict intimacy and expand personal space to depict isolation, try creating a dance that does the opposite. Use overlapping personal space to depict isolation and expanding personal space to depict intimacy. Typically an isolated person would not allow anyone to come near him. That person has an expanded bubble that moves with him that he will not allow anyone to enter without extreme discomfort. You expand personal space by placing the dancers far away from each other. Hint: Try creating an intimate duet with overlapping personal space and then have the dancers spread out across the room and repeat the same movements alone, as if someone was there. Have them perform this at the same time. Do the same with isolation. Create a duet with the dancers far apart, and then place them very close together. Ask them to attempt the same choreography. You may have to make a few adjustments to accommodate the changed spacing.

2. Try creating a feeling of static space by using a lot of dancers moving in general space. Also try creating dynamic space using one dancer in self-space. Hint: Energy is created by the perceived effort of the dancers.

REFLECTIVE QUESTIONS   How was the intent (intimacy and isolation) affected by reversing the traditional use of personal space? How might you use this in your choreography in the future? • Is it possible to create a static effect using a lot of dancers moving through general space? If so, what are some choices for movement that seem to work? • What must you consider as a choreographer when creating a solo in order to develop spatial energy?

 ## Essential Question

Why do line and shape affect intent in choreography?

Warm-Up

1. Lie on the floor in any position you like. Close your eyes and take a few moments to focus your concentration inward. Slowly curl your body up into as tight a shape as you can. Feel the curves in your body. Identify where the curves are happening, such as your spine and your arms. Anywhere else? Now slowly stretch out your body so that your hands and feet are as far away from the center of your body as possible. Feel the shape that has been created. Notice the straight lines that resulted from stretching out. Slowly draw up into a tight shape again, feeling the curves as they form. Again, slowly extend into a stretched-out shape, noting the straight lines as they form. Continue alternating between tight and curved to stretched out and straight, getting gradually faster each time you repeat the sequence. You need not return to exactly the same shape each time. Explore various ways to go from tight to stretched out, but remain at a low level on the floor. Once you explore moving from one to the other in approximately one count, begin to slow down again gradually until you come to a stillness. Wait for the others to complete their movement.

2. Beginning from a standing and very stretched-out shape with straight lines, repeat the prevous warm-up by gradually folding into a tight curved shape. Your tight shape may still be at a high level supported by one leg, or you may return to a low level on the floor. Try exploring ways to change levels in each shape, finding curved tight shapes at low, middle, and high levels and finding straight stretched-out shapes at high, middle, and low levels. Increase your speed gradually, then decrease and find a stillness, waiting for others to finish.

REFLECTIVE QUESTIONS   How do you feel when you are moving into a tight curved shape? How do you feel when you are moving into an open stretched-out straight shape? • How does the timing affect how you feel? • How do these shapes affect the intent of your movement?

Improvisations

1. Working in self-space in any level you like, create shapes with your body that include all curved lines. If you have a mirror available, you may want to use it at this point to check the visual effect of the shapes you are making. Sometimes curves feel straight, and straight lines feel curved. If you do not have a mirror, work in pairs and help each other create shapes that include only curved lines.

   Note: It is easy to create curved lines in the torso, because the bones in the spine are small with many tiny joints between each. However, the arms and legs have long straight bones with few joints that move. Giving the appearance of a curve with long straight bones is more difficult. You have to be careful not to create angles. After exploring many curved shapes, you should be able to find a curved shape without looking in the mirror or without the aid of a partner. Since you are creating static shapes, this is one improvisation where you may stop and think and plan rather than move continuously.

REFLECTIVE QUESTION   What visual and emotional effects are created by curved lines?

2. Repeat the previous improvisation using shapes created with straight lines.

REFLECTIVE QUESTION   What visual and emotional effects are created by straight lines?

3. Beginning in self-space, but allowing yourself to move through general space, create a curved shape as a starting position. Explore moving from one curved shape to another, acquiring a constant flow to your movement and continuing to move through curved shapes at all times. Do not allow the body to transition through straight lines. Explore tight curved shapes as opposed to open curved shapes. Try undercurves (a curve that forms a bowl under something above you is an undercurve) and overcurves (a curve that forms a dome over something under you is an overcurve).

REFLECTIVE QUESTION What is the difference between the effect of an overcurve and the effect of an undercurve? As a choreographer, when would you choose curved lines as you create?

4. Repeat the previous improvisation using straight shapes that travel through general space. Explore long straight lines and shorter lines that create angles.

REFLECTIVE QUESTIONS What is the difference between the effect of a long straight line and a short angular line? As a choreographer, when would you choose straight lines as you create?

5. Group **sculpture**: One person enters the performance space and creates a curved shape. The next person joins the first and creates a curved shape that is complementary to the first shape. Continue this process until you have five or six dancers in the sculpture. Each dancer entering the sculpture must find a shape that belongs in the sculpture and creates added interest. Use one of the following methods to make sure your shape is complementary to the group. Imitate the lines created by another dancer with one or more body parts. Create parallel lines that are pleasing to the eye. Or continue a line created by another dancer. For example, if a dancer has created a half circle with his or her torso, you may complete the circle either with your torso or with another body part. Or you could reverse the curve and create an S curve between you. Another method that does not relate directly to line and design but helps to unify a sculpture is to enter the sculpture by creating intent. For example, you may notice a dancer caressing the air with an open circular shape created with the arms. You may enter that space between that dancer's arms and be a person that dancer is caressing. Continue creating sculptures with the class until everyone has been involved in viewing and creating.

REFLECTIVE QUESTION What is the overall effect of a group sculpture that contains all curved lines?

6. Repeat the previous group sculpture using shapes with straight lines.

REFLECTIVE QUESTION What is the overall effect of a group sculpture that contains all straight lines?

7. Group sculpture combining lines: Repeat the group sculpture improvisation, but allow each person to choose a shape that is curved or straight, rather than dictate one or the other. Make sure the sculpture stays unified and pleasing to the eye without confusion.

REFLECTIVE QUESTION How does the use of line and shape help to create a unified effect in a group sculpture? • What happens when many kinds of lines are created in a dance sculpture? When is this effective and when is it not?

Discussion of Key Concept

Line and shape are the primary choreographic concepts used in developing design in dance. That design is also instrumental in the development of emotional content. The reason for this is our innate ability to read body language. By analyzing the shapes people create during various emotional states, you can use those shapes to create emotional content in your choreography.

Creating design for your dance may be very simple or extremely complex. Simple and coordinated lines within a shape may be read by an audience clearly and may guide the eye as it travels through the choreography. Complicated lines that are random and askew may be chaotic and confusing to the eye, resulting in a lack of **focus** and an agitated audience. Both of these may be valid according to the choreographer's intent. They could also have a negative effect toward the intended outcome. Oversimplification may be predictable and boring. Yet choreography that is too busy may be difficult to watch.

It is important not to spend endless hours creating material for your choreography without regard to the lines and shapes that are being created, both within the individual dancers and for the dancers in relation to each other and to the stage space. If you create material as is habitual for technique classes, you may discover movement that feels great but has no contribution to the spatial design of your work. Because technique classes are focused on individual perfection, usually little attention is given to the relationship between dancers. Most "performances" in class take place in unison, with all dancers performing exactly the same combination at exactly the same time. This may or may not be optimal for your choreography. You need to analyze the combination for line and shape in order to determine its value as choreographic material. And you need to consider how these lines and shapes fit together as you **arrange** combinations of movement.

Interestingly enough, unison dancing does provide a very simple way to acquire **complementary lines**, which is why it is used so often in recitals and why Marius Petipa used it to extreme in his full-length ballets. Petipa (1818-1910) was artistic director and primary choreographer for the St. Petersburg Ballet from 1862 to 1903. He was known for his evening-length ballets, the most famous of which are *Swan Lake* (in collaboration with Ivanov; see figure 4.5), *Sleeping Beauty*, and *La Bayadère*. However, it is also important to note that pure unison dancing that is effective in its simplicity is very difficult to obtain and usually requires many rehearsals and the competence of well-trained dancers. A choreographer who uses unison to provide simplicity, stability, and balance must consider the dancers' size, structure, and ability. Not everyone can dance *Swan Lake* effectively. Nor can most student dancers be precise in executing new choreography given to them by a peer with a limited amount of rehearsal. For this reason and for reasons discussed in chapter 10, you are encouraged to use unison dancing sparingly in your early attempts at choreography.

Figure 4.5 *Swan Lake.*

It is worth discussing a few simple rules when using line and shape to depict emotional content. Overcurves and forward curves connote introversion. These shapes are usually protective and pull into the body's core. You think of someone who is slumped forward in her stance as being sad, shy, or inferior. Or an overcurve may be protective, as a mother curves over a child (see figure 4.6). Undercurves and curves that lean backward connote extroversion or an open and welcoming feeling (see figure 4.7). Undercurves that reach to the sky may beckon a spiritual guidance or welcome a gift with thanks. The suggested energy created by these curves is gentle, comfortable, and flowing. A backward curve of the torso, particularly when accompanied by strength and energy and the eyes focused high, connotes confidence and pride.

Long straight lines usually connote extroversion. The eye is directed in straight lines away from the center of the body with strength and power (see figure 4.8 on page 66). These can be used to show anger that is ready to strike out or a boldness that is ready for action. Short and **acute angles** (less than 90 degrees) may connote potential energy, like a cat ready to spring.

Mixing lines can show internal conflict of one or more dancers. If the torso is placed in an overcurve with the head and arms in an undercurve, you might interpret that dancer to be struggling internally and searching for help. Changing from curved to straight may communicate indecision (see figure 4.9 on page 66). A mixture of curved and straight lines in the same shape might show two separate intents at the same time, such as being protective but wanting to escape.

If you create shape with your intent in mind, you will usually come up with the right shape without thinking about the lines you are using. But if you are having trouble coming up with a shape that works, you may try these simple rules to see if it helps you find a shape that communicates the intent you desire. You may also use these rules to evaluate a shape you have selected for a particular intent. If it is not working, these rules might tell you why.

Lines and shape do not have to have an emotional intent to be effective. Just as a visual artist draws and paints lines and shapes on a page, a dancer creates lines and shapes in the performance space. There are an infinite number of possibilities in creating designs using curved lines (see figure 4.10 on page 66) and straight lines (see figure 4.11 on page 66) to define your shapes. A great number of dances are created with design as the main intent of the work. Which designs are effective and which are not must be explored and evaluated according to the context in which they are created. Design is usually most effective when it is simple but with interesting variations and contrast (see figure 4.12 on page 67). An entire dance may be created around

Figure 4.6 A protective overcurve.

Figure 4.7 Undercurves are welcoming.

Figure 4.8 Straight lines and angles suggest power.

Figure 4.9 A shape that includes straight and curved lines might suggest conflicting emotions. This undercurve welcomes or searches for an answer while the straight lines show movement away from the searching, not wanting to know the answer.

Figure 4.10 These curves are created for the sake of design rather than meaning.

Figure 4.11 Straight lines may connect dancers by design rather than intent.

a diagonal line aimed in one direction in the stage space. The dancers' shapes may all be created in parallel lines complementary to each other as they travel through the space or find new levels and places on the stage. A surprising curve interspersed in the choreography may add contrast and interest, while the rest of the shapes remain similar in their variations on the original diagonal. The first movement of Alvin Ailey's *Revelations* is a beautiful example of simple design. The straight arms aimed toward the sky create strong emotional intent but also contribute to simple variation in design broken with surprising curves. (A video of *Revelations* is available on VHS: *An Evening with the Alvin Ailey American Dance Theatre*, presented by RM Arts, The Classis Performance Collection, 1986.)

Movement Studies

1. Think of some simple event that occurred to you recently that changed your feelings emotionally. You may have been anticipating a low grade on a test and discovered that you did very well. Or perhaps you were excited about going to a movie and discovered it was all sold out. Think of anything in which you can label two opposite emotions that occurred within

Figure 4.12 Group sculpture created with straight and curved lines.

a short span of time. Create a dance using lines and shapes to depict these emotions through a narrative. Do not concern yourself with acting out the actual story. Abstract the emotions from the story and turn those emotions into lines and shapes. Begin and end with a still shape, and create many shapes within the choreography that depict your emotions and the transitions as they change. You may create the shapes independently, but make sure they fit together logically in a dance with a beginning, middle, and end.

2. On a piece of paper, draw a combination of curved and straight lines that you find pleasing to the eye. Keep this simple. Make it an improvisational drawing—no one will evaluate it. Do not draw too many lines. Ask yourself this question as you create this drawing: Where does the eye look first? How does the eye travel across or around the drawing? You will use this information in creating your movement study. After you have completed your drawing, create a solo dance using the same lines from your drawing. Think first of the place where the eye begins in your drawing. If that is a straight line, then you should begin your dance with a straight shape similar to the one on your page. As the eye moves around the page to take in all the lines, create movement to coordinate with all the lines on the page. Focus on body shape rather than pathways of movement, because pathways will be discussed later in this chapter. Make sure your dance has a beginning, middle, and end and that all your transitions are logical.

Assessment

Use these assessment tools in evaluating your progress toward understanding line and shape as key concepts in choreography.

Class Critique

- Begin by identifying the lines and shapes in the work you observe. Discuss if and how these shapes contribute to emotional content in the work.

- If the work is abstract design without emotional contact, discuss what makes the design work and what might make the design more interesting.

- Since both of these movement studies are solos, discuss how the solos might be expanded to include group work. What would you have to consider as far as line and shape are concerned to expand the work for more than one dancer? Would this add or detract from the original solo?

Rubric

Following is a sample rubric that you may use in evaluating the first movement study for line and shape. Try filling in evaluator comments for yourself and for your peers, or create your own criteria according to what you believe to be important in the understanding of line and shape.

Rubric for Line and Space

Criteria	Strong evidence	Little or no evidence
Shapes clearly communicate emotional content through the use of curved and straight lines		
Logical narrative with smooth transitions and an obvious beginning, middle, and end		
Total: (maximum 4 points)		

Documentation

Videotape your work, save it to your computer, and choose individual still photos from the video to represent the collection of shapes you chose for your work. Use a software program such as PhotoStory (a free download from Microsoft) to create a slideshow with these frames. Add commentary for each slide that explains the lines used and the intended emotional content, if any. Save it in a folder with a copy of a completed rubric to evaluate your work. Add comments that describe the class critique as well. Include everything in your digital portfolio.

Drawing Conclusions

Breaking the Rules

1. Create a dance that depicts a shy character using shapes with all long straight lines.

2. Create a dance that depicts a bold character using shapes created by over-curves and forward curves.

REFLECTIVE QUESTIONS Why does shape communicate mood? What other choreographic concepts may be used to communicate mood? (Hint: Think about other spatial concepts and energy concepts.) • What happens when different elements communicate contrasting moods?

 Essential Question

Why would you choose to use either symmetry or asymmetry in your choreography?

Warm-Up

1. Repeat the warm-up as in chapter 3, item 2 in the Dynamics section (page 31). Repeat this swing continuously about 10 times or until you are well warmed up. Focus on keeping the right and left side of your body exactly the same at all times. This movement would be considered **flip symmetry**, if you consider the right side of your body symmetrical to the left side (see figure 4.13).

2. Keeping the body fairly straight, swing both arms together from side to side. Swing both arms right, then left, then right, and continue the swing into a circle over the head and down to the left and swing back to the right. Repeat the entire sequence, beginning left. This movement is a rough application of slide symmetry (see figure 4.14). It is rough because the body has depth and the elbows must bend in order for the arm to cross the body. If the body were completely flat and you could do this with completely straight arms, it would be precise in its slide symmetry.

3. Standing straight again, place your right arm high overhead and the left arm low at your side. Keeping your arms in front of you at all times, swing the arms forward to change places or until the left arm is high and the right arm is low. Repeat this swing several times. This movement is a good example of turn symmetry (see figure 4.15 on page 70).

4. Finish your warm-up by doing 16 jumping jacks. For those who may not have done these in school, begin with the arms down at your sides, standing with your feet together in first position. Jump out to second position with your feet, while your

Figure 4.13 In flip symmetry, shapes are mirrored, as if a page in a book is flipped. Triangles show oppositional direction of symmetry.

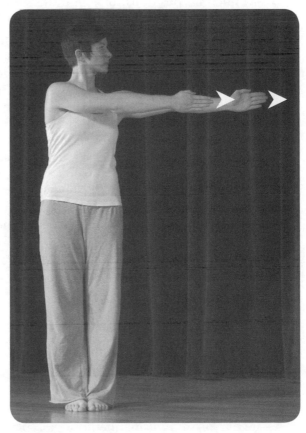

Figure 4.14 Slide symmetry, as in warm-up 2. Triangles show parallel direction of symmetry.

arms swing out to a high side position. Jump back to first position and bring the arms to your sides in the same path they came from. This movement is an example of **rotational symmetry**, if you consider a point in the center of your torso as the point of symmetry (see figure 4.16).

Improvisations

1. Choose a partner as close to your height as possible. This is the familiar mirror improvisation used in dance and theater to develop awareness of your partner. This time, you should focus on interesting symmetrical positions. Choose a leader. Stand facing each other and move together slowly, with the follower acting as the leader's mirror. While you are facing your partner, mirroring is fairly easy. Progress to working side by side, but make sure your symmetry is oppositional, or flipped, and not parallel, or slide. The line of symmetry is an imaginary line between you and your partner, where the mirror would be. Repeat with the other person leading. Make a mental note of some of the most interesting symmetrical positions you found, and show them to the rest of the group.

2. Again with a partner and with a line of symmetry between you, this time you will explore slides. The easiest way to begin is to stand side by side, facing the front. **Slide symmetry** is created when you do everything exactly the same as the other person. If the leader's right arm moves, your right arm moves. And it moves in exactly the same direction. The line of symmetry is the imaginary line that exists between you and your partner. Slide symmetry is created automatically when dance is in unison. Try turning to face a side wall. The follower must turn to face the same wall. Be careful not to revert to mirror (flip) symmetry.

3. Lie on the floor on your back side by side with a partner. Now only you turn yourself around, leaving your feet in the same spot, but your head is now 180 degrees from its original position. This is **turn symmetry** (see figure 4.17). The line is an imaginary horizontal line separating your feet and perpendicular to the vertical line of your bodies. Explore positions that use this form of symmetry. Begin by using the floor as a plane and move along it. You may have to talk to

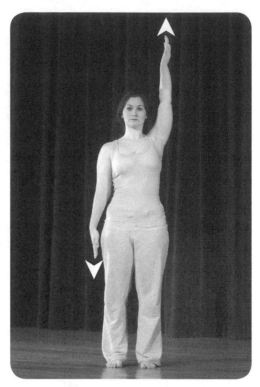

Figure 4.15 Turn symmetry, as in warm-up 3. Triangles show the direction of symmetry.

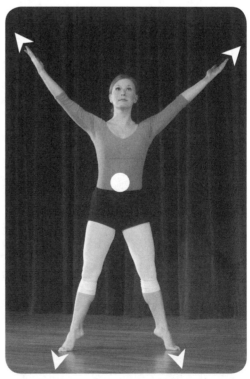

Figure 4.16 Rotational symmetry, as in warm-up 4. Point indicates point of symmetry. Triangles show direction of symmetry.

Figure 4.17 Turn symmetry for improvisation 3. Dotted line indicates the line of symmetry.

each other or sit up to look at each other and plan, because you cannot see each other from this position. Your movements should look opposite to each other horizontally, but they are really the same. For example, if you extend your left arm to the side, your partner should also extend his arm out to the left side. If you sit up in this position, you will be facing your partner and you can see well enough to do parallel movement that looks oppositional. Again, remember that the apparent oppositional movement in this case means you are really moving exactly the same way, only you are facing each other, so it looks opposite rather than the way it would look in a mirror. Next, consider how this might be done from a standing position. Can you think of any positions you might be able to sustain in a vertical plane that have turn symmetry?

4. Work in groups of five or six. Begin by lying on your backs on the floor with everyone's feet close together. Keep the distance between everyone the same so that your bodies make a kind of starburst shape. Then everyone sit up and reach the right arm to one side. This is rotational symmetry (see figure 4.18). The symmetrical movement rotates around a point, or the center of the small circle created by your feet. Explore ways in

Figure 4.18 Rotational symmetry for improvisation 4.

which the entire group can move in rotational symmetry. You need not stay sitting on the floor, although you should begin there until you get used to following each other. Everyone must do the same movement using the center of your circle as your front. Be careful also to keep equal distances between you and the next person around the circle as you explore movements away from the center.

REFLECTIVE QUESTIONS   How would you define symmetry, in general? (That is, how would you define it to include all types of symmetry?) • Which forms of symmetry have you seen used most often in dance? Relate what you now understand as the four types of symmetry to choreography you have seen in the past. • What effects are created when using symmetry? • What emotional content is created by these manipulations of line and design? • Why do some types of movement and shapes work better than others when creating symmetry?

5. Alternate between symmetry and asymmetry: Begin in a grouping of rotational symmetry as in the previous improvisation. After establishing movement using rotational symmetry, work as a group to logically, without stopping the improvisation, break the symmetry and move into a group sculpture that is not symmetrical. Make sure the transition into the new group shape is part of your improvisation. Do not stop the intent of your work. After holding a stillness in the group sculpture long enough to establish a strong intent, gradually change shapes individually and cooperatively to create a group sculpture that uses flip symmetry. You will do this by finding someone on the opposite side of a center line in the group in order to mirror their shape. If you have an odd number of dancers, at least one of you will have to create a symmetrical shape on the center line. Create interest by using lines and contrasting levels. Choose one side of the group to remain in place while the other side changes to new shapes, creating a total-group sculpture that once again is without symmetry. Hold this sculpture until everyone has established a new shape. As a group, decide on one person to imitate; everyone except that person changes shape to be exactly the same as the chosen shape. Try to do this without talking. If you move slowly enough, you will be able to follow each other easily.

Note: If this improvisation becomes confusing, return to the beginning and start again. It will become easier as everyone understands what is expected.

Once everyone has obtained the same shape, follow the "leader" in slow unison movements, which illustrate slide symmetry. During these slow sustained unison movements, each dancer may choose to break out and create different movement every so often but then return to the group, continuing the unison movement. Continue to do this more and more often until everyone is doing something different and contrasting to the original unison movement. Work in contrasting levels, amounts of energy, and shapes. Keep going until your instructor cues you. When your instructor says stop, everyone freeze in a shape.

REFLECTIVE QUESTIONS   What challenges do you face when working with symmetry? How do those challenges change when you are allowed to work without symmetry? • What differences did you observe between the overall effect of a symmetrical shape and the overall effect of a shape without symmetry? • What do you have to think about to make an effective symmetrical shape? What do you have to think about in order to create an effective shape without symmetry?

Discussion of Key Concept

Because of its nature of repetitive forms, symmetry automatically creates balance. Some forms of symmetry seem more balanced than others, particularly in dance when you consider that human beings are steadier when supported by their feet than when they are standing on their hands or heads. But a balance in design is created because shapes and movements are the same in all parts of the symmetrical design. All lines will be complementary and nothing will clash. It is a tool that creates interest in movements by providing some variation without having to vary movement. Busby Berkeley (1895-1976) was a film director and choreographer who used hundreds of showgirls all dressed alike and filmed from above to form kaleidoscopic effects using rotational symmetry. Berkeley used rotational symmetry to great advantage in his spectacular musicals that were filmed in the 1930s. It is easy for a choreographer to teach a sequence or phrase to a group, all at the same time, and then ask the group to perform the phrase together as a group, all facing the same way (slide), facing each other moving as a mirror (flip), in opposition (a form of turn that may be used more easily in dance so you do not have to stand on your head), or in a circle (rotate). *Slide, flip, turn,* and *rotate* are math terms rarely used in dance or choreography. Dance more often uses the terms *unison* for slide, *mirror* for flip, and *circle* for rotational symmetry. And dance rarely uses turn symmetry. However, by using a mathematical understanding of symmetry, you open up your concept of symmetry to many unusual possibilities you might otherwise ignore.

Because symmetry is such an effective tool in providing variation with complementary lines, it is often overused in choreography. It is important to remember that symmetry provides balance, stability, comfort, and even stasis; it is not appropriate for creating intent that is less comfortable, such as anger, frustration, fear, instability, excitement, surprise, or passage of time. If it is used often in a long work, it can become boring and predictable to the audience. Many choreographers use symmetry to begin and end a piece. It is an overused symbol that says, "I am about to repeat the same picture you had at the beginning so you will know this is the end." If the intent is to show a stable situation at the beginning and end, then the use of symmetry is appropriate (see figure 4.19). But if your intent is simply to leave the audience with a pretty picture and punctuate your work, you should think further about the intent of the work and what you want to say at the end. It is possible to punctuate and create beautiful, memorable pictures without using repetition and symmetry. You may want to consider stage

Figure 4.19 Group symmetry creates balance expressing stability that may be static.

balance instead. Anything that is not symmetrical is considered asymmetrical, or without symmetry. Stage balance is achieved through asymmetry when the size and number of dancers on one side of the stage seem to balance visually with those on the other side of the stage. They do not have to be equal or exactly the same. Many elements determine the visual weight of a dancer. A dancer using high energy would carry a lot of visual weight. A dancer moving in slow motion with very little energy would not carry very much weight regardless of size. Two small female dancers making a shape together in two different levels downstage left might balance one large male dancer upstage right. This is what is meant by balanced **asymmetry** (see figure 4.20). It is a good idea to keep your stage balanced regardless of whether you are using symmetry. It is not necessary for the stage to be balanced at every moment, but as your dance progresses, you will want your audience to perceive a balance of your use of stage space. The only exception might be a particular intent that intentionally created an off-balance feeling for your audience. All asymmetry creates an energy on the stage because it seems to suggest movement rather than stasis. Rather than encourage the eyes to settle in a central location, asymmetry moves the eyes around the stage space.

Movement Studies

1. Create a duet by building 10 symmetrical positions and creating transitions for the dancers to move from one position to the next. Use varied types of symmetry. Add the use of dynamics, energy flow, size, body parts, and levels to provide variation in your dance, especially during transitions. Be sure it has a beginning, middle, and end and that it is created with intent.

2. Create a duet. First create one short phrase of movement. Then create variations in your dance by implementing all four forms of symmetry. Do not use new material. Manipulate only the original material by finding variations in symmetry.

3. Create a group work that alternates between symmetry and asymmetry. Try to maintain a balance of stage space during the asymmetrical parts of the work. Again, create with intent and make sure you have a beginning, middle, and end.

Figure 4.20 Asymmetry may also be balanced but is usually dynamic, suggesting movement.

Assessment

Use these assessment tools in evaluating your progress toward understanding of symmetry and asymmetry as key concepts in choreography.

Class Critique

- Identify and evaluate the symmetrical shapes used in the choreography. Are these shapes interesting, or do you have suggestions for adding interest while preserving the symmetry?

- Is the choreographer able to create intent for the movement while maintaining a focus on design?

- Can you identify places where the intent is lost and suggest ways it might be added? Is the choreographer able to create interest in a work that is completely symmetrical? Why or why not?

- Identify moments when the stage space is balanced and when it is not. What suggestions do you have for creating balance in places where it is missing?

Rubric

Following is a sample rubric that you can use in evaluating the third movement study for symmetry and asymmetry. This is an example of a four-point rubric and shows a larger range in the evaluation of each criterion than previous samples. You may wish to use these criteria or create your own according to what you believe to be important in the understanding of these key concepts. See table 1.3 on page 14 for a sample of this rubric with evaluator comments.

Rubric for Symmetry and Asymmetry

Criteria	Strong evidence (4 points)	Some evidence (3 points)	Little evidence (2 points)	No evidence (1 point)
Clear use of symmetry and asymmetry				
Balance of stage space				
Clear movement intent				
Beginning, middle, and end				

Total: 9 (maximum 16 points)

Documentation

Record your work on video and save it as is, accompanied by a completed rubric. Also, in a separate folder, isolate the symmetrical shapes and the asymmetrical shapes as still photos in a slide show. Label them according to the type of symmetry they represent, or as asymmetry. Add the folder to your portfolio labeled as "examples of symmetry and asymmetry."

Drawing Conclusions

Breaking the Rules

1. Create a dance about frustration using all symmetrical design.

2. Create a dance that communicates stability, serenity, and stasis without using any symmetrical design.

REFLECTIVE QUESTIONS Why might you use symmetrical design to communicate instability and unbalanced mood in dancers? Is it even possible to communicate these states with the use of symmetrical design? • Why would you ever choose to use asymmetry to communicate stability, serenity, and stasis? Does it work?

 *Essential Question*

Why would a choreographer want to be aware of negative space in his or her choreography?

Warm-Up

1. Begin lying on the floor completely supine (on your back with legs straight) with arms a little open and flat against the floor. Take a few moments to find an internal focus, relaxing the joints and breathing freely. Begin to notice the spaces that are open between you and the floor: under your neck, your lower back, your knees, and so on. One at a time, try to squeeze out that space by pressing the body part above that space toward the floor. Then release and allow your body to return to normal. Now, by lifting parts of your body slightly, create new spaces under you, and then gently lower that body part, squeezing out the space. Try a different body part. Try your torso. You may allow yourself to roll and turn to find different ways to create space underneath you and then gently squeeze that space out by lowering yourself again to the floor. Gradually make the spaces bigger, which will lift you into the middle level. Always be aware of the space that is created and its shape before lowering and squeezing the space out. Continue to increase the spaces until you are actually lifting into a high level and then return back to the floor, still with the focus of empty space being created underneath you that you can squeeze out as you return to the floor. Create the space under you one more time, taking yourself to a high level. This time, stay at your high level and focus on the empty spaces around your body that you are making with the shapes of your arms, legs, torso, and head. After everyone is still, relax but remain standing.

2. Moving in general space, explore ways to sculpt the empty space around you. Slice, scoop, and mold the air around you. Allow yourself to change levels as you travel around the room. Use your arms, legs, torso, hands, head, or any body part to sculpt the space. Create curved empty shapes. Then try creating straight empty shapes. Be very aware of the space around you as you move through the space. Continually be aware of the shapes you are creating with the empty space around you. Eventually come to a conclusion with your movement and remain still until all the dancers in your group have completed their movement.

REFLECTIVE QUESTION   How does the intent of your movement change when you are focused on the space around you rather than the shape you are making internally with your body?

Improvisations

1. With a partner, sculpt some empty space around you. Without communicating verbally, spend some time creating an air sculpture together. This sculpture may be large or small and may have many parts extending throughout the room. You may work together on some parts and work individually on others. Remember to use parts of your body other than your hands to create your sculpture. Also use various amounts of energy. Imagine that some parts of the air are difficult to cut through and others may be sliced through with ease. Your sculpture may overlap the sculptures of others working in the space. After you have finished creating your sculpture, be still and wait for the others to finish.

REFLECTIVE QUESTIONS   How was your movement connected to that of your partner? • How was your focus on the space between you different from previous improvisations when you had to focus on the positive shape your partner was creating?

2. This time on your own, use the shapes around you in the room, combined with the shape of your own body, to define some empty shapes (see figure 4.21). Your focus will be on the space between you and other structures in the room, such as the floor, barres, chairs, and dance bags. This improvisation works extremely well outdoors if you have a safe and comfortable space to explore (see figure 4.22). There, you may find trees, fences, pathways, and walls. Try to make your transitions similar to your second warm-up where you sculpt empty space around you until you find an object or structure to partner with in making a new empty shape. Pause to focus on this new shape and then continue on to another one.

REFLECTIVE QUESTIONS   How does using shapes in the environment around you extend or limit your choices for creating shapes of your own? • If you were able to take this improvisation outdoors, how did the size of your environment affect your movement and design choices?

3. With a partner, define some interesting shapes between you. Focus on the empty spaces made by your bodies. The spaces do not have to be closed. For example, an extended arm horizontal to the floor may define a line that continues across the room. That line may be captured by your partner by completing the line with a leg reaching along the same line from the other side of the room (see figure 4.23), or by interrupting the line with an opposing line, such as the vertical line of the body. Your body lines define the empty space around you. Although you are making shapes with your bodies, which are considered positive space, your focus should be the shapes created in the empty space around you, which are considered negative space. Your transitions should continue to be smooth, as in your second warm-up. Extend this improvisation to include three dancers. Try it with four dancers.

REFLECTIVE QUESTIONS   How does using a partner help you define negative space? • What happened to the improvisation as you increased the number of dancers?

Figure 4.21   Using studio structures to create interesting negative space.

4. Create body sculptures with a focus on negative space: One person enters the center of the performance space and creates a still shape. The dancer should create interesting shapes in the air around, under, above, and through the body shape. The second person who enters the sculpture must note one of the empty shapes created by the first dance and change or extend it in some way. Empty spaces may be filled, imitated, extended, or focused on as if there were something inside the space. Continue to add dancers as long as the sculpture remains interesting. If it begins to become confusing and chaotic, start over. Each person may decide if the shape needs to start over before adding to the sculpture. However, do not use this as an opportunity to avoid difficult choices. As long as the sculpture is working, you should attempt to add something to it that also works.

Figure 4.22 Creating parallel lines with outside structures in order to emphasize negative space.

REFLECTIVE QUESTIONS How did you decide when the sculpture needed to start over? What made the sculptures work, and what created confusion? • How does a choreographer encourage the audience to focus on negative space?

5. Create dance movement that indicates the following intent: Imagine there is a bright light in one of the upper corners of the room in which you are dancing. Make a shape with your body that focuses on that light. You may either use your eyes for that focus or create a shape that acknowledges the light is there, even if you are not looking at it. Imagine the light is getting brighter and very, very hot—so hot that you are able to feel the warmth. Begin moving in reaction to the heat. Now it is getting unbearably hot—so

Figure 4.23 Capturing a line across negative space. The dancer on stage right uses her arms to capture the line sent by the leg of the dancer on stage left.

much that it is beginning to burn you, and you need to get away from it. Create movement that indicates this intent. Now the rest of the room is getting so cold that you need to move closer to the light in order to get warm. The only source of heat in the room is the light and you know the warmth is there, but the room is so cold that you can just barely feel it. You know if you could get closer, you would be warmer. Suddenly there is a loud screaming siren coming from the light. It is so loud that you can hardly bear it. Now someone is beginning to talk through a loudspeaker close to the light. You know that person is saying something important, but you cannot hear it well enough to understand it. You wonder if you are the only one who cannot hear it. Suddenly a strong spray of water is coming out of the light. The water is so forceful that you cannot remain where you are, but it is pushing you backward. Now there is a powerful vacuum in that upper corner next to that light. It is sucking everything into it, including you. You try to resist it. Find a shape that depicts that resistance and hold it until everyone has found a still shape.

REFLECTIVE QUESTION Why would a choreographer want to create meaning about an area of performance space that has nothing in it?

Discussion of Key Concept

Negative space in dance is all the space that is open and defined by solid structures, such as performance structures, sets, props, or dancers. These solid structures form what we know as **positive space**. The empty space that is surrounded by positive space or is pointed to by a positive shape is called negative space (see figure 4.24). Parallel lines in body shapes automatically define the space between the two lines. A focus on empty space may occur, whether or not the choreographer is conscious of that intent. Some dances are so busy that it is impossible to focus on any particular shapes or space, either positive or negative. Dances with very simple lines create negative space almost automatically. Complementary lines between dancers encourage the audience's eyes to focus on the space defined by those lines.

If you are still struggling with understanding the concept of negative space, the employment of negative space in the M.C. Escher lithograph (1944) *Encounter* may clarify the concept for you. Please view this print at the M.C. Escher Web site at www.mcescher.com. On the wall in the back of the lithograph, the light, positive shape of the optimist also defines the negative, dark shape of the pessimist. Depending on your focus and concentration, you either see the optimist as the positive shape or the pessimist as the negative shape. Your eyes must alternate between the shapes and it is difficult to see them both at once. However, by the time these figures leave the wall, you may focus on both figures at once as positive shapes. Your focus is no longer drawn to the empty space between the figures but to the figures themselves. In choreography, you may draw the eye to negative space or positive space. Lighting effects

Figure 4.24 The negative space defined here is heart shaped.

can enhance this process but are not discussed in this text. When spaces between positive shapes are clearly defined, as you see on the back wall of this print, your audience is more apt to note the negative space that has been created. When it is not clearly defined, or when it is busy, like the shapes between these figures in the foreground of the print, the eye is more likely to stay with the positive shapes. Effective simple shapes allow the eye to travel back and forth between positive and negative space. If you as a choreographer remain aware of the shapes being defined as both positive and negative, you will expand your opportunities to create visually appealing choreography.

Negative space, or empty performance space, may be given a symbolic meaning in dance. You explored this idea somewhat during the first improvisation in this section as you made air sculptures with your partner. You defined shapes in the empty space that took shape and form but were completely imaginary. But they did not necessarily have meaning. **Symbolic space** is negative space that is given some kind of meaning in your choreography. The meaning of the space becomes more important than the shape of the space, although sometimes the shape of the space must be defined before the audience can understand the symbolic meaning. The best examples of the use of symbolic space occur in theater. A mime may define a box to be confined in, a chair to sit in, a bicycle to ride, and stairs to climb that are not really there. The mime spends a great deal of time practicing the art of defining shapes in negative space in order to act out a scene without any scenery. Dance is usually less literate, and symbolic space often indicates a feeling or a concept, such as the past or the future. How a dancer reacts to space gives it its meaning and creates the intent for the choreography (see figure 4.25). A liturgical dancer will use the space above the dance to indicate the presence of God. The movements embrace, beckon, and welcome the space above. Someone else might become burdened by the space above to represent oppression. Alvin Ailey (1931-1989) used these techniques in his seminal masterpiece, *Revelations*. (Ailey founded the Alvin Ailey Dance Theatre in 1958. His company, with primarily black dancers, was influential in changing American dance at a time when most major companies included only one or two black dancers. *Revelations*, taken from his "blood memory," is still being performed by the company 50 years after its first performance.)

Figure 4.25 These dancers create symbolic space by focusing the emotion of fear in one direction.

Negative space may also be dynamic. It may act on the dancer. You explored this concept in chapter 2, when inspiration for movement came from outside the body. If something unseen actually creates movement in the body by applying imaginary force to the dancer, dynamic space is created. When the actions from the dynamic space suggest meaning, then the space becomes both dynamic and symbolic. Donald McKayle's (1930-) "Rainbow 'Round My Shoulder," available for performance by students as "Rainbow Etude," employs dynamic space that is also symbolic. Imaginary chains are wrapped around the legs of the dancers, restricting their movement as they drag their legs in a backward walk. (Donald McKayle is a prominent modern dancer and choreographer who trained with the New Dance Group, Martha Graham, Merce Cunningham, Nenette Charisse, Karel Shook, and Hadassah. "Rainbow Etude" is available from the American Dance Legacy Institute. For more information, go to the American Dance Legacy Web Site at www.adli.us/productaz.html.)

Movement Studies

1. Create a duet or group dance focused on the use of negative space. Explore the use of levels and stage spacing to add dimension to your work.

2. Create a duet or group work in an environment other than the dance studio. Use the environment in your dance to create a focus on negative space.

3. Take a combination from your dance class and focus on the negative space that is created in that combination. Play around with it. Make the shapes bigger or hold them longer to emphasize them. Add dancers and change their positioning in order to extend the negative space. You are using the combination as material, but you may change the order and timing, and you may even repeat it to create this new focus on negative space.

4. Create a dance using symbolic space. The symbol may be literal or abstract, but your movement should not be too literal. Even though dance may encompass theater, explore the special opportunities for movement that extend beyond theater that are provided by dance in this movement study. You may allow that symbolic space to be dynamic or static, or it may change during the movement study.

Assessment

Use these assessment tools in evaluating your progress toward understanding negative space as a key concept in choreography.

Class Critique

- Identify the negative space evident in each work.
- Discuss how the dancers were able to create a focus on the space to bring it to your attention.
- Identify the positive shapes that are used to define negative space, particularly in an outdoor environment.
- Are there any limitations to the size of the negative space that may be defined in dance?
- Identify the negative space in the combination from the dance class before it was manipulated and changed.
- Evaluate the success of the choreographer in drawing attention to increased negative space as this movement was manipulated. Make suggestions about what you might do to create more focus on negative space.
- Identify the use of symbolic space and how the choreographer created it.
- Reflect on the meaning of the symbolic space.

Rubric

Following is a sample rubric that you may use in evaluating the fourth movement study for negative space. This is another example of a four-point rubric that shows a range in the evaluation of each criterion. Try filling in evaluator comments for yourself and for your peers, or create your own criteria according to what you believe to be important in the understanding of negative space that is symbolic.

Rubric for Negative Space

Criteria	Strong evidence (4 points)	Some evidence (3 points)	Little evidence (2 points)	No evidence (1 point)
Good focus on negative space				
Clear meaning established for symbolic space				
Clear movement intent				
Beginning, middle, and end				

Total: (maximum 16 points)

Documentation

Continue to record all your work on video. It may be more difficult to capture negative space on video, so make sure you are comprehensive in your comments about your work. Use more detailed descriptions and include some of your experiences recorded in your journal from the reflective questions.

Drawing Conclusions

Breaking the Rules

Create a movement study that gives the appearance of having no negative space at all. (Hint: You may want to extend your options for positive space by using scenery, props, and quite a few dancers.)

REFLECTIVE QUESTIONS What is the effect created by a work that seems to have no negative space at all? Is this even possible?

 Essential Question

How will variations in the use of direction affect the intent of movement?

Warm-Up

1. Walk forward through general space. You may make your steps small or large, slow or fast, but always walk forward. Be aware of others around you. Be aware of the pathways you are making through the space. When are they straight? When are they curved? Now walk sideways. Always walk to the right of the way you are facing. You may change your facing direction to alter your pathways. Again, be aware of the people around you and the pathways you are making. Create straight pathways. Create curved pathways. Change the size and timing of your steps. Explore ways to find variations in moving sideways. Change to moving to your left and continue this exploration. Now walk backward. Be careful. Take care of yourself and others around you. Begin slowly. Move faster as you see empty space behind you. Change the size of your steps. Be aware of the pathways you are making. Vary between curved and straight. Come to a stillness and wait for the others in your group to stop around you.

   REFLECTIVE QUESTION What is the difference in the kinesthetic sense of the body when it travels forward, sideways, and backward?

2. Staying in self-space, stand at a high level, and explore all the space in front of you with your arms and legs. Move your arms forward through space and return. Swing one leg forward and return to a natural position. Change legs. Explore different ways of moving other parts forward. Move your head, hips, elbow, and knee to keep exploring. Try swinging, sliding, jabbing, floating. Now explore moving things into the space behind you. Remember not to travel; you are working in self-space. Explore different ways to move the arms backward, both high and low. Explore ways to move the legs backward without moving the torso. Then allow the torso to move. How far can you move the leg backward without moving the torso forward? Try other body parts. Now explore ways to move your extremities sideways. Feel as if you are moving in a flat plane, as if your body were placed on a flat piece of paper. Move only that plane. You can move your extremities straight side, side low, and side high and any variations in between. Try different qualities of moving sideways. Explore many body parts. Find a stillness and wait for others in your group to complete their explorations.

   REFLECTIVE QUESTION What is the difference in the kinesthetic sense of movement that extends forward from your center of gravity, sideways from your center or gravity, and behind your center of gravity?

3. Select a point in the room at eye level, and focus on it. On your instructor's cue, walk directly to that point and create a straight shape with your body that is focused on that point. Be aware of others around you. If they are in your straight pathway, do not change your pathway. Slow down or wait until they have moved out of your pathway and then continue on. Your pathway must move directly to the point you have selected. Ready, go! Select another point. Go! Select another point. Go! Now do the same thing, only this time you will walk sideways to that point and create a straight shape that focuses on that point sideways. You must make a straight path to the point but move along it sideways. Keep the point to your side and make a straight shape that focuses on that point. Go! Find another point. Walk sideways again. Go! Select another point. Go! Repeat this process walking backward.

REFLECTIVE QUESTION   What intent do you feel when you walk directly to a particular focal point?

4. Stand in the middle of the room and imagine that you are being pulled in many directions by many points in the room all at the same time. Begin walking forward, side, back—any way that the strongest point pulls you, only do not allow one point to pull you more than a moment and then go another direction. Move faster and faster in many directions, then get slower and finally make a curved shape that is focused in many directions at once (so there is no clear focus for the shape you are making; it should still look like you are being pulled from many directions at once). Do this several times until you have explored the idea of having no definite focus but many focal points that act on your body and your shapes all at the same time.

REFLECTIVE QUESTION   How does it feel to be pulled in many directions at once?

Improvisations

1. Select a point across the room that you will travel to. Using movement and body shapes that include only straight lines and angles, move directly to that spot by transitioning through many shapes that are focused on that point. Change your levels and facing directions so that sometimes you move forward, sometimes sideways, sometimes backward, but always move directly to the point. When you get there, hold a shape that is directed toward the point. Continue to explore moving in straight paths across the space to selected points across from you. Use your own timing; each time you arrive, hold your shape a few moments. Then turn, select a new point, and move toward it. Find a logical conclusion to your improvisation and wait for the others in your group to complete their exploration.

REFLECTIVE QUESTION   What intent is created with movement and shapes that are directly focused toward a particular point in the performance space?

2. Repeat the fourth warm-up exercise using many focal points with a variation. Instead of walking, begin by creating a curved shape in any level. Allow that shape to transform because it is being pulled in many directions. You will stay in self-space because all the points are pulling you at the same time and not allowing you to travel. You may, however, change your facing direction and your levels. Try moving slowly and quickly, with just a little energy, and with a lot of energy. Finish your exploration in a new curved shape.

REFLECTIVE QUESTION   What intent is created when movement and shapes have no specific focus but move in many directions at once?

3. Be sure that you have an opportunity to view others during this improvisation, because the visual effect is more important than the kinesthetic effect. In trios, select a focal point that is downstage left. Begin in upstage right and use straight shapes and a direct pathway to reach the focal point downstage left; move together and in relation to each other. You do not have to move in unison. Explore moving at various levels and at various tempos, but maintain a strong focus downstage left (see figure 4.26 on page 86).

4. Repeat this improvisation from upstage center to downstage center (see figure 4.27 on page 86).

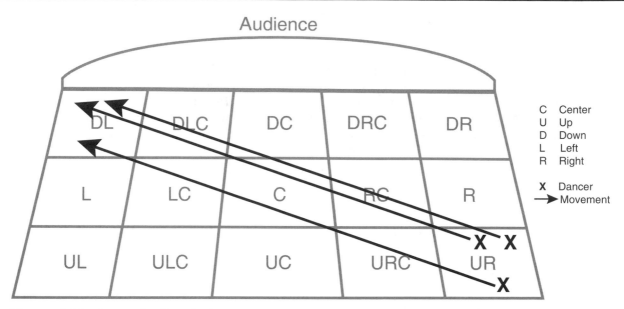

Figure 4.26 Improvisation 3: floor pattern for three dancers moving from upstage right to downstage left.

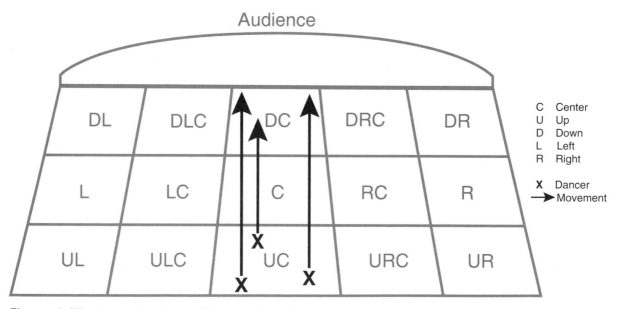

Figure 4.27 Improvisation 4: floor pattern for three dancers moving from upstage center to downstage center.

5. Repeat this improvisation once again from upstage left to downstage right (see figure 4.28). Try to keep the movement the same as you change the pathway.

6. Repeat the improvisation one last time. Change the focus at least five times during the improvisation, causing the pathway to curve along the floor with no fixed focal point (see figure 4.29).

REFLECTIVE QUESTIONS During the improvisations 3 to 6, what was the difference in the visual effects created with these pathways? How might you use this knowledge in your choreography in the future?

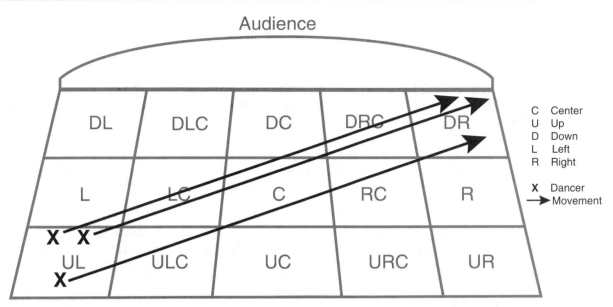

Figure 4.28 Improvisation 5: floor pattern for three dancers moving from upstage left to downstage right.

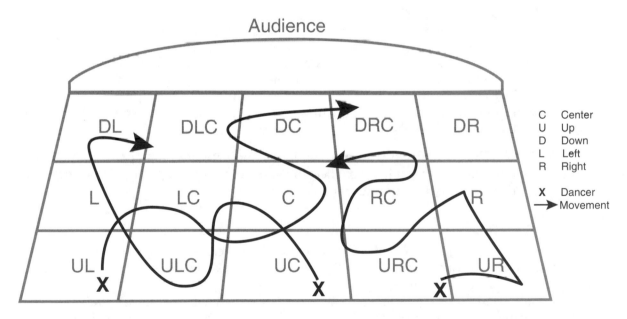

Figure 4.29 Improvisation 6: possible floor pattern for three dancers moving with no fixed focus or floor pattern.

7. Again, make sure you have an opportunity to view this improvisation. Dance in partners and assign one partner a straight direct path while the other does a curved path. The person using the curved pathway should stay close to the person on the direct straight pathway so that both dancers move across the space together. Remember to vary levels, shapes, energy, and body parts. After crossing the floor, change places to allow the other person to do the straight path.

REFLECTIVE QUESTION How do variations in floor patterns affect relationships between dancers?

8. Straight pathways and curved pathways are possible not only as pathways on the floor but also as pathways through space. In self-space, move your right hand in a straight direct pathway from a low position behind your body to a high position in front of you. Make sure your hand takes a direct path through space. This will require you to bend your elbow. Try again, moving your hand from a position beside you level with your shoulder to a position over your head. Do not make an arc, which will happen if you do not bend your elbow. You must bend your elbow in order for your hand to travel on a straight path through space. Explore other ways that your hand may travel through space on a straight path. You may move the rest of your body to accommodate that pathway by turning or ducking to get out of the way. Explore with the other hand. Explore straight pathways through space with other body parts: foot, head, hip, elbow, knee. Try different energy levels and speeds in your movement.

REFLECTIVE QUESTIONS How is your kinesthetic sense affected by movement that defines straight pathways through space? What visual effects are created by these movements?

9. Repeat the previous improvisation with curved pathways through space. Curved pathways are most natural because the arms attach to the body by rotating joints. Swinging the extremities creates a natural curved pathway in three-dimensional space. Remember to explore all body parts and various levels of energy as you explore curved pathways.

REFLECTIVE QUESTIONS How is your kinesthetic sense affected by movement that defines curved pathways through space? What visual effects are created by these movements?

10. Explore traveling on a straight pathway on the floor while defining straight pathways through space with your body. Then travel on a curved pathway while your body moves through curved pathways in space. Then try mixing them up. Travel on a curved pathway while your body defines straight pathways through space. Travel on a straight pathway while your body defines curved pathways in space.

REFLECTIVE QUESTIONS How do various combinations of floor patterns and movement through pathways in space affect the intent of the choreography? How might you use this discovery in your future choreography?

Discussion of Key Concept

Direction in dance may refer to the direction a dancer travels on the floor or the direction a body part travels through space. Tracing the directions a dancer travels on the floor or the direction a body part moves through space creates pathways. Curved and straight pathways may create effects and meaning similar to those created by shapes with curved and straight lines. A straight pathway is direct and strong, whereas a curved pathway is calm and graceful. A pathway that changes direction often indicates indecision, frustration, and impatience. Circular paths may symbolize eternity and unity. Many dancers following the same pathway may provide an emphasis for that pathway, as if the dancers must follow an invisible lane.

Doris Humphrey defined stage space and pathways as tools for meaning in choreography, which are well worth reviewing. She considered the two upstage corners as "significant beginnings" (1987, p. 74). She noted the pathway from upstage right to downstage left as the most powerful diagonal on the stage. This may be true in the Western world, where we are taught to read a page from left to right, and where our eyes are accustomed to tracking in that direction. However, in the Eastern cultures, where the eyes track from right to left, the opposite diagonal may be stronger. This is just one small way culture may affect the meaning or interpretation of your choreography. I have noted that most students have an innate sense of where dancers should be placed on stage for a particular intent. It is hardly necessary to emphasize a particular rule in this regard. What is often illuminating is to ask students to place dancers in a different place from what may seem natural for a desired effect. Often what is unplanned and outside the initial instincts of the choreographer provides a depth of possible interpretations that may be surprising yet appropriate to the work.

Direction also includes focus. Focus in dance need not be only what the eyes are seeing. It may be a part of the body other than the eyes that is focused on a particular point, as if that part of the body had eyes. It may be when a combination of lines made by the dancer seems to point to a particular spot. **Direct focus** occurs when there is only one focal point and a direct line of attention toward that point is created. The attention might be detected in the eyes, but it might also be a knee or an arm. It might be a part of the body that moves directly toward a focal point without meandering or arcing through space. Direct focus is usually something that directs the eyes of the audience to single point. **Indirect focus** is based on many focal points all at once rather than only one (Dell, 1977). Movement with indirect focus causes curved, meandering pathways both as floor patterns and as body shapes through three-dimensional space.

The movement a dancer performs along a pathway may take on the quality created by the direction of the pathway. A curved pathway will encourage curved movement above, but movement that contrasts may show some confliction of purpose. What direction you move in and what direction you give your attention to as you move say a great deal about your intent for the movement. For example, coordinating straight direct lines in pathways, in body movement, and in shape, combined with direct focus, offers the ability to create one of the strongest visual effects in choreography.

Direction in dance has the ability to make a movement or a focal point very prominent. The direction of movement in relation to the performer and the focal point, whether it is forward, backward, sideways, up, or down, may say something about the relationship of the dancer to the focal point. A movement that pushes forward toward a focal point may seem aggressive, whereas a movement sideways toward or away from that point might be entreating, and a movement backward may show only slight attention to an unimportant but nagging focal point. Movements upward may simulate growth and strength, whereas movements downward may simulate shrinking or weakening of spirit. Subtle distinctions in relationships between dancers may be varied by a simple change in the direction of their movements.

Movement Studies

1. Draw some interesting floor patterns that include some curved lines and some straight lines. Remember that curves may include arcs, circles, S shapes, and snake patterns. Straight lines may include zigzags, squared corners, and sharp angles. Using this drawing as a map, create a dance that covers the floor pattern you created. Pay attention to the kind of movement you place over these floor patterns to create intent in your work.

2. Create a movement study of contrast that alternates between direct and indirect focus. Be sure to include intent to your movement so that the changes in focus are logical.

3. Create a dance around a single focal point. Explore directional movement as a means of indicating the relationship of the dancer to the focal point. Allow the relationship to change throughout the piece by using changes in direction.

Assessment

Use these assessment tools in evaluating your progress toward understanding direction as a key concept in choreography.

Class Critique

- Identify the directions employed in the work you see. Remember to look for floor patterns, pathways of body parts through space, and movement in relation to one or more focal points on the stage.

- Notice floor patterns in relation to the front of the stage space from the audience's point of view. Discuss how these directions in the work you view affect the intent of the movement.

- Make suggestions for more variation or change of direction when appropriate. Try these changes and repeat the studies for a second evaluation.

Rubric

Following is a sample rubric that you may use in evaluating the third movement study or direction. Try filling in evaluator comments for yourself and for your peers, or create your own criteria according to what you believe to be important in the understanding of direction.

Rubric for Direction

Criteria	Strong evidence (4 points)	Some evidence (3 points)	Little evidence (2 points)	No evidence (1 point)
Clear focal point				
Interesting variations of directional movement				
Changing relationships created by directional movement				
Total: (maximum 12 points)				

Documentation

Continue to record your work on video. Try to place the camera directly center and in front of the performance space so that you may easily determine the directions intended for the movement in this work. Make sure you also write a description of the work so that you will be able to interpret it accurately at a future date. Add evaluations to accompany your video and place it in your digital portfolio.

Drawing Conclusions

Breaking the Rules

1. Create a dance with no particular focus, no particular floor patterns, and no particular directional movement. Also, do not pay attention to any front of the stage. View the dance from many angles as you create it.

2. Create a dance with movements that are intended to create a strong impact, but instead of bringing them forward from upstage, have them recede to upstage. Take movements that are intended to be weak and have them travel in the strong diagonals. Go against everything you have learned about floor patterns and patterns in space. Try to create the opposite of what might be expected.

Why would a choreographer choose movement that is created without any directional intent? • Why is it helpful to attempt creating movement that is in complete opposition to the rules of the craft? What personal discoveries did you make as you tried this?

Drawing Conclusions

Critical Thinking Essays

Choose one of the following topics: Discuss the use of space in order to create emotional content, or discuss the use of space to create an abstract work focused on design. Use the critical thinking model from chapter 1 for your essay.

    I. Introduction: Summarize the key spatial concepts in choreography.

   II. Discussion

        A. Analysis: Identify key concepts that affect emotion or design.

        B. Reflection: Reflect on why these concepts affect emotion or design and intent.

        C. Integration: Relate your experience in creating this way by highlighting key learning moments.

  III. Conclusion: Summarize and evaluate the effectiveness of key spatial concepts for creating emotional content or interesting design.

Time

Chapter 5

Initial Inquires

How can we make the statement "That dancer has great musicality!" even when the dancer dances in silence? • Is it true that some people have better rhythm than others? • If a student has no rhythm, is it possible for that student to learn to dance? • Why are musicality and dance so closely linked? • Which do you think came first—rhythm or dance? Is it even possible to separate the two? • What is musicality, anyway?

Dance is an art form that exists in space and time. **Time** is the measured or measurable period during which an action, process, or condition exists or continues. The way time is measured is arbitrary and changes depending on our purposes for measuring. Days, weeks, and years seem to help us keep track of our time on earth. Our watches help us to coordinate our arrivals at meetings so that we can convene for a particular purpose. People at sea measure the tides to determine the best times to fish in the shoals without getting stuck in the sand. So why does a dancer measure time, and what purpose do those measurements have for a choreographer?

Dance borrows its measurements of time from the art of music. I cannot say which came first, music or dance, but I do know that in the Western world, music was formalized and notated long before dance. Dance was the servant of music, always coordinating and expressing the feelings offered by playing musicians. But in today's world, dance has matured and broken its tethers from music. It is now possible to create movement without music, or at least independently of music. But music and dance come from the same part of the soul. Whether or not they are created together, dance and music intersect time in the same way, with patterns and **accents** and beats. The people who defined musical time for us provided dancers with a great system. It is not necessary for us to reinvent our own. And besides, if we are going to work with composers at all, it is nice to speak the same language.

This chapter leads you through explorations of tempo, meter, and rhythm. You will learn some music terms and discover the way dancers count, which is often very different from the way musicians count. Although the terms I use are borrowed from music, the application of those terms in this chapter is specifically for dance. The structure of this chapter is the same as those that precede it. After each exploration you will read about the key concepts, perform movement studies, and assess your work. Your critical thinking essay at the end will help you draw conclusions about your relationship to time as a choreographer. It may be true that some people are more musical than others. But everyone is capable of learning how to be musical as a choreographer.

 Essential Question

Why is it important for a choreographer to understand opportunities for variations in the timing of movement?

Warm-Up

1. Begin walking around the performance space at a normal pace. Walk anywhere you like and do not follow the pathways of anyone else. Focus on the timing of the steps and allow yourself to conform to the timing of the group. Create your own pathways. Changing gradually and staying together, everyone begin to walk more quickly. Continue to increase your speed until you are walking so quickly that you are almost running, but you are still walking. Remember to stay together with the group. There should be no leaders. Now gradually slow down as a group until you are once again walking at a normal tempo. Gradually slow down even further until everyone is just barely moving. Your steps should be extremely slow, as slow as possible without actually stopping. What is the slowest timing you can possibly perform and still produce a walk? Once again, gradually speed up your walk until you are walking at a normal pace. When I clap, freeze.

2. Standing in self-space, begin to explore the space around you with one arm very slowly. Explore different ways of moving your arm in straight lines and curved lines. Gradually increase the speed of your arm movement until you are finally moving it as fast as you possibly can. Then gradually decrease the speed of your movement until you are just barely moving. Be patient and explore just how slowly you can move without actually stopping. When you think you have discovered the slowest possible movement, find a stillness and wait for the others in your group to finish. Try this warm-up with several other body parts.

REFLECTIVE QUESTIONS How might you use speed to create intent in choreography? • What intent is created by very slow movement? • What intent is created by very fast movement? • Which speed is more comfortable for you? Why?

Improvisations

1. Perform one movement in 8 slow counts. Try to keep it as one movement and not a movement **phrase,** which is a combination of several movements. Perform one arm circle or one leg lift, one contraction, or one swing. You decide. Repeat it. Practice it until you are very familiar with everything that happens in the 8 counts. Make sure your entire body is part of the performance, even if you are using only one body part. The rest of your body should be engaged in the movement through intent and focus. Now perform the exact movement in 4 counts. Practice it again. Keep practicing until 4 counts are comfortable. Alternate between performing the movement in 8 counts and performing the movement in 4 counts. Now perform the movement in 2 counts. Practice until you are sure you can complete the entire movement correctly in 2 counts. Now randomly change from 8 counts, 2 counts, and 4 counts, changing whenever you like, repeating whenever you like. (You may choose to have someone call out the counts at random here for everyone to follow.) Use the slower movement to recover from the faster movement. Change the movement to 16 counts. Make adjustments as necessary to make it possible to perform well, such as adding a balance before a step or fall so that you are able to suspend time. Add the 16-count movement to your choices. Now do the movement in 32 counts. Try to keep moving all the time and evenly space the movement through all 32 counts. Add the 32-count movement to your choices and explore changing from 32-count to 16-, 8-, 4-, and 2-count movements, not necessarily in that order. Finally

try completing the movement in one count. Practice until you have this mastered it, and add it to your choices as you change back and forth from 32-, 16-, 8-, 4-, 2-, and 1-count movements. Keep exploring ways to do this. Find a logical conclusion to your exploration and wait for everyone to finish.

Note: It helps to have something to keep a constant beat or time in this improvisation. Someone beating a drum may be useful, although this may encourage movement that is always sharp in quality. Using the voice to count works well because the quality of the voice may change as the counts stretch out or speed up. Whoever is leading may experiment with various qualities of the voice and see how that influences the movement of those performing. Music that is soft and unobtrusive yet maintains a beat may also be used. (See Soft Dynamics in the Music Resources section near the back of this book.) If you have a musician to play for your class, you might ask that person to maintain the beat and continually change the quality of the music to keep the dancers from getting tied to a particular quality in their movements. Make sure they understand not to accent any beats so the dancers are free to change from one length of movement to another without having to fight with a strong accent in the middle of a movement. Also, make sure the musician has the ability to maintain a particular tempo as the quality of the music is changed. This may be as difficult for the improvising musician as it is for the dancer.

2. Repeat the previous improvisation with different movements. Try some that are full-body movements and some that are focused on single body parts.

   REFLECTIVE QUESTIONS   What effect does a change in the speed of a movement have on its intent? • Identify some images and emotions that are created by various speeds of movement, such as lazy, anxious, excited, and carefree. • What adjustments have to be made to change the speed of a movement? • Is it possible to change the speed of any movement?

3. Body halves: Explore ways to move the lower body very slowly while moving the upper body very quickly. Begin by concentrating on the lower half—everything in your body from your waist down, which includes your hips, should be moving very slowly. You may move in self-space or general space. After you have established a certain speed of movement in the lower half of your body, begin adding some very quick movements with an upper part of the body while you continue to move the lower body at the established speed. Start with something small that you can easily focus on, such as a finger. Continue to add quick movements over the slow movements until you are moving everything above the waist very quickly and everything below the waist very slowly. If you lose focus or get frustrated, go back to just the slow movement and begin again. Remember that you may change levels.

4. Repeat the previous improvisation in reverse. Begin with very quick movements in the lower half of the body, and add slow movements with the upper body gradually.

5. Repeat the previous improvisations dividing the body into right and left sides rather than upper and lower.

   REFLECTIVE QUESTIONS   What effect is created when different speeds of movement are used in different parts of the body? • Can you identify any movements that you have practiced in a technique class that involve different speeds of movement in different body parts? What effect is created with those movements?

6. In a group, begin exploring movement that is extremely slow. Try movement in all levels and try changing the amount of energy you are using. Sometimes use a lot of energy to move slowly, and sometimes use very little. Once the group has established a way of working very slowly together, anyone may make a choice to move very quickly for

short periods. Pay attention to the entire group and move quickly only when you feel there is a need for the quick movement as a contrast to the slow movement, and then return to the slow movement. You may want to react to someone else's movement as inspiration for your changes in speed. Remember to change your energy also in the fast movements. You may be fast and strong or fast and weak. Allow the improvisation to build in speed this way until everyone is moving quickly together for a short time, and then gradually diminish the quick movements until no one is moving quickly anymore. As this happens, the entire group should make the choice to find a stillness together.

REFLECTIVE QUESTIONS How do changes in speed create interest and variation in group work? • What worked really well in this improvisation, and what was not effective?

7. With a partner, explore movement that contrasts in speed. If one dancer is moving quickly, the other must move slowly. Explore gradations of speed between slow and fast, but try to always have a different speed from that of your partner. Set this up as a conversation in speed between you. Again, remember to use variations in levels and energy as well.

REFLECTIVE QUESTION How do changes in speed affect relationships created through movement?

8. Acceleration and deceleration: Begin moving very slowly through space. Explore full-body movement in slow motion. Gradually increase the speed of your movement. Take your time to change so that it is barely noticeable that your speed is changing. Continue to increase your speed until you come to a point where you could not possibly go any faster. Relax—you do not have to be strong to be fast. Now gradually begin to decrease your speed. Take your time slowing down until you finally come to a stillness.

REFLECTIVE QUESTIONS What effect is created by gradual changes in the speed both as they are felt kinesthetically and as they are perceived by an audience? What images are produced?

Discussion of Key Concept

Dance is temporal. It exists in the moment. We create a movement in time and then it is finished. We can no longer change it. We can repeat it, and alter the repetition, but the actual opportunity to change the movement at that particular moment is past. But the mind has memory, anticipation, and a sense of relativity, which offer the opportunity to create the illusion of altered time. Real time marches on, but we may generate environments that slow it down, speed it up, or even make it stand still. These are illusions that become the tools of the choreographer. And they are necessary for creating particular effects. If there is something important that you, as a choreographer, want to establish for your audience, you must slow down time to give them an opportunity to see it. Quick movements may disappear before the eye has even had time to notice it on the stage. It is easy to mistakenly relate quick to strong. To make an emphatic point, you may produce a strong quick accent, hoping to project a strong response from the audience. More often than not, a majority of the audience will miss the movement entirely because it was too quick. The audience is not given enough time to observe the strength in the movement. Especially if there is a chance the audience is looking away from where you intended to create a strong effect, by the time you draw the eye of the audience back to the focal point where a quick, strong movement is taking place, it is over. The full effect is missed. Note that real time almost always needs to be exaggerated for an audience in order to be effective.

Tempo is an Italian term that means time. In both music and dance it is an indication of speed or duration. Tempo has to do with how long it takes to complete a particular movement. If it takes a very long time to complete a movement, the tempo of the movement is slow. If you are able to complete a movement in a very short time, then the tempo of your movement is quick. An infinite number of tempos exist between the slowest possible tempo and the fastest possible tempo. Dancers rarely explore the extremes, so practicing extremely fast and extremely slow movement will enhance your ability to be expressive in your movement. Some people are more comfortable moving slowly, while others are more comfortable moving quickly. Much of this has to do with individual body type and metabolism. It can also say much about personality. We all know the lethargic personality and the hyper personality. If you take time to notice people around you and observe the speed in which they move, you will begin to collect ideas for establishing mood and character in your choreography.

In the story of our lives, there are many reasons we choose to move slowly or quickly or in any of the myriad tempos that exist in between. If you are tired, you tend to move slowly; if you are excited, you may move more quickly. But even the choices of movement that result from similar circumstances may vary. Being in a hurry because you are late or being hesitant to enter a room because you are fearful someone will notice that you are late are two contrasting speeds resulting from the same cause: that you are late (see figure 5.1).

Music, having been classically formalized in Italy, uses Italian terms to indicate particular variations in tempo. They are commonly used in dance as well, and it is good to become familiar with them as a choreographer, especially if you intend to communicate with musicians and composers. **Andante** indicates a normal walking tempo, and everything else is placed in relation to that middle point. **Adagio** is a bit slower, **largo** is very slow, and **grave** is extremely slow. **Allegro** is fast, **presto** is very fast, and **prestissimo** is extremely fast. More specific terms and definitions are shown in figure 5.2.

Most dance techniques require perfection of movement that employs various speeds of movement in various parts of the body. Tap has quick and isolated movement in the feet sometimes accompanied by loose and slower movements in the torso and arms. Classical ballet usually employs slow lyrical movements of the arms, regardless of the speed of the steps.

Figure 5.1 Contrasting tempo: lingering and hurrying.

Grave	Largo	Larghetto	Adagio	Adagietto	Andante	Moderato	Allegro	Vivace	Presto	Prestissimo
Very, very slow and solemn	Very slow and broad	Not quite as slow as largo	Slow	Not quite as slow as adagio	Walking tempo	Moderate, or medium	Fast	Lively and brisk	Very fast	Very, very fast

Figure 5.2 Tempo variations.

These isolated speeds of body movement take a great deal of practice to master. You will find that if you are trained in one particular technique, you have acquired an ease in dividing the body into sections and performing separate speeds of movement in these areas. However, as you switch them around and go against what is usual for that technique, it may be very challenging for you. Do not dismiss it for that reason. Exploring unusual movement will expand your movement vocabulary and even your choreography in the technique you have practiced.

What have been your personal discoveries as you have both performed and observed variations in the speed of movement? Have you discovered your comfort zone as a dancer? How does that comfort zone relate to the choreography you both create and observe?

Movement Studies

1. Create a movement study that uses all the tempos listed in figure 5.2. Begin your exploration for the study by walking at a normal tempo and establishing what that tempo is. Find other movement that may occur at a walking tempo. Then create a movement that moves as fast as you possibly can and call that prestissimo. Find movement that moves as slowly as you possibly can and call that grave. Create all the other tempos in relationship to those three. Put these movements together in a movement study. They do not have to be in any particular order, but your piece should have a beginning, a middle, and an end.

2. Create a movement study that explores varied tempos in divided body halves. Use improvisations 3 to 5 under Tempo on page 96 as a beginning exploration and set a movement study with a beginning, a middle, and an end.

3. Create a sequence of movement that is taken from a particular technique that you have studied in a class. Put these movements together in a phrase that has a beginning, a middle, and an end. Then change the movements in the phrase by altering the speed of the movements. Make sure all the movements that were fast are changed to slow and all the movements that were slow are changed to fast. Try to find the largest possible contrast in speed for each movement. You may decide to repeat the movements that were slow, as you make them faster, in order to take the same amount of time. However, your

new creation does not have to take the same amount of time as the original sequence. In fact, you may play around with a number of repetitions of the entire phrase to create your study. This will be awkward at first, but continue to manipulate the tempos until you have something quite different from the original, yet something that works as a movement study. Rehearse it well so you can show it and get feedback from your peers.

Assessment

Use these assessment tools in evaluating your progress toward understanding tempo as a key concept in choreography.

Class Critique

- Comment on the ability of each dancer to show clear variations in tempo.
- Identify different tempos in different body parts.
- Identify tempos that are natural to particular techniques and comment on what happens as these tempos are altered.
- Discuss how tempo and energy may or may not be linked.
- Make suggestions to help anyone who is having trouble finding the extremes in tempo variations.

Rubric

Following is a sample rubric that you may use in evaluating the third movement study for tempo. Try filling in evaluator comments for yourself and for your peers, or create your own criteria according to what you believe to be important in the understanding of tempo as a key concept.

Rubric for Tempo

Criteria	Strong evidence (4 points)	Some evidence (3 points)	Little evidence (2 points)	No evidence (1 point)
Clear definitions of tempo in original movement phrase				
Good contrast in tempos during manipulations				
New unique material				
Clear beginning, middle, and end				

Total points: (maximum 16 points)

Documentation

Record your work on video and review your use of tempo while watching the recording. Make comments to evaluate your use of tempo. Include the previous rubric after it is completed, or use your own criteria. Include comments from your journal that compare your understanding of tempo with the description of the key concept. Add this to your digital portfolio.

Drawing Conclusions

Breaking the Rules

Create a movement study that includes absolutely no variation in tempo. Whatever tempo is used in the beginning must be maintained throughout the work and for every body part. There will be no contrast in tempo.

REFLECTIVE QUESTIONS   What challenges did you encounter in trying to create movement without any tempo variations? • What is the effect created by movement without tempo variation? • Is there ever a time that you might want to use this effect in your choreography? Why or why not?

 Essential Question

How does meter in movement affect a dancer's performance?

Warm-Up

It is helpful to have a leader with a drum to keep the class consistent in timing. A stronger tap on the drum may indicate the beginning of each count sequence.

1. As a group, begin walking around the room at a normal tempo until everyone has established a common walking tempo (andante). The instructor will clap on the first of every eight steps. Follow this clap: X-2-3-4-5-6-7-8-X-2-3-4-5-6-7-8. When you are comfortable with this tempo and the counts, join the instructor with a clap on the first step. Now stop and listen. This time, clap with your hands up high without taking a step, and then take seven steps away from the spot where you begin. You may walk in any direction you like, and you may add any other movement with the upper body and arms. You may even change level from middle to high, but do not change your means of support because you must keep walking. When you finish your seven steps, you must stop and clap with the arms high again and then repeat the seven steps away from the spot where you clapped. All walking should stop as you clap. The counts will be the same as before. X-2-3-4-5-6-7-8-X-2-3-4-5-6-7-8. Begin by clapping with your instructor. Now go.

2. Repeat the previous warm-up in 6 counts: X-2-3-4-5-6-X-2-3-4-5-6. Then in 4 counts: X-2-3-4-X-2-3-4. Then one more time in 3 counts: X-2-3-X-2-3-X-2-3-X-2-3.

3. Select a strong, quick movement to perform instead of the clap and move any way you like through the rest of the counts (not necessarily walking), and repeat the previous exercise. Always perform a strong quick movement on the first count.

   REFLECTIVE QUESTIONS How did the kinesthetic feel of your movement change as the number of counts changed between the claps (or the strong quick movement)? • How did the 8 count feel? The 6 count? The 4 count? The 3 count?

4. This improvisation still involves walking, but this time you will travel across the floor with a partner. You will walk across the floor counting in 2s. On the first count, or clap, you will step strong and as low as possible; on the second count you will step light and get as high as possible so that you are down low on one step and up high on the other. Your partner will walk in 3s at the same time. Your partner will step down strong and low on 1 and as light and high as possible on 2 and 3. This will be similar to the modern dance triplet. Allow the rest of your body to shape into these low and high areas. You may use your arms and torso any way you like. Cross the floor together. Have an accompanist play constant beats on a drum to keep you together, but the accompanist should not play any accents on the drum. The accents should be reflected in the movement and will be different for each dancer. Without changing your own performance, become aware of how your timing relates to that of your partner. Try this with other groups of counts, such as a 4 against 3, or 7 against 4.

   REFLECTIVE QUESTIONS What relationships develop when you perform with someone who is performing to a different grouping of counts than you are using for your performance? • How does this relationship of counts affect the intent of your movement together?

Improvisations

1. Pick any movement that takes 8 counts to perform, and practice performing it over and over in repetition. Make sure it is only one movement and not a movement phrase. Pick another movement that takes 8 counts and practice it as well. Now perform these two movements in sequence. Repeat this sequence, alternating from one to the other. Keep your timing exact with no extra counts to transition from one movement to the other. Try this with a third movement so that you are performing three 8-count movements in sequence repeatedly. And finally, do this with a fourth movement so that you are performing four 8-count movements in sequence and in repetition. As you do this improvisation, allow yourself to place your accents wherever you like. You need not be tied to the first count of each movement, but make sure you complete each movement in 8 counts. Repeat these four movements over and over to establish a pattern.

2. Repeat the previous improvisation using the same movements, but shorten the timing to 6 counts for each movement. Repeat the four movements again, performing them in 4 counts each, then 3 counts, and finally 2 counts. Keep your counts consistent in timing. Do not allow them to speed up or slow down even though you do have to speed up the movement.

   REFLECTIVE QUESTIONS How did the kinesthetic feel of your movement change as the number of counts changed for each movement? • What was the difference in the feel of the patterns of movement that formed during the repetition of the movements? • What happened to the tempo of the movements themselves?

3. One person in the room will play the drum in 4 counts, tapping the drum more strongly on the first beat of every 4 counts. This person must remain consistent in the timing of the beats. Explore moving to this beat. It is not necessary to perform a strong movement on every strong beat, but your movement should express this timing and grouping of beats in some way. You may change levels, energy, floor patterns, shapes, and so on. Find variations in your movement that fit the 4-count accompaniment. Explore various ways of using the counts by reflecting all of them separately in your movement or allowing your movements to flow together through the counts. However, when your movements flow, you must still reflect the 4-count grouping in some way. Take turns with the drum. As you play the drum, observe the rest of the dancers in your group.

   REFLECTIVE QUESTIONS What are some choices that were made in order to reflect the 4-count timing other than using a strong accent on the first count? • Were some choices more effective than others? Why? • Were some choices more interesting than others? Why?

4. Repeat the previous improvisation using a 3-count accompaniment on the drum. Every first count of 3 counts will be stronger on the drum than the rest of the counts. Explore moving to this accompaniment. As before, find different ways to solve the problem of reflecting the feel of this 3-count grouping of beats.

   REFLECTIVE QUESTIONS How is the kinesthetic feel of the 3-count grouping of beats different from that of the 4-count grouping?

5. Repeat the previous improvisation alternating between the 4-count grouping and the 3-count grouping.

   REFLECTIVE QUESTIONS What happened to the kinesthetic sense of the movement when you explored mixed groupings?

6. Dance with a partner. You dance with movement that reflects a 4-count grouping as your partner dances to a 3-count grouping. Explore movements together that reflect the grouping of counts assigned. Try this first with a very strong movement on the first count of every grouping. You may have to stop and start several times because it is difficult for you to keep your own timing while dancing with someone who is using a different timing. The person playing the drum for you should not accent any counts; this will avoid confusing you. After you are comfortable working with a strong accent on the first count, try placing your accents in different places, but maintain the feel of your assigned grouping of counts. Also try to be aware of your partner's timing as it relates to yours, but be careful not to change your timing as you do this.

REFLECTIVE QUESTIONS What happens to the relationship between two dancers when they are dancing to different counts?

7. Special challenge: Assign a 4-count grouping to your lower body while performing a 3-count grouping with your upper body. The best way to start this is to set up a simple walk in 4 counts with an accent on the first step. Then create your 3-count movements with your arms. Reverse this with a 3 count in the lower body and a 4 count in the upper body. Then explore splitting body parts any way you want.

REFLECTIVE QUESTION What effect is created visually and kinesthetically when body parts split apart in the timing of the performance?

Discussion of Key Concept

Meter in music is the organization of stressed and nonstressed beats arranged in units called measures or bars. In more simple terms, meter is a grouping of beats. Because one beat is by itself and does not constitute a group, you will never have a 1-beat meter. The only meters possible are groups of 2 and groups of 3, and combinations of 2 and 3, because everything else can be a multiple of one of these numbers. Whereas the determination of these groupings often occurs by placing the strongest accent at the beginning of a measure, there are times when one or more strong accents may take place in the middle or at the end of a measure, fooling you into thinking that the next measure is starting earlier than is actually written or planned. This is called **syncopation** and is discussed under rhythm. Groups of 2, or a multiple of 2, are considered **duple meter**. Groups of 3, or multiples of 3, are considered **triple meter**. Duple meter is common for dancers using steps to mark time because we have two feet, and an even number of steps feels balanced and normal. Triple meter is more difficult when marking time with steps. Think about how difficult it is to learn a **waltz** step, especially if you must dance with a partner. Grouping steps in 3 counts requires you to switch feet with each grouping, and if you have to coordinate this with a partner, it magnifies the complexity. However, this shifting of weight from one foot to the other encourages a sway in the upper body, resulting in a lilt or lyrical quality to the movement that is not possible with a duple meter. If you listen to various pieces of music and identify the meter as being duple or triple, you will also notice the difference in the quality or feel of that music, and this will help you understand the kinesthetic feel of these meters in your movement (see figure 5.3).

A grouping of 6 beats provides an opportunity for a choice between duple and triple meter. It may be performed as three groupings of 2 beats, or it may be performed as two groupings of 3 beats. If it is a very quick 6, it is often performed as two groupings of 3, but it feels like duple meter because the accents are placed on the 1 and the 4 and the rest of the counts are very minor, such as in a tarantella. Whatever the music is behind the movement, the movement itself has a feeling of meter depending on how it is performed that may or may not coincide with music or sound score that accompanies it. That is why dancers and choreographers assign their own counts to the movement, which often confuse musicians. It is the source of much consternation and botched relationships between dancers and the musicians they work with. This is explored further in chapter 7.

Figure 5.3 Contrasting meter: dancers on stage right dance to a march (duple), while the dancers on stage left dance to a waltz (triple).

A grouping of 5, 7, or 11, which you have not yet explored, is usually a combination of duple and triple placed in sequence, which was briefly explored in improvisation 5. You will have to listen carefully to these odd meters because it is easy to think of these as even meters and miss a count somewhere within the group. This is especially true when accents within the measure keep shifting. A grouping of five may be a sequence of 3 and 2, or 2 and 3. A grouping of 7 could be a sequence of 3-2-2, 2-3-2 or 2-2-3. A grouping of 11 simply offers a more complex sequence of duple and triple meters, with more choices for that sequence. All of these **mixed meters** create interesting **rhythms**, which are discussed later in this chapter. These odd-numbered meters may also retain the feel of length without subdividing into smaller units, as was the case when we explored the length of an 8-count meter in the first improvisation. If the long measure is truly drawn out without more than one strong accent, then we could say it truly had the feel of a meter of 7 or 8 or even 12. A meter of 8 is still considered a duple. Meters of 5, 7, and 11 are odd or mixed meters; 3, 6, and 9 are triple meters.

Regardless of how you want to recognize these groupings, the grouping of counts creates meter in your movement, and different meters will provide an infinite number of possibilities as you choreograph. Each choice you make will create a unique kinesthetic feel. It is often interesting to create opposing meters in your movement that do not necessarily coordinate with the music that accompanies your work. Coordinating beats and opposing meter, such as a triple-meter movement against a duple meter in music, can give a feeling of pulling against the music, or pulling against time. This is explored further in chapter 7.

Movement Studies

1. Create a movement study in duple meter (any multiple of 2). Explore the difference between movement that marks each count and movement that flows through the counts, but stay true to the duple meter.

2. Create a movement study in triple meter (any multiple of 3). Again, explore the difference between movement that marks each count and movement that flows through the counts keeping true to the triple meter.

3. Create a movement study that uses both duple and triple meter. Make sure that it is evident to the audience when the change occurs between the two. You may wish to alternate between duple and triple, or you may choose blocks of movement that use one before changing to the other. Or you may assign different dancers different meters. Explore several possibilities.

4. Choose an irregular meter, such as 5, 7, or 11, and create a movement study using this meter. Explore multiple ways of breaking up the meter into duple and triple, but also show some movement that remains true to the length of the meter.

Assessment

Use these assessment tools in evaluating your progress toward understanding meter as a key concept in choreography.

Class Critique

- Identify the meters used in the choreography.

- Are the dancers clear enough in their timing for you to recognize the meter? Identify some of the ways the dancers used the meter, either by accenting the first beat of each measure or by using some of the other techniques you discovered during improvisations.

- Evaluate the way the choreography used meter to create interest in the work.

Rubric

Following is a sample rubric that you may use in evaluating the third movement study for meter. Try filling in evaluator comments for yourself and for your peers, or create your own criteria according to what you believe to be important in the understanding of meter as a key concept.

Rubric for Meter

Criteria	Strong evidence (4 points)	Some evidence (3 points)	Little evidence (2 points)	No evidence (1 point)
Obvious duple and triple meters				
Interest created by changes in meter				
Clear intent				
Clear beginning, middle, and end				

Total points: (maximum 16 points)

Documentation

Record your work on video and review your use of meter while watching the recording. Make comments to evaluate your use of meter, particularly changing meter and mixed meter. Include the previous rubric after it is completed, or use your own criteria. Include comments from your journal that compare your understanding of meter from the improvisations and the discussion of the key concept. Add this to your digital portfolio. If you have time, include some video of your improvisations. These might help you with your movement studies in the future.

Drawing Conclusions

Breaking the Rules

Create a movement study that has no meter. Make sure that observers are not able to discern a pattern of grouped beats in your work.

REFLECTIVE QUESTIONS   What process did you use to create movement without meter? • If you think you were successful, what effect did a lack of meter have on your work? • Why might you want to create this way in the future?

 Essential Question

How do accents and the duration of movement within a meter affect the feel or quality of choreography?

Warm-Up

1. Breath rhythm: While lying on the floor with your eyes closed, focus on your breathing. Allow yourself to relax and breathe naturally until you notice that your breathing has settled into a constant sequence of time. Pay attention to that timing of your breathing. Exactly how long does it take to breathe in, and exactly how much time does it take to exhale? Is there any hesitation between these transitions? What is that timing like? Where is the greatest amount of energy in your breathing? When do things speed up? And when do things slow down? Become very familiar with every aspect of your breathing. Now take one arm and move it through space in the same timing as your breathing, gathering energy as you gather air while you inhale and releasing energy as you release the air as you exhale. Make sure you include any hesitation in your timing that you noticed with your breathing. Practice this several times to make sure you are consistent with your timing. If you need further information as you begin to create your movement, feel free to go back to just breathing to gather that information. Add another body part. Continue to add body parts and develop your movement until you are doing full-body movement at all three levels using this breath rhythm. Find a logical conclusion by employing one final release, and rest until everyone is still.

2. Faster breath rhythm: To prepare for the next warm-up and exploration, you need to run very fast for about 15 to 30 seconds. You can do this by running back and forth across the studio floor and blocking with your hands against the walls to break your momentum. Run back and forth until you feel somewhat winded. Then find a space in the center of the room and stop. Standing with your eyes closed (or with an internal focus, if you are dizzy), be aware of the timing of your breathing. Try to capture the timing of your breathing as you first notice it, because it will change as you continue resting. When you notice your breathing has begun to slow down, repeat the running. Do this several times until you have memorized the precise timing of your breathing when you are stressed or winded. Once you have memorized this timing, explore movements that reflect that timing. You may start with a small body part, but continue to explore many movement possibilities.

REFLECTIVE QUESTIONS What was the difference in the quality of your movement from the slow breath rhythm to the quick breath rhythm? What were the similarities? • When might you choose to use one or the other in your choreography?

Improvisations

1. Create movement that illustrates triple meter by placing a strong accent on the first count of every 3 beats. This strong accent should be very visible to an audience. Make a strong accented movement on that count each time you come to it. You may do this with sound accompaniment if you like, but it may be better to set up the meter in your own timing in your head. Keep your tempo moderate to slow. After you have established this rhythm, add another accent on the third count. Keep the original accent on 1, and make the second accent on 3 lighter than the first. Continue exploring movement with this new rhythm. Next, do a shaking movement on the second count each time you come to it. Do not change the amount of time you give each count. The shaking movement requires more movement in a short time than the single accented movement. Your rhythm is now *strong-shake-weak*. Keep practicing this until it is comfortable and consistent.

2. Everyone in the group begins by standing in a circle. One person starts by clapping a 4-count rhythm four times. The rest of the group responds by clapping the same rhythm 4 times and then performing a movement to the rhythm four times without clapping. A simple way to get started is to first clap 4 counts with an accent on the first beat. The first clap should be the loudest, and the other three are softer. The movement response should clearly illustrate the rhythm in the same timing with the same accent on the first count. The movement response is also repeated four times, but the clapping stops to allow the body to establish the rhythm. The next person to create a rhythm will be the one counterclockwise from the one who began. This person claps any 4-count rhythm four times. Everyone responds by clapping the same rhythm four more times and then moving to the rhythm four times. Continue until everyone has had at least one turn in creating a new rhythm. Do not repeat a rhythm that was used before you. Create something new. Rhythms may change by changing the space between claps (such as only two claps in the 4 counts, clapping on 1 and 3 only or 1 and 2 only), by subdividing the counts (clapping two, three, or four times in place of 1 count), and by changing the accents within the 4 counts (such as making the third clap the strongest, or even making one of the subdivided counts the strongest). Combining these possibilities leaves an infinite number of possibilities for changing the rhythm, because any part of the 4-count meter may change. It is not necessary to think about exactly how you are creating the rhythm with longer notes or subdivided notes. I have found that everyone is capable of creating interesting rhythms and repeating them without knowing how they are created. If you are unsure, ask someone in your group who understands rhythm to begin and the rest of you will follow immediately. Once the rhythm is selected, make sure the movement you use clearly reflects it.

   REFLECTIVE QUESTION   How is the quality of movement affected by the rhythm within the meter?

3. Break into groups and choose a leader. The leader establishes a repeated rhythm in movement. It may be any meter that dancer chooses, but the rhythm must be visible in the movement. The leader continues to repeat the rhythm with movement until the rest of the group recognizes the rhythm and begins to move with the same rhythm. When the leader sees that the rest of the group is moving, the leader stops to watch and decides if the rhythm the rest of the group is dancing is the same rhythm the leader established first. If the group has picked up the correct rhythm, then the leader begins again with a new rhythm. The others stop what they are doing, watch the leader, and try to pick up the new rhythm. If the group has not picked up the rhythm correctly, the leader must repeat the first rhythm until everyone has reflected that rhythm correctly in their movement. Note that the movement itself does not need to be repeated, nor should it be. It is better to explore different movements that have the same rhythm.

   REFLECTIVE QUESTIONS   How is rhythm established and perceived in movement? • What suggestions do you have to help dancers establish clear rhythms in their movement?

4. Rhythm sing: By using your voice, you will set up a sound score that directly reflects the rhythm of the movement performed by your partner. You will use vocal sounds that mirror the quality, accent, and timing of the movement you see. For example, a swinging movement might be reflected in the voice by a long sustained "ahhhhhhhh" that changes **pitch**—high at the beginning and end and low in the middle. Four quick sharp movements might be reflected by a strong and sharp "ba, ba, ba, ba." Gliding movements might be reflected with sustained "shhhhhhhhh" sounds. The sound score produced by your voice should be similar to a conversation without real words and with a great deal of change in pitch, quality, and timing, depending on the movement that

your partner performs. As you perform together, one moving and the other creating the sound score, make sure you are coordinated, that you pay attention to the other person, and that you perform a timing that may be coordinated. The dancer should not go so fast as to make it impossible for the "singer" to follow. You may need to go back and repeat something in order to get it right. Setting up simple repetitions in movement, especially at the beginning, is helpful to your partner in order to practice creating the sound score before progressing to more complex choreography. Be sure to change places so each of you gets a turn at creating a sound score with the voice and choreographing. Concentrate on the rhythms. It is not necessary to focus on any one meter. Meter will happen automatically without thinking about it, and the meter may change many times throughout this improvisation.

REFLECTIVE QUESTIONS What challenges did you have in creating the sound score for your partner? • How did you feel about the sound score that was created for your movement?

5. Repeat the previous improvisation, except this time the person creating the vocal sound score establishes the rhythms that must be performed by the dancer.

REFLECTIVE QUESTIONS What challenges did you have in creating movement from your partner's sound score? • How did you feel about movement that was created by your partner for your sound score?

6. Explore ways to go back and forth between moving and "singing" with your partner. You may both move and both vocalize, or one may vocalize while the other moves. There may even be times when you both move in silence. The movement may inspire the vocalized sound score, or the sound score may inspire the movement. Continue to explore ways to combine rhythmic movement and rhythmic vocalizations that are interesting to perform, to hear, and to watch. Whenever it gets too complex to understand what is happening between you, stop and begin again. Remember to start simple and build complexities as you go. Eventually come to a logical conclusion with stillness and quiet.

   Note: This improvisation can become noisy and confusing, so it is best for just one or two couples to work at a time while others watch. Observing this process is beneficial even if everyone does not get a chance to try the process. This could be a movement study for those who do not have an opportunity to perform during the exploration.

REFLECTIVE QUESTIONS Which moments in this improvisation seemed to work for you? Can you reflect on why? • Which moments did not work? What happened? • Explain the meaning of the statement "A performer who dances with musicality makes the body sing."

Discussion of Key Concept

In his book *Rhythmic Training for Dancers*, Robert Kaplan (2002, p. 5) defines rhythm as "The animating element of all music. The element of music that deals with the duration of notes in time. The feeling of movement in music comes from its rhythm." We can think of rhythm in dance as being a specific arrangement of movement with specific durations. For example, in ballroom dancing, the American tango is composed of steps that are slow, slow, quick-quick, slow. (For an in-depth study of time, I recommend Kaplan's text. As a musician who has worked with dancers for many years, Kaplan has bridged the all-too-prevalent gap between musicians and dancers.)

The tango takes place in a meter of 4 counts. A slow step takes one full count as opposed to a quick step, which takes half a count. It might be counted as 1, 2, 3-and-4. This rhythm of the tango remains constant in relationship to any possible changes in rhythm that occur in the music. Interesting rhythms in dance are created within a meter by either sustaining movement through more than 1 count, holding still, or subdividing the counts into small quick movements. In music, rhythms are created with notes and rests of varying duration. For example, in a triple meter, which would be counted 1-2-3, a rhythm may exist that you might count "1 and-2 de and a-3." In music, counts are usually divided in half, so 1 count may be divided into 2 or 4 or even 8 and 16 subdivisions. In the previous example in triple meter, the first count has two subdivisions, and the second count has four subdivisions. These subdivisions are twice as fast as the single count and four times as fast as the single count.

You began exploring interesting rhythms with subdivisions in improvisation 2, perhaps without realizing it. Understanding these rhythms and writing them down require knowledge of music notation. For this you need to actually study music theory. If you have not already done so, I recommend that you plan a course of study in music theory. Every choreographer should have an advanced understanding of music in order to create interesting movement and in order to avoid mistakes when coordinating movement to music.

Accents also create rhythm. Shifting the accent around within the meter will help to create variation in your movement and keep it from being predictable. The mazurka, which is a triple meter, traditionally has its accent on the second or third beat rather than on the first beat, and often alternates between the two. The quality of a mazurka is strong, fun, and surprisingly impish. The shifting accents are teasing. The polonaise, which is also a triple meter, always has the accent on the third beat, which changes the usually lilting triple meter to a strong and regal dance, almost like a **march**. These examples illustrate how changing the rhythm and accents within a meter can completely change the quality of the music. You can also do this with the movement you create.

Syncopation, a technique used by jazz musicians, is created when an accent occurs on a part of the music that is not typically accented or on a subdivision of a beat (see figure 5.4). Syncopation in movement is acquired the same way: accenting a movement that is not typically accented in the meter or accenting a very quick movement that is off the beat. It is important to establish rhythms in your choreography and to be clear about these rhythms in the performance of them in order to create movement with musicality. It is not necessary to perform movement with music in order to be musical. It is necessary for the movement to "sing" in order for the movement to be musical.

We usually learn to dance by dancing to music. The music often dictates the rhythm we set up in our dancing. If you are lucky enough to have live accompaniment in your classes, then you receive variation in the accompaniment to your dancing, and you are continually inspired and challenged by new rhythms and new qualities in the music to employ in your dancing. An exceptional accompanist who has a good working relationship with a dance teacher will pick up on the rhythms the teacher requests and mirror that in the music to help the dancers acquire the **musicality** in their movement that the teacher is projecting. Unfortunately for many, the cost of live accompaniment is prohibitive, and many students practice with recorded music. With recorded music, there is no partnership between teacher and musician.

Figure 5.4 Jazz dance uses strong, sharp movement to visually enhance the syncopation in the music.

Not only is the recorded music created independently of the movement being taught, but often the same music is used over and over so that students stop listening for intricate rhythmic patterns and music quality and instead use the music only to establish meter and tempo. Movement often becomes even, balanced, and boring. It becomes unmusical because dancers are not required to listen to the music or use its rhythmic quality in their dancing. Dancers become slaves to the 8-count phrase, and even when they are waltzing to a meter of 3, they think they are dancing to an 8. This occurs because almost all music that is recorded for dance classes is phrased in 8s and most teachers teach in 8-count phrases of movement.

To be musical in your dancing and your choreography, you must learn to break away from the 8-count phrase to discover new rhythms created by movement independently of any accompaniment. These rhythms must be clear and strong and well established in the movement itself. Once these rhythms are established, then it will be possible to make choices about how these movements may be partnered with music or a sound score. There is no doubt that much of dance is created with music or a sound score in the mind of a choreographer. An advanced choreographer is able to create movement rhythms independently of the sound score while listening to it, and not be a slave to its structure. Good choreography will always stand on its own without accompaniment, so a good test for this is to remove the music or sound score and watch the movement in silence. If the movement is still interesting to watch, then the choreographer has usually been successful in creating interesting rhythms in the movement that have musicality. When movement is dependent on a sound score to create interest, and the movement is no longer interesting when the music or sound score is removed, then the choreography is usually without rhythm and will be deemed mediocre. Your choreography needs to sing on its own.

Movement Studies

1. Create a clapping rhythm in 4 counts as in improvisation 1. Explore various rhythms until you find one that you really like. Be clear about where the accents occur in the rhythm. Repeat it until you are sure you remember it well and that it is interesting to you. Create another rhythm to 4 counts that is very different from the first one you created. For example, if the first rhythm has many subdivided counts in it, think of creating a rhythm that sustains through the counts or places a rest on a count. Again, explore until you find one you like and repeat it until you are sure you can remember it. Now create a solo in a meter of 4 that includes only the two rhythms you have created. You may repeat them and alternate them, placing them in any order you like. Do not repeat the same movement for each rhythm, but design your choreography to flow naturally from one rhythm to the next, using the rhythms to explore variations in movement. Remember to create accents in your movement to coordinate with the accents in the rhythms you created. (You may want to decide on a sequence for your rhythms and record them on a sound tape. Then choreograph to the sound of the claps on the tape. However, make sure you remember the sequence, because you should be able to share your movement study without the use of the clapping so that the rhythms are observable in your movement.) Your work must have a beginning, middle, and end; also watch out for intent.

   This would be a good movement study to add music to after it is created. You will have to be careful to find examples of music in a duple meter that is in a similar tempo to the movement you created.

2. Create a duet that uses rhythm as a "conversation" between the two dancers. Establish a rhythm in the movement of one dancer that may be read by the other dancer who will either pick up the same rhythm or answer with a contrasting rhythm. You might want to begin by directing an improvisation in this way, but eventually you must set something that is interesting and has a beginning, middle, and end.

3. Repeat improvisation 6 on page 110, only plan it and set it. Make sure it is complex enough to be interesting but simple enough not to be too confusing for the audience. You may

wish to use silence as a recovery for too much noise. The rhythms of the voice must relate to the rhythms in the dance. Remember to create a beginning, middle, and end.

Assessment

Use these assessment tools in evaluating your progress toward understanding rhythm as a key concept in choreography.

Class Critique

- Identify the rhythms you observe in the work. Which rhythms are clear, and how could the dancers make those that are not clear more evident? How do these rhythms add interest to the movement, or how might they be designed to create more interest? Which rhythms seem the most interesting to watch?

- Are the dancers able to consider intent as they work in specific rhythms? Why is this easier for some than for others?

- For the dance that includes voice, do the voices coordinate logically with the rhythms in the movement? Does the combination of voice and movement work for you? Why or why not?

- Watch for an obvious beginning, middle, and end in each work.

Rubric

Following is a sample rubric that you may use in evaluating the third movement study for rhythm. Try filling in evaluator comments for yourself and for your peers, or create your own criteria according to what you believe to be important in the understanding of rhythm as a key concept.

Rubric for Rhythm

Criteria	Strong evidence (4 points)	Some evidence (3 points)	Little evidence (2 points)	No evidence (1 point)
Obvious rhythm in movement				
Obvious relationship between rhythm in voice and rhythm in movement				
Clear intent				
Clear beginning, middle, and end				
Total points: (maximum 16 points)				

Documentation

Record your work on video. Record the rhythms you used as well and save them in a file with your video recording. Evaluate the relationship between the rhythms you recorded and the dance you created. Include comments, journal entries, class critique, and rubrics with your video in your digital portfolio.

Drawing Conclusions

Breaking the Rules

Create a dance that has an obvious beat but no variations in rhythm or accents. The only rhythm will be the underlying beat. Be careful to maintain one tempo and one beat without adding any variation.

REFLECTIVE QUESTIONS How is it possible to indicate a beginning, middle, and end without variations in timing? • How is it possible to create interest in your movement without varying the rhythms in your movement? • As a choreographer, why would you decide to use the technique of no variations in rhythms?

Drawing Conclusions

Critical Thinking Essay

Write an essay that discusses your understanding of how choreography is affected by tempo, meter, and rhythm. Use the critical thinking model described in chapter 1. An outline is provided to help you get started.

I. Introduction: Define tempo, meter, and rhythm and make a statement about their importance for a choreographer.

II. Discussion

A. Analysis: Describe key moments of learning, including tempo, meter, and rhythm; you may want to include improvisations and movement studies as examples.

B. Discuss the effect these concepts have on your work.

C. Integrate: Relate things you have noticed about other work as it relates to these three concepts (during peer critique or as you have reviewed choreography on tape or in live performances).

III. Conclusion: Evaluate your progress in the understanding of these key concepts of time. Include personal conclusions that are not offered from this text.

Chapter 6

Quality of Movement

Initial Inquiries

Why is it that some dances just don't seem to connect with your feelings? • Why is it that sometimes when you know you are supposed to understand a story as you watch dance, it just doesn't make sense? • Have you ever been to a performance and read the program notes and noticed that what you expected to see wasn't there? • Do you have to understand dance in order to enjoy it? • What do you have to do with your choreography to help the audience understand your work? • All art is a form of expression. What does dance express well?

You have explored energy, space, and time as separate entities, but you know that not one of these elements can exist by itself. In this chapter, you will explore how these elements work together to create the specific intent that you desire in your work. Whether you are the kind of choreographer who likes to express issues that deal with the human condition, or whether you are the kind of choreographer who likes to play with dance in an abstract way and enjoy movement simply for the sake of movement, you will need to focus on the quality of the movement you create. The quality of the movement will help you express your intent to the audience. In this chapter, you will explore emotions, Laban's effort actions, and the use of language to inspire movement quality. These are not the only approaches to movement quality, but they will start you on a path of discovery that you will continue as you explore more advanced techniques in part IV of this book. Since this entire chapter deals with movement quality from various perspectives, you are asked to wait until the end of the chapter before attempting to complete your movement study on breaking the rules. As before, you are offered forms of assessment after each exploration, and you will be asked to begin to evaluate your own development as a choreographer in the critical thinking essay.

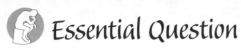

Essential Question

How does a choreographer express emotional content?

Warm-Up

1. While sitting on the floor with the eyes closed, focus on the way you are currently feeling. Think about the things that happened before you arrived in the dance studio today. How much sleep did you get last night? How did your breakfast make you feel? What is the weather like, and to whom have you been talking? What have you been talking about? How do you feel about everything that is going on around you? Has anything in particular happened to you to affect the way you are feeling? Become very aware of your feelings at this moment; now create a shape with your body that communicates that feeling. You may create your shape at any level. You do not have to remain sitting. Your eyes may be open or closed, but they should reflect the way you are feeling. Now explore moving through space with that feeling. Allow the energy and tempo of your movement to reflect the feeling you are trying to project. You may continually pause to find new shapes that reflect your feelings. Move out of that shape into movement to expand your expression. As you move, notice how you employ concepts of energy, space, and time. Eventually settle into a final shape and wait for everyone in your group to find a stillness.

2. Repeat the previous warm-up, only this time select a feeling that is in complete contrast to your current feelings. Take a moment to decide on that contrasting feeling and focus on how your body might react to that feeling. Now create a shape that reflects that feeling. Expand the feeling by exploring movement that travels throughout the space. Again, you may pause once in a while in new shapes and alternate between stillness and movement to project this new feeling. Develop an awareness of the choreographic elements you are using. Eventually find a stillness as a conclusion and wait for others to complete their exploration.

   REFLECTIVE QUESTIONS How do the choreographic concepts in energy, space, and time suggest particular moods or feelings? What happens to those elements when you go from one mood to a contrasting mood?

Improvisations

1. Take a simple emotion, such as sad. Create a shape that reflects this emotion. Now begin to move, keeping that same emotion for a short time. Now explore different forms of sad and reasons for being sad, and allow your movement to reflect those nuances of sad. How many kinds of sad are there? What subtle differences can you express in your movement? What other words can you use in place of *sad* that will help you find new movement? What about *discouraged, forlorn, listless, lonely, helpless, feeling left out*? Keep thinking of new words and change your movement to fit the new words. Repeat this process with *angry, happy*, and *afraid* so that you have explored many variations in these simple emotions.

2. Create emotion statues. One person begins by going to the center of the room to establish a shape that communicates a particular emotion. The next person must add to the statue in an interesting way by changing levels, paying attention to focus, creating parallel or opposing lines, and creating intent. This new dancer must create the same emotion that was established or enhance it with this new shape. Continue adding to the statue until five or six dancers are included. Once the statue is finished, the dancers in the statue

should find a way to move out of the statue and offstage with the same emotion that was created in the statue. Repeat with other emotions. The first person always establishes the emotion.

REFLECTIVE QUESTIONS How does dance communicate emotion? • Why would you use choreography to communicate emotion rather than explain the emotion with words?

3. Play some music that has a great deal of variation in dynamics. Listen to the music and imagine emotions that are reflected in the music. Create movement that reflects the emotional content of the music. Do not use music with words, because that will cause you to become too literal. (See Emotional Content in the Music Resources section near the end of this book.)

REFLECTIVE QUESTIONS How do we interpret emotional content from music? What are the musical elements that communicate emotion?

4. Create an abstract movement phrase. Abstract in this sense means no literal or suggested narrative or emotional content. Use movement vocabulary that is from a particular dance technique, such as ballet or jazz. Make sure the phrase has a beginning, middle, and end. Practice it a few times to become familiar with it. Then choose an emotion and perform the phrase again expressing that emotion. Instead of only placing a new feeling on top of the movement as you perform it, make choices to change the movement to express the mood more clearly. Do you need to change the timing? The shape of a particular movement? The direction? The energy? The level? Feel free to make these changes, but hold on to the original choreography in some way.

REFLECTIVE QUESTIONS Why would you want to be able to communicate emotion through an abstract formal technique, such as ballet or tap? • How is it possible to maintain the integrity of the technique while adding these emotions?

Discussion of Key Concept

As a choreographer, you need to know what dance is good at expressing and what it does not have the ability to express well. This will help you be more successful in your attempts. For example, I do not recommend that you attempt to tell the story *Alice's Adventures in Wonderland* even if you are choreographing for children. Although it is a familiar story and has been created in many media, the charm of the story is in the written language. Although the characters are interesting, they are interesting because of the way they speak, not because of what they do. It is possible to create interesting costumes for these characters, because they are unusual, but it is impossible to project the play on words that is so critical to Lewis Carroll's success with this story.

So what does dance do well? Martha Graham (1894-1991), one of the pioneers of American modern dance, was a very expressive choreographer. Her work focused on the psyche of the human mind and spirit. Although you might see Graham's work as dated, you cannot deny that she, along with others during her time, discovered the ability of dance to tell the innermost secrets of the human condition. And although she told stories, the story was not the focus of her work, but the subtle psychological turmoil that each of her characters experienced.

Dance uses the body as an instrument. Body language can be exaggerated and abstracted in dance to project an infinite number of feelings, subtle moods, and emotions (see figure 6.1). Many choreographers, especially those rebelling against what they thought was the overly dramatic early modern movement, have ignored this side of choreography and embraced only the abstract craft of movement. Today it is important to recognize both sides of the spectrum and to be able to create both with abstract craft and with literal emotion, especially as a beginning choreographer. Eventually you will discover your personal strength and passion for creating movement, and you will lean in one direction or the other. But as a student, you must explore both methods of intent.

There is no getting around it: The body tells stories about the feelings of human beings. George Balanchine believed that it was not necessary to apply emotion to choreography. Choreography uses the human form, and an art form that is connected to the human form will tell a human story regardless of whether you intend to create a story. Audiences naturally read emotion and feeling when watching someone move on the stage (see figure 6.2). Balanchine focused on creating abstract movement and expected his audience to read stories and emotional content from the work, even though he never layered it there himself. And true enough, many of his pas de deux were read as complex emotional relationships.

Working with emotion and dance can be a trap, which is the reason Balanchine, Merce Cunningham (1919-2009), and Alwin Nikolais (1912-1993) tried to separate emotion from their work. It is easy to become melodramatic and clichéd. Although exaggeration has its place, too much drama can be insulting to an audience. Emotion that is layered on top of movement rarely works. And facial expressions that are superficial and disconnected to the choreography lack impact. A golden rule for portraying emotion is "Let the movement tell the story." Antony Tudor (1909-1987), known for his psychological ballets, related his experience at American Ballet Theatre, where his ballet *Pillar of Fire* was so successful that it was being repeated often. The dancers had performed it many times, and Tudor felt it was losing its impact. He discovered that his dancers knew the story too well and were feeling every emotion deeply in the emotionally charged work. Tudor

Figure 6.1 A dramatic expressive dance.

Figure 6.2 A partnership created without emotion and with a focus on design and effort may still suggest emotion to the audience.

asked the company not to think about the emotions in the next performance. They were simply to do the steps as beautifully and as accurately as possible because emotion was already built into the movement. The next performance was the best performance of the ballet. After following Tudor's instructions, the dancers came off stage completely drained emotionally. The movement had told the story, and even the dancers had listened.

So what are these tools that may be used to express emotion through dance? You have already explored the elements of time, space, and energy and made discoveries about the way these elements communicate. You have learned that curved shapes are soft, comforting, and welcoming, whereas straight lines are usually strong, sometimes intimidating, and menacing. The best way to find movement that expresses a particular feeling is to imagine the feeling you want to express and improvise movement that seems to express that feeling. To ensure that it is movement that is expressing the emotion and not you as an actor, ask yourself to express the emotion in different body parts. How would your head move? Your torso? Your arm? Your big toe? If you are still having trouble, go back to your notes and look for the elements of dance that you have identified to express a particular mood; use those elements first. Then fine-tune the movement by adding the nuances you need for a particular statement.

When creating choreography with an intent for expressing an emotional landscape, it becomes imperative that you never "drop the ball." You should not go from expressive movement to abstract, getting caught up in the design of the movement and forgetting the original intent of the work. This will cause the audience to lose their place, so to speak, in the sequence of emotional events. Also, you must never jump from one emotion to the next without allowing for a logical transition that may be read by your audience. The journey on which you take your dancers and that you expect your audience to follow must be clearly created through the elements of choreography that will express your intent (see figure 6.3).

Although expressive dancers are wonderful to work with and a joy to watch, you should not depend on a particularly expressive dancer to carry your story. The responsibility of telling the story lies with the choreographer. That dancer may help you define the choreographic elements you need for your intent. For example, you may wish to tell your dancer a story in order to obtain a particular mood. But then you must watch the performance to decide which choreographic elements work and which choreographic elements do not work. If you want your choreography to be lasting, you must be able to switch dancers without losing your choreographic intent.

Figure 6.3 Expressive dance uses strong emotion to create movement quality.

Take a moment to record in your journal any personal discoveries you have made concerning the way movement is able to express emotional content. After you have reviewed your thoughts, the following sequence of projects will take you through a process of personal discovery as you translate your emotions to movement that you create on yourself as the expressive dancer.

Movement Study

This movement study has three parts. Part 1 involves drawing. Part 2 requires building a wire sculpture. Part 3 involves creating choreography. This movement study is taken from Eugene Loring's choreography classes at the University of California at Irvine in the late 1960s and early '70s.

Part 1

You will need a large pad of newsprint and a strong crayon (I like to use the husky crayons because they are less likely to break). Think of an experience you have had that was very emotional and is still vivid in your memory. There is no limit in amount of time this experience took, but make sure you can recall all the details of the experience, what happened when, and how you felt each step of the way. You will not have to share the actual experience with anyone, but you should be able to work with it for a long period. Therefore, do not pick something that has not yet been resolved or that may be painful for you to dwell on for long periods. Once you have selected your experience, spend a few minutes reviewing it in sequence. Think of it as a story and recall each part of that story in your memory. Focus on the places that are vague and see if you can bring them back. Notice the places that changed your feelings or attitude and make sure you remember these transitions well. Now sit on the floor in front of your newsprint with a crayon in your hand. Close your eyes and draw the experience from beginning to end. Use the first extended improvisation in chapter 4 as a guide for this activity. Instead of using the music to inspire your drawing on paper, you are using the emotions from your experience to create the lines on your paper. Place the crayon on the paper for the beginning and draw your emotions on the page while you imagine the entire sequence of events. You may want to do this several times until you are happy with the reflection of your experience on the paper. You may realize on your first try that you have forgotten some transition or important occurrence in the experience. Or you may have been perfectly happy with your first try and go with that.

Part 2

Now you will take the line drawing you created and transpose it into three dimensions by creating a wire sculpture. You will need some pliable wire, such as picture-framing wire, or electrical wire. Coat hangers are too hard to bend. You will also need something to anchor your wire at the base. It could be a small block of wood or a box top or a plastic container. An old CD will work if your wire is not too heavy. Looking at the lines you created on your paper and thinking of your experience again, make a line sculpture with the wire, beginning at one end of the wire and molding it through space, until you come to the end of the experience. Make sure you reflect your emotions through the shapes made in space by the wire. When the wire sculpture is completed, bring it to class and share the sculpture by describing the emotions in the experience while pointing out your interpretation of those feelings in your sculpture. You do not have to share the details of the experience, only the feelings that were involved.

Part 3

Create a movement study that reflects the entire experience. Use the drawing and sculpture to give you movement ideas. Remember to use body shape, floor patterns, and movement patterns through space. Think about how your wire sculpture may be translated through movement with energy, space, and time. The sequence of your drawing, your wire sculpture, and your dance should be the sequence of your experience. Pay particular attention to the transitions in the experience, the points when your emotions change. Do not rush to complete the dance. Explore each important moment in your experience.

Assessment

Use these assessment tools in evaluating your progress toward understanding emotion as a key concept in choreography.

Class Critique

- First look at the drawing and wire sculpture in relation to the choreography and see if the relationships between all three seem logical to you. To clarify, have the choreographer describe the creative process of all three creations (the drawing, the wire sculpture, and the dance). After hearing the explanation, make suggestions of where things need to be clearer or where you are confused, paying particular attention to transitions or changes in emotion.

- Identify the choreographic concepts that were used to portray particular emotions, and evaluate their success. Make suggestions for change and try them.

- Since this is a narrative form (something that follows a sequence of events), there should be strong evidence of a beginning, middle, and end. Evaluate this form in each work.

Rubric

Following is a sample rubric that you may use in evaluating all three parts of the movement study on emotion. You may use this rubric in evaluating your peers, and your peers can complete rubrics for you. If you wish, you may change the criteria to be more in line with what you believe to be important content for this movement study.

Rubric for Emotions

Criteria	Strong evidence (4 points)	Some evidence (3 points)	Little evidence (2 points)	No evidence (1 point)
Logical relationship between emotional content and drawing				
Logical relationship between emotional content and wire sculpture				
Logical relationship between emotional content and choreography				
Interesting and varied use of choreographic concepts to express emotion				
Strong narrative form with beginning, middle, and end and logical transitions				
Total: (maximum 20 points)				

Documentation

Write comments on your drawing that explain where the emotional content is depicted throughout the experience. Write a description of your wire sculpture, explaining the relationships between the sculpture and the emotional content in the experience. Save all of your work in a safe physical location to be included with your digital portfolio. Or you may want to photograph both your drawing and your wire sculpture to include in your digital portfolio. Make sure you take photos of the wire sculpture from multiple perspectives so that you can see the entire sculpture when viewing it. Record your choreography and include a description of the relationship of the choreography to the emotional content in the event. If you have the software necessary, add narrative to the video so that you can be very clear about the connections between the event and the choreographic content. Evaluate your work by including comments from your peers and mentor.

 Essential Question

Why do specific combinations of energy, space, and time create movement quality?

Warm-Up

This includes a review of previously explored key concepts in time, space, and energy using a focus on Laban terminology.

1. Time (tempo): quick. Choose a large movement with your right arm. Practice it a few times until you are familiar with the entire movement. Now perform that movement as quickly as you can and freeze the action at the end so that the quick movement is followed by a stillness. Repeat this several times until you get the feeling of a very quick, sudden movement. Now explore this kind of movement with another body part. Complete a movement very quickly and halt that movement so that the movement starts and stops very suddenly.

2. Time (tempo): sustained. Explore movement that is continuous and in slow motion without any obvious beginning or ending. Begin by exploring the first large arm movement that you created in the previous warm-up. Begin the movement very gradually and end the movement very gradually so that the beginning and ending are hardly noticeable. Now explore this kind of sustained movement with other body parts and with full-body movement.

REFLECTIVE QUESTIONS How does changing the tempo of a movement change its intent? What qualities are created by the extremes of quick and sustained movement?

3. Focus (space, direction): direct. Find a point in the room to focus on. Walk directly to that point and stop. Create a shape that is focused directly on that point. (Same as in chapter 4, direction.) Find a new point to focus on. Walk directly to it. Repeat a new shape that is focused directly on that spot. Now create movement that moves directly toward a focal point in the room. Allow the movement to be isolated into small body parts and expand to include full-body movement. All movement should be making direct pathways toward a focal point in the space.

4. Focus (space, direction): indirect. Stand in the middle of the space and react to a feeling of being pulled in many directions at once. You are being pulled first one way and then the other. This causes you to wander through the space in no particular direction, continually changing your pathway, your facing direction, and even your level as these forces pull you up and down, side to side, forward, back, around, everywhere at once. Rest. Now begin swinging one arm in no particular direction. Allow it to wander around in space. Add a second arm, include head, then torso, and so on until a full meandering swing is accomplished. Continue to create curved pathways through space with no particular focal point. Steady yourself and rest.

REFLECTIVE QUESTIONS How does changing the focus of a movement change its intent? What qualities are created by the extremes of direct and indirect movement?

5. Weight (energy, dynamics): strong. Begin walking around the room. Imagine you are walking on the beach in the sand and you are trying to make very deep footprints. Use your entire body to create the deepest footprints possible by gathering all your strength behind each step. Now explore further by using all your strength to make holes in the space around you. Use different body parts. Try various tempos, but keep your energy high.

6. Weight (energy, dynamics): light. Again, imagining you are on a beach, walk as if you are trying to leave no footprint at all. You must just barely touch the sand with your feet in order not to leave a print. After you explore this feeling of walking very lightly, explore moving other body parts very lightly in the space around you. And move though the space while touching other dancers very lightly and using different parts of the body to make very soft, light contact.

REFLECTIVE QUESTIONS How does changing the dynamics of a movement change its intent? • What qualities are created by the extremes of strong and light movement?

Improvisations

These improvisations combine specific concepts within the elements of time, space, and energy as practiced in the warm-up in order to form the eight Laban **effort actions**. The effort actions are labeled at the end of each improvisation.

1. Combining direct, quick, and strong: Establish movement that is direct. This movement must establish a focal point and move directly toward it. The focal point does not always have to be away from your body. It may be a point close in to your body, requiring the movement to come directly into you. Keep changing the focal point, but make sure your movements always travel directly to it. Explore this with various body parts and with full-body movement. Remember to keep your movements in a direct line. Now continue these direct movements, but do them quickly. Make each movement with an obvious beginning and ending, and stop for a moment at the end of each movement so that the movements are sudden. Finally, add a great deal of energy to each movement so that your movements are strong. This combination of focus, time, and weight creates the effort action called punch. If you make a fist and perform a punch in space, you will see that it is direct, quick, and strong.

REFLECTIVE QUESTIONS What quality is created by the effort action of punch? How might you use this quality to achieve intent in your choreography? What emotional content might be expressed by using this effort action?

2. Combining indirect, quick, and strong: Establish movement that is indirect. This movement should have no particular focal point and should wander through the space, usually in curved pathways. Again, explore with different body parts and with full-body movement. Now perform these movements very quickly with obvious starting points and stopping points so that all your movement is sudden and quick. Finally add a lot of energy so that these sudden, indirect movements are also strong. This combination of focus, time, and weight is the effort action called slash.

REFLECTIVE QUESTIONS What quality is created by the effort action of slash? How might you use this quality to achieve intent in your choreography? What emotional content might be expressed by using this effort action?

3. Combining direct, sustained, and strong: Again, establish movement that is direct. Find many ways to move in a direct pathway with a direct focus. Remember that the focus can be in as well as out. Now change your tempo to very slow movement. Sustain that movement so that there is no beginning or end to the movement; one movement transitions into the next movement without a perceptible stop or start. Now add a great deal of energy to this slow, sustained direct movement. This effort action is called press.

REFLECTIVE QUESTIONS What quality is created by the effort action of press? How might you use this quality to achieve intent in your choreography? What emotional content might be expressed by using this effort action?

4. Combining indirect, sustained, and strong: Establish movement that is indirect. There is no established focus. Move very slowly through space so that there is no perceptible beginning or ending to your movements. Now add a great deal of energy to your movements. This combination of elements is the effort action called wring. If you think of your body as a wet washcloth and perform a movement that simulates the action of wringing the water out of you, you will be using indirect, slow, and strong movement.

   REFLECTIVE QUESTIONS   What quality is created by the effort action of wring? How might you use this quality to achieve intent in your choreography? What emotional content might be expressed by using this effort action?

5. Combining direct, quick, and light: Establish direct movement through space, change the timing to quick and sudden, then make sure you are using very little energy so that your movements are very light. This effort action is called dab.

   REFLECTIVE QUESTIONS   What quality is created by the effort action of dab? How might you use this quality to achieve intent in your choreography? What emotional content might be expressed by using this effort action?

6. Combining indirect, quick, and light: Establish indirect movements in space. Perform them so that they're quick and sudden. Then make sure you are using very little energy, as if you are brushing things away lightly in space. This effort action is called flick.

   REFLECTIVE QUESTIONS   What quality is created by the effort action of flick? How might you use this quality to achieve intent in your choreography? What emotional content might be expressed by using this effort action?

7. Combining direct, sustained, and light: Establish direct movement in space. Now make sure the movements are slow and sustained, and use very little energy in your movement. This combination creates the effort action called glide.

   REFLECTIVE QUESTIONS   What quality is created by the effort action of glide? How might you use this quality to achieve intent in your choreography? What emotional content might be expressed by using this effort action?

8. Combining indirect, sustained, and light: Establish indirect movement that wanders through space. Make sure you are moving in slow motion with no beginning or ending to your movement. Perform with very little energy, as if you were very light and meandering through space. This last effort action is called float.

   REFLECTIVE QUESTIONS   What quality is created by the effort action of float? How might you use this quality to achieve intent in your choreography? What emotional content might be expressed by using this effort action?

Discussion of Key Concept

Effort actions are mathematical combinations of the extremes within the dance elements of space, time, and energy as defined by Rudolf von Laban. Within this system of defining effort, Laban selected focus (space), time (or tempo), and weight (or energy) to combine and determine possible efforts in movement. You will note from our exploration of these three elements that there are many other key concepts, such as line and shape in space, rhythm in time, and flow in energy. Laban used these additional concepts in his complete system of **effort shape**, but this discussion of effort actions is limited to the specific concepts of tempo, focus, and dynamics. Note that the specific terms he used for these three concepts are time, focus, and weight. Time really indicates tempo and includes the two extremes of quick and sustained. Focus includes the extremes of direct and indirect, which were explored in chapter 4. Weight really indicates dynamics, or the amount of energy used in performing a movement. Weight includes the extremes of strong and light. Combinations of these six extremes are specific to the Laban system of movement analysis and provide a very concrete way of looking at movement according to the effort it takes to accomplish it rather than approaching the movement according to its intent. However, as the terms assigned to each combination suggest, intent is very apparent in each effort action. Emotional content as well as narrative content may be projected very effectively using these effort actions as vocabulary for choreography. Table 6.1 shows each effort action and how it is created through combinations of focus, time, and weight.

It is easy to become self-indulgent while creating emotional content or drama for a piece of choreography, especially if the content is personal. This may happen when something is strongly felt and you are very close to the situation. Movement may become predictable and clichéd because you are determined to communicate the literal side of your story. You may be tempted to use movements such as placing the hands to a crying face or slamming fists into the floor. You may rely on facial expressions too heavily. Effort actions may help you abstract an emotion and find its true essence, and they allow you to find new and unusual vocabulary for expressing that emotion. In contrast, sometimes when an emotion is strongly felt, you may have difficulty placing yourself at the point of view of the audience. Because you already feel the emotion, you may miss the opportunity to express that emotion to the audience. The movement will fall short without your realizing it because the emotion is so real for you personally. Effort actions can bring your emotion to life, again by abstracting that emotion into action. You may take that action into unusual body parts and find unique ways to express something that may seem ordinary (see figure 6.5 on page 128).

I have also found effort actions to be helpful in creating movement appropriate for particular characters or pieces of music. By using them, you may avoid falling into the usual traps. For example, if you want to choreograph to Prokofiev's *Peter and the Wolf*, you may be tempted to find movements that you think are birdlike for the bird. You will try to find unique ways to flap your wings or scurry along a branch or soar through the air because you are thinking literally of a bird. However, if you listen to the music after you have become very familiar with effort actions, you will be able to hear effort actions in the music for the bird. Those actions might be flick and glide. If you stop thinking of the bird and create movement that uses these two effort actions traveling through every body part, you will be surprised at how birdlike your movement has become. Of course the music helps here, because Prokofiev was a master at creating an accurate quality in the music for each of his characters. But this is a good way to find an interesting and unique relationship to any music.

Table 6.1   Effort Actions

FOCUS		WEIGHT		TIME		
Direct	Indirect	Strong	Light	Quick	Sustained	Effort action
×		×		×		Punch
×		×			×	Press
×			×	×		Dab
×			×		×	Glide
	×	×		×		Slash
	×		×	×		Flick
	×	×			×	Wring
	×		×		×	Float

Figure 6.5 From stage right to stage left (left to right in photo): flick, punch, dab, press, wring.

I have worked with very young students who have never danced before. I've asked them to dance a story using effort actions to create their characters. I am always amazed at how much variety of movement I get from those inexperienced dancers. Because effort actions are built on strong contrasts of time, space, and energy, they provide opportunities for variation that are interesting to watch, even in abstract form without emotional content. And I am pleased at how quickly the inexperienced students leave the realm of acting and start dancing the qualities of the characters, which is what dance is all about.

Movement Studies

1. Pick three effort actions and create a movement study using only those effort actions. It will help if you do not select all strong or all light or all fast or all slow. Select contrasting effort actions to create variation in your work.

2. Decide on an emotional sequence for a dance. Assign one or more effort actions to fit each emotion and create the dance using the effort actions rather than the emotions to create the dance.

3. Listen to a piece of music you would like to choreograph to. (Do not use music with words.) Assign possible effort actions to the music as you listen to it. Create movement that fits the effort actions the music suggests independently of the music. Add the music back after you have completed the choreography.

Assessment

Use these assessment tools in evaluating your progress toward understanding effort actions as a key concept in choreography.

Class Critique

- Identify the effort actions that you observe in the work. Are they clearly defined? Talk about any interesting contrasts you notice.
- Discuss any emotional content that seems evident. Does the emotional content come from the effort actions? How?
- If you complete the third movement study, how do the effort actions relate to the music? How does the music contribute to the choreography? How does the choreography contribute to the music? Does it work for you? Why or why not?

Rubric

Following is a sample rubric that you may use in evaluating the first movement study on effort actions. You may use this rubric in evaluating your peers, and your peers can complete rubrics for you. If you wish, you may change the criteria to be more in line with what you believe to be important content for this movement study.

Rubric for Effort Actions

Criteria	Strong evidence (4 points)	Some evidence (3 points)	Little evidence (2 points)	No evidence (1 point)
Clear performance of at least three effort actions				
Good contrast in movement				
Clear beginning, middle, and end				
Total: (maximum 12 points)				

Documentation

Record your work. Attach a narrative to the work that identifies the effort actions used, or create a slide show of still photos. Include a rubric and comments from class critique to record an evaluation of your work. Include comments from your journal to record your learning process.

 ## Essential Question

What is movement quality and why does a choreographer need to be aware of it?

Warm-Up

1. Begin walking through the space. Find your own pathways. Be aware of others around you, and keep to your own personal space. Vary your walk in some way. Change any of the elements you have learned about energy, space, and time. Now find a new word to describe the way you are walking. You are no longer walking; you are _____. (If you have slowed down and added stillness in a halting fashion, your word might be *hesitating*.) Now go back to walking. Vary your walk in another way. Find a new word or combination of words. Keep doing this several times until you have collected a few descriptive action words. Write them in your journal. Remember to begin by changing an element of movement first. After the movement has changed, think of a word to describe the movement. Go through a list of concepts: dynamics, energy flow, size, level, body part, self-space, general space, and so on.

   REFLECTIVE QUESTIONS   How did changing the key concepts affect your walk? What challenges did you have in finding words to describe your movement? Why do you think these challenges exist?

2. Perform a full-body movement in self-space that changes level. Find a short sequence that can be repeated several times, and practice it. Now take the first word you created from the previous warm-up and apply it to this movement. If your first word was *hesitating*, you would probably perform this movement with different timing. You might need to change the shape of the movement. If it was extroverted and open, you might want to close your shapes. Think of your word and try to do everything you can to express that word in your movement. Repeat this with another movement and your second word. Keep going until you have explored all the words you created in the previous warm-up.

   REFLECTIVE QUESTIONS   What were your challenges in creating new movement from the descriptive words as cues? Why do these challenges exist?

Improvisations

1. Begin alone in the performance space. Think of a quality that may be expressed through movement. It can be anything. It does not have to be an effort action or an emotion. It can be any quality you like. Keeping that quality in your head, begin moving in the performance space with that quality. The next person will enter the performance space mimicking the quality you have established but performing his or her own choice of movement. The quality should be maintained, but the movement vocabulary may be quite different. Continue to add dancers until five or six are dancing together at the same time. Once the whole group is moving, find a logical way to conclude the improvisation and find a stillness that connects in some way to the established quality. At the end of the improvisation, solicit ideas for words that might match the quality that was performed. Write the words in your journal. Repeat this improvisation many times, continually changing groups to allow some to observe and some to dance, always changing the quality with each improvisation.

   REFLECTIVE QUESTIONS   What were your challenges in creating movement that matched the quality of other dancers? • How did you observe quality? What did you look for in order to decide on the quality to use?

2. Choose a partner. This person will be your collaborator in creating an action defined by the words in table 6.2. Using the list of action words that connote quality, have someone call out a word at random. The duet must create movement together that depicts the action word given. Continue to explore more words. Try to find more than one solution for each.

REFLECTIVE QUESTIONS   Was it possible to create more than one movement quality for each word? Why or why not? • How many variations in energy, time, and space may be used in creating the same action?

3. As a solo, repeat the previous improvisation using the words in table 6.2 that depict states of mind. Again, as each word is called out, explore as many variations in time, space, and energy as you can for that word, keeping true to that particular state of mind.

REFLECTIVE QUESTIONS   How is your performance of states of mind different from your previous performances of descriptive action words? • How did you use the elements of movement to achieve the movement quality you needed?

Table 6.2 Words   That Suggest Quality

Action words			State-of-mind words	
Admire	Frolic	Scamper	Alienated	Friendly
Annoy	Fumble	Scratch	Angry	Frustrated
Bend	Fume	Separate	Anguished	Furious
Boast	Glide	Shake	Annoyed	Generous
Catch	Grab	Simper	Anxious	Grateful
Chomp	Grapple	Skitter	Apprehensive	Guilty
Chop	Grieve	Sink	Arrogant	Haughty
Claim	Grind	Skid	Astonished	Hostile
Climb	Grope	Slice	At ease	Humble
Clutch	Hide	Slide	Blissful	Impatient
Collide	Hinder	Slink	Boastful	Irritated
Command	Hinger	Slither	Bold	Jealous
Cram	Jab	Smash	Bothered	Loathing
Cringe	Juggle	Snatch	Buoyant	Longing
Crush	Liberate	Sneak	Careless	Modest
Curse	Lunge	Soar	Cautious	Playful
Dab	Manipulate	Spill	Cheerful	Pretentious
Deliberate	Meander	Spin	Content	Proud
Direct	Mirror	Spiral	Courageous	Relieved
Drip	Mix	Spread	Delighted	Saucy
Drop	Order	Spring	Desperate	Shy
Dunk	Patter	Squash	Disgusted	Skittish
Fight	Pity	Squeeze	Dissatisfied	Snug
Flatter	Plunder	Stare	Distressed	Sorrowful
Flinch	Plunge	Swagger	Dreamy	Spirited
Float	Pry open	Sweep	Enthusiastic	Timid
Flutter	Pull	Swirl	Envious	Tortured
Forage	Punch	Taunt	Estranged	Vain
Force	Push	Tease	Excited	Weary
Forgive	Repel	Tempt	Fearful	Yearning
Fracture	Resist	Threaten	Feeling of loss	
Freeze	Restrain		Fiendish	

4. Now combine words, using one state-of-mind word and one action word. Pick them randomly and explore movement that expresses both words simultaneously. Examples are *haughty flutter* and *irritated skid*. You may wish to leave this to chance by placing these words on strips of paper in two baskets. Choose one word from each basket and perform the combination.

    REFLECTIVE QUESTIONS What were your challenges in creating movement that matched the quality of these words? How did you interpret the qualities from the words into movement?

5. Take the previous improvisation one step further by creating duets. Each person selects two words (one from each list) and then uses these words to interact in a duet. Each person must stay true to the qualities that have been chosen and must create a "conversation" using that movement quality with a partner. Conversation means that you must relate to your partner as if you are talking to each other, but you are using movement to talk instead of speech.

    REFLECTIVE QUESTIONS How does movement quality affect a duet? How do you think movement quality will affect a group dance?

Discussion of Key Concept

Quality is what makes a particular movement unique. All movement may be qualified by describing its attributes. If you describe the energy, the spatial elements, and the timing of a movement, you are analyzing it. When you consider the effect of all these attributes together, the resulting effect is the quality of the movement. Usually quality is perceived by the senses. How does it look? What does it look like? How does it feel? What does it feel like? Every movement has quality, but often the intent of a choreographer is to create a particular quality of movement. In this case, it is necessary to understand how each element of movement may affect the overall quality of the movement that results. We have discussed quality as we explored each key choreographic concept independently. Even the words for dynamics suggest quality: *strong* and *light*. We talked about curved lines as being nurturing, protective, and welcoming. You cannot separate quality from movement any more than you can separate movement from time. However, you can analyze a particular quality for its key attributes in order to make it easier to create the quality you seek. For example, vibratory movement is something that is often used in creative movement classes. What does vibratory mean? What actually is a vibration? Something that is vibrating is almost still. But within that stillness is an extremely small yet fast and continuous back-and-forth movement. As you begin to perform this movement, you will discover that it is bound, because it takes a lot of energy to perform, yet you must restrict the size of the movement. A good choreographer will be able to break up a movement into all of its attributes for two reasons: to communicate it to the dancers and to create many variations of the same quality by altering other elements.

Texture in choreography is created by the variations in **movement quality** used within the work. We think of texture as something we can actually feel with our fingers. But qualities can be felt through our eyes and through our kinesthetic sense. We can feel movement that is sharp and movement that is smooth. We can see bubbly movement and movement that is harsh. An infinite number of possibilities exist for combining subtle differences in energy, space, and time in movement, therefore creating an infinite number of possibilities for movement qualities, much more than could ever be described through language. This is what makes dance and all the arts a very special and mysterious way to communicate. The arts are above language. It is possible for us to understand the communication of these qualities without ever being able to describe them with words. Dance has its own unique set of attributes that govern the way it communicates.

You will notice from the previous explorations that I believe in the ability of dance to communicate emotions, states of mind, and actions. I do not believe in its ability to be precise in the telling of a story or the humor of a pun. For this reason I have focused your explorations in movement quality on emotional content, effort actions, and words that connote states of mind and action. Even though dance is above language, descriptive language can be a tool for exploring new ways to create movement quality. The mere fact that I have asked you to find more than one solution for each word should be a clue to the expectations I have for dance as an infinite means of communication that goes beyond these words. That is why it is often hard for people to describe a performance they have seen. It is often easier to break down the elements of energy, space, and time and analyze their use individually than to describe the overall effect, which has created quality and texture in the work and contributed to its intent.

If we are capable of understanding extremely subtle differences in quality when observing dance, why is it that people have different interpretations after watching the same dance? Heinrich von Kleist (1777-1811), a German author, poet, and dramatist, would tell us there is no "innocent eye." Each audience member will come to the performance with a unique set of experiences with which to relate your work. The actual quality of the movement you intended to produce may be perceived as a completely different quality by the viewer (see figure 6.6). So, although you may make every effort to be precise with intent, and you should be, the audience will expand the interpretation of that intent to encompass the experience of every member in the audience. Because we are human, there are commonalities among our experiences and interpretations. And although we may not be able to vocalize these commonalities, they do exist. For this reason, we strive for an understanding of our work. We strive for that common interpretation or common experience. That is what we mean when we say we want people to be able to relate to our work. So it is important to be precise about your intent while you create by being precise in the subtle qualities you use in creating something that you hope will relay a personal understanding.

Figure 6.6 Three subtle differences in quality: excited, delighted, and cheerful.

Movement Studies

1. From table 6.2, choose three contrasting action words that connote quality. Use one to create the beginning of your work, one to create the middle, and one to create the ending. Make sure that your transitions from one to the next are logical by concentrating on the intent of the work. Ask yourself why the quality and action change here. Make sure you answer this in your movement. Remember to explore multiple solutions for each word and select the solutions that will work best for your movement study. Be prepared to defend your movement choices.

2. From table 6.2, pick three contrasting state-of-mind words that connote quality. Create a movement study using these words in the same way as described in the previous movement study. Again, be prepared to defend your movement choices.

3. From table 6.2, pick three combinations of action and state-of-mind words and create a movement study in the same way as described previously.

Assessment

Use these assessment tools in evaluating your progress toward understanding movement quality as a key concept in choreography.

Class Critique

- Identify the qualities evident in each work. Is it possible to discover which words were used as inspiration by the choreographer? Why or why not?
- Identify the moments of transition from one quality to another. Are the transitions logical? Do they work for you? Why or why not?
- Was the choreographer able to support the choice of movement for each quality? Do you have suggestions for making the quality more clear or interesting?

Rubric

Following is a sample rubric that you may use in evaluating any one of the three movement studies on movement quality. You may use this rubric in evaluating your peers, and your peers can complete rubrics for you. If you wish, you may change the criteria to be more in line with what you believe to be important content for this movement study.

Rubric for Quality Language

Criteria	Strong evidence (4 points)	Some evidence (3 points)	Little evidence (2 points)	No evidence (1 point)
Logical relationship between words and movement qualities				
Interesting variations within each movement quality				
Good support for movement choices				
Logical transitions between movement qualities				
Total: (maximum 16 points)				

Documentation

Record your work on video and attach a narration that labels the movement qualities that you chose to work with. Write a defense of your movement choices and include it with your video in your portfolio. Also include a completed rubric and comments from class critique. Rate yourself on your understanding of movement quality.

Drawing Conclusions

Breaking the Rules

Try to create a movement study void of quality. You will use no emotion, no effort actions, and no quality words to help you create. Try to be completely abstract. This may be virtually impossible, since movement without quality may be considered a quality on its own. However, try to limit your focus on movement quality and see what happens.

REFLECTIVE QUESTIONS   How does working this way affect the final quality of your work? Is this a valid way to create choreography?

Drawing Conclusions

Critical Thinking Essay

Explain your use of movement quality and how this relates to your developing style as a choreographer. Some choreographers are much more abstract than others. Some are comfortable developing movement by thinking only of the individual design and kinetic effects created by movement, whereas others are very focused on emotional or physical qualities of their work. What about you? An outline follows to help you get started:

I. Introduction: Define movement quality and make a statement about your comfort level working with it.

II. Discussion

   A. Analysis: Discuss your use of emotions, effort actions, and descriptive vocabulary to inspire your work. Highlight key moments of learning about movement quality.

   B. Reflection: Discuss why you believe you can be successful or unsuccessful working with these options for movement quality.

   C. Integration: Compare your work to that of others in your class.

III. Conclusion: Evaluate your strengths as a choreographer. How does your understanding of movement quality affect your work?

Part III

Exploring Synthesis

Chapter 7

Sound

Initial Inquiries

What kinds of sound may be used to accompany dance? • Is dance ever truly in silence? • How does what we hear affect the way we feel about the dance we see? • If you like a piece of music, are you willing to forgive a mediocre piece of choreography? Or are you more likely to be upset if the choreography does not meet the expectations of the music? • It you do not like the music, are you able to appreciate the dance? • How do composers work with choreographers? Who gets to make the decisions about how the work will be created? • How can a choreographer help dancers relate to the sound that accompanies their movement? • How does a choreographer make sure the relationship that is intended is performed accurately by the dancers?

*D*ance and sound or music are often closely interwoven. The best way to explore the relationship between sound or music and movement is to employ musicians to work with you. Often, because of a lack of funding, hiring live musicians is a challenge. If you are working in a college or university that has a music department, this would be a good time to begin collaborating across disciplines. Both you and the student musicians will benefit from the experience. However, I recognize that overcoming this challenge may be unrealistic, especially as you consider scheduling. I have therefore included many opportunities for you as the dancer to become a musician. You will do this by creating sounds and vocalizing. This is a great challenge for dancers, but it's one that dancers should overcome. Dancers' vocalizing during performance has become an accepted and often exciting practice. You should realize that this is an interesting option for you to explore as a choreographer. And dancers should practice vocalizing with confidence, because they might be asked to perform for choreographers who require it.

The relationship between dance and music is a natural one, yet it can be very complex. And music is not the only sound that may accompany dance. Even dance in silence offers background noise from the environment of the performance space and sounds made by the dancers to accompany the dance. Only those people who are unable to hear sound may experience dance in true silence. This chapter explores the relationships you may develop with sound. You will explore how you can create movement to reflect the sound (**music visualization**) or how you can create sound to reflect the movement (**movement auralization**). And you will explore ways to combine these two, choosing to alternate or to actually strike out in new and independent directions in an ultimate conversation between the two. You will also have an opportunity to explore the complexities that are offered with the addition of text to your work. After these explorations, you will have an opportunity to decide what relationship works best for you in your critical thinking essay.

Finally, a special section in this chapter is titled Working With Music and Sound Scores. This section is not an exploration but a method for mapping counts and graphing sounds as tools for analyzing the structure of your music or sound score. It also includes a discussion of copyright because, in this time of easy access to information, it is imperative for dancers and choreographers to respect the rights of composers as artists.

 Essential Question

Why would a choreographer want to make music visible through movement?

Warm-Up

1. Choose a slow warm-up sequence that can be performed in one minute. Choose something that you are familiar with and that you know works well for you, or create your own warm-up. Include movement that begins isolated and progresses to full-body movement. Take a few minutes to practice your warm-up sequence.

2. Play some music that is moderately fast and that is written in the meter you need for your movement. (See Moderato in the Music Resources section.) Repeat your warm-up to this music, ensuring that you make the movement fit the music. If you are working with musicians, ask them to improvise something that is allegro, and follow their lead. Ask them not to follow *your* lead, which they may be tempted to do. Make your movements faster to match the tempo in the music.

   REFLECTIVE QUESTIONS How does the change in tempo in the music affect your warm-up exercises? What adjustments did you have to make? How did the quality of the movement change?

Improvisations

1. Pick a piece of music with a strong pulse (see Strong Pulse in the Music Resources section) and play it while you sit on the floor and close your eyes. Allow yourself to feel the music within your body. React in a natural way by allowing your body to move to the music. The first reaction is usually to the pulse of the music. Once you have allowed yourself to fully engage in the pulse of the music with your movement, begin to react to other aspects of the music—quality, energy, pitch, rhythmic structure, and so on.

   REFLECTIVE QUESTIONS What movement choices did you make to reflect the music? How did music quality become movement quality?

2. Pick a piece of music that has variations in dynamics from loud to soft (see Variations in Dynamics in the Music Resources section). Translate the dynamics of the music to movement. Improvise ways to express the dynamics of the music with your movement. You may choose any interpretation you like, but make sure the dynamics of your movement are parallel to the dynamics in the music.

   REFLECTIVE QUESTIONS What movement choices did you make to reflect the music? • How do you perceive energy in music? • How did the dynamics in the music become dynamics in your movement?

3. Pick a piece of music that has variations in timing (see Mixed Meter and Tempo Variations in the Music Resources section). Listen to the music first to identify meter, tempo, and rhythmic structure. Improvise to this music, being careful to reflect every change in the timing provided by the music. Reflect tempo, meter, and rhythm precisely the way it is structured in the music.

   REFLECTIVE QUESTIONS What were your challenges in making sure your movement reflected the timing of the music? • How did this music structure affect your movement?

4. Pick a piece of music with a solo instrument that is not a piano or keyboard instrument. (Look for a piece of music that has only one "voice." See Solo Instrument in the Music Resources section, or invite a musician to your classroom.) Listen to this music several times, paying attention to the timing, energy, and quality of the music created by this single instrument. Think about how this music might be translated to movement. Play the music again and improvise movement to reflect the music created by this instrument. You must stay true to the timing, energy, and quality of the instrument you have chosen. You want to do more than simply keep to the correct timing, which is practiced so often in dance classes. This time you must make sure your movements are as varied as the instrument you are following. Consider spatial elements as well. Since music does not have actual spatial elements in it, you must create spatial elements through suggestions you hear in the music. For example, high pitch, which does not exist as a dance element, might be reflected by movement at a high level. You decide. You want to reflect every aspect of that instrument's journey in your movement. Also, make sure you have an opportunity to watch others in this improvisation. Since you are trying to create a visualization of the music, it is important for you to see what that visual interpretation is. Music delivers an automatic kinesthetic response. It is interesting to see the visual effect of that kinesthetic response.

   REFLECTIVE QUESTIONS   What movement choices did you make to reflect the musical elements you heard? • How is it possible to perceive spatial elements in music? • How do you perceive quality?

5. Find a piece of chamber music (see Chamber Music in the Music Resources section), or music that uses three to five instruments. Listen to the music and identify the sounds created by each instrument. Try to follow one of those instruments while listening. Identify the timing, energy, and quality of the instrument. Think about ways to depict this sound in movement. Then divide into groups. Have each person in the group choose one instrument to dance to. It is okay to have more than one person assigned to an instrument, but try to make sure that each instrument in the piece of music is represented by at least one dancer. Play the music again, and improvise to the music as a group. You must stay true to the timing, energy, and quality of the instrument you have chosen. Make sure your movements are as varied as the instrument you are following. Also, pay attention to the relationship between the sounds of each instrument in the music. If you think the instruments are interacting, then you should interact with another dancer in your group in the same way. Repeat this improvisation several times with the same music (or musicians) and the same dancers. It may take a little practice to realize all the opportunities presented by a particular instrument in a piece of music. If enough dancers are present so that others can watch, ask them to give you ideas in between the times you work. Have them tell you what part of the music you are reflecting well and suggest things that are happening in the music that you might be able to reflect better.

   REFLECTIVE QUESTIONS   How does moving to music help you to understand the structure of the music? • How does watching others use music visualization while creating to music help you understand the structure of the music? • What is the effect of mirroring your movement precisely to the music?

Discussion of Key Concept

The first relationship between music and movement must have occurred kinesthetically. The earliest instrument—the drum—provides a strong internal response in the listener that is hard to ignore and naturally produces movement. If you have ever had the opportunity to listen to a strong African or Caribbean drum group perform, you know that it is nearly impossible to remain still while listening to a well-played drum. And so the first forms of choreography must have been closely related to music.

As dance became formalized in the Western world, the relationship between dance and music was limited to the timing. Often strong orchestral works would overpower the movement that occurred onstage. During a mime sequence that had very little movement other than hand gestures, there might have been a section of music to accompany it that used every instrument in the orchestra with very loud dynamics. This was traditional practice that was regarded as correct, and certainly we would have a hard time arguing that the relationship between Petipa's choreography and Tchaikovsky's music in *Swan Lake* was unbalanced and inappropriate. These have been established as the quintessential works of their time and have lasted well into our current century.

However, in the late 1800s, one man explored in depth a different relationship between music and movement. Emile Jaques-Dalcroze (1865-1950) was a Swiss composer and music teacher who invented eurythmics, a system that helped music students develop a sense of rhythm through translating music to physical movement. Jaques-Dalcroze attracted the attention of dancers at the time who were rebelling against the formalization of Petipa and the Russian ballet. Serge Diaghilev (1872-1929), founder of the Ballets Russes in Paris in 1909, became infatuated by a demonstration by music students and brought Marie Rambert to work with Nijinsky in his setting of the ballet *Le Sacre du Printemps*. Other dancers directly influenced by Dalcroze were Mary Wigman (1886-1973), considered the originator of modern dance in Europe; Hanya Holm (1893-1992); and Kurt Jooss (1901-1979), principal dancer for Rudolf von Laban and choreographer of *The Green Table*, a political commentary on the futility of war. The late 1800s and early 1900s saw a movement of true music visualization in dance. Isadora Duncan (1878-1927) is often credited as the originator of American modern dance and was an influential figure in the feminist movement. Loie Fuller (1862-1928) enthralled audiences by waving silk fabric while illuminated by newly developed electric stage lighting. Russian Anna Pavlova (1881-1931) was considered the greatest ballerina during the early 20th century. Ruth St. Denis and Ted Shawn established Denishawn, a dance school in Los Angeles, in 1915. The school was considered fertile ground for developing the pioneers of American modern dance.

Following the nuances of music precisely with your movement may be the most natural and fundamental way to work with music. It is also the most predictable, so it is perhaps not always the best choice. You must ask yourself, "Why do I feel it is necessary to make a statement with my movement that has already been made through the music?"

Whereas it may no longer be optimal to follow the music precisely in your choreography, it is wise to know your music well, with all the nuances of timing, quality, texture, and dynamics. It is definitely true that by setting movement to the music precisely, you learn the structure of the music. As you choreograph, you will make choices of when to mirror the music and when to go against it. Knowing and understanding the structure and quality of the music will enable you to make informed choices. Ignoring the music structure may cause relationships to be implemented that do not follow the intent of your work and may even be offensive to your audience members, especially if they are musicians.

Movement Studies

1. Find a short piece of chamber music and create a group work in which each dancer is assigned to dance to one instrument. Reflect the music judiciously. Perform the dance with the music first and then without. Try performing the same dance with different music. Discuss the relationships between the dance and the music in each version and decide which performance you think works best and why.

2. Find or create a sound score. A sound score is a collection of sounds organized in sequence. You may wish to collect environmental sounds by recording them, or you may wish to solicit the help of other dancers to pound a block with a hammer, crinkle paper, rub sandpaper together, or make other noises with props. It is best to record these

sounds to create your score so that it is set in a particular order and timing. If you create your own sound score, try to find sounds with various qualities and dynamics. You may also choose to have the dancers in your work create the sounds as they dance. They may use **body sounds** by slapping, clapping, and brushing (see figure 7.1). They may also use vocal sounds, but do not have them actually sing a melody. Now set movement that reflects the sounds. Coordinate the movement precisely with your sound score. Again perform it three ways, with the sound score, in silence, and with another sound score or other music. As you change the accompaniment, try to stay true to the original sound score in timing and quality.

Assessment

Use these assessment tools in evaluating your progress toward understanding music visualization.

Class Critique

- Identify movement choices made to coordinate with specific elements in the music, including timing, dynamics, and quality. Which choices do you think were most effective? Why?
- Identify any moments that did not seem to reflect the music precisely.
- Evaluate this process of choreography. Does this process work for you?

Figure 7.1 Body sounds are created by hitting or slapping the body to create rhythms.

Rubric

Following is a sample rubric that you may use in evaluating any one of the three movement studies on music visualization. I encourage you to use this particular rubric because it asks you to evaluate your precise reflection of the music, which is the purpose of music visualization.

Rubric for Music Visualization

Criteria	Strong evidence (4 points)	Some evidence (3 points)	Little evidence (2 points)	No evidence (1 point)
Accurate reflection of timing in the music				
Accurate reflection of dynamics				
Logical movement choices for quality of music				
Overall ability to reflect the music with logical movement choices and good movement intent				
Total: (maximum 16 points)				

Documentation

Record your work on video. Make sure that your recording has good sound quality. Label these recordings as "Music Visualization" and include the completed rubric as an evaluation of your work. You may want to add comments that list any challenges you faced and suggestions on how you might overcome those challenges in the future.

 Essential Question

How is it possible to translate movement into sound?

Warm-Up

1. Begin lying on the floor with your eyes closed. Focus on your breathing. As you breathe, begin to add vocal sound to your breathing so that everyone can hear your breathing in and out. You will need more than the sound of air entering and leaving your lungs. Add voice to it. Now begin moving to this **breath rhythm**, continuing to make vocal sounds with your breathing. You may want to start with just one body part, but expand your exploration to eventually include full-body movement that uses all three levels in space. Reflect the changes in your movement by changing the quality of your vocalizations. Add new qualities to this rhythm and reflect that as well in your vocalizations. If your movement is smooth, your voice should be smooth. If your movement is strong, your voice should be strong. Find a logical conclusion to your warm-up and remain quiet while waiting for the others to finish around you. If you have musicians working with you, you may wish to ask them to create music or sound to accompany your breath rhythm rather than vocalize yourself.

2. Travel around the room doing swinging movements. Add vocal sounds to the swinging action to reflect the energy, size, and quality of your movement. Remember to vary the spatial elements for your swings, such as size, direction, body part, and level. Make the sounds you create vocally reflect the variations that occur in the energy, timing, and quality that result from your variations in spatial elements. Again, if you have musicians, have them create the sounds for you.

   REFLECTIVE QUESTIONS   How did it feel to vocalize your movement? • Did vocalizing affect your movement choices at all? If so, in what way? • How did it feel to have musicians mirroring your movement? Again, did this affect your movement choices? Why?

Improvisations

1. Begin at one side of the room and move across the floor with gliding actions. If you do not have musicians, have a dancer in your group make vocal sounds to accompany your gliding. The sounds created should precisely mirror the quality and timing of your movement. If you are working with musicians, have them create "gliding" music that matches your movement. They should watch you in order to create the music and mirror your movement precisely. Repeat this with all the effort actions: glide, flick, float, dab, press, punch, slash, and wring.

   REFLECTIVE QUESTIONS   How were you, as the dancer, able to create variety in the music or sounds that accompanied you? • What were your challenges in making your movements clear enough for the vocalists or musicians to interpret your movement through sound?

2. Improvise using a focus on levels. If you are unable to secure musicians, have one dancer in your group vocalize your movement. Or select two or three vocalists. If you have musicians, have them interpret your use of levels by translating their visual impressions into the music. It can be interesting to have more than one musician playing different instruments.

   REFLECTIVE QUESTIONS   Why are some choices in sound or music more successful than others in reflecting changes in spatial design in movement? • What choices worked best for you, and why?

3. Improvise using a focus on variations in timing, including meter, tempo, and rhythm. Begin with meter and see if you can communicate meter to a musician or vocalist without speaking. Once your accompanist has picked up on meter, begin to vary the tempos of your movement. After your accompanist has become accomplished with reflecting the meter and tempo of your movement, begin to vary the rhythms of your movement. Give the accompanist time to see and reflect what you are doing by repeating rhythms until the accompanist has recognized it and reflected it accurately. Be very clear about the timing of your movement.

   REFLECTIVE QUESTIONS   How were you able to make meter, tempo, and rhythm clear enough in your movement to be interpreted by a vocalist or musician?

4. Be the conductor: Gather a chorus of vocalizers in one location in the room, or if possible, gather a group of musicians. Find another spot in the room with a lot of space around it and place yourself in that spot facing your chorus or musicians. Beginning very still, start to move one body part very slowly. The chorus or musicians must follow your movement with sound (see figure 7.2). Explore ways to move that will change the sound that you hear. Find ways to build in dynamics and create variations in the sound. Listen carefully, and if the sound is not changing, find ways to make it change by creating new and different movement. Remember that you can include silence in your sound score, so you may wish to have some stillness in your movement. Make your last stillness evident that it is the end of the improvisation.

5. Repeat the previous improvisation with a group of three dancers. You will need at least three musicians, preferably playing different instruments; if you are using a chorus, divide your chorus into three groups. Assign each musician to a dancer, or each choral group to a dancer. Each dancer will control the sound or music created by the chorus members or musicians assigned to that dancer in using the same process as the previous improvisation. The dancers should listen carefully to what they are creating and use that listening to guide their choices of movement. For example, if the sound gets chaotic,

Figure 7.2   Dancers may use music to create movement, and musicians may use movement to create music.

the dancer must choose whether chaotic is the intent of the improvisation; if not, the dancer should scale back the movement to something simpler.

REFLECTIVE QUESTIONS What kinds of movement choices make interesting sound scores or music? What kinds of choices do not work? • As a dancer, how does it feel to control the accompaniment you are using rather than being controlled by your accompaniment?

Discussion of Key Concept

Movement auralization is a term I have coined to indicate the translation of movement to sound. It is something that is perceived through the sense of hearing. Just as music visualization is translating music to make it visible (with movement), movement auralization is translating movement to make it audible (with music). Although the term does not appear in the dictionary, this practice often happens in a modern dance class when live musicians are available and musicians and dancers are asked to improvise together. The musicians will watch the dancers, often picking up on the timing and quality of their movement and using that to create the music. I have spoken to many musicians who get a great deal of satisfaction working with dancers this way. If they are composers, they often find this gives them inspiration to compose new and interesting music that they might not have discovered on their own. True collaborations between artists can be quite exhilarating.

Allowing yourself the opportunity to influence the way music is created can be quite empowering. As a dancer, you are certainly accustomed to allowing the music to take the lead in your relationship. When you discover that something you do may influence how the music sounds, you are well on the road to realizing that a relationship to music may be much more sophisticated than a simple visualization of the music. You will note that even if you are choreographing to music that is already composed and recorded, your movement may be placed in such a way that it looks like the music is reacting to your movement. And if you have an opportunity to collaborate with a composer on a production, the process of listening to each other and reacting to each other may give you material that may eventually become parts of your choreography or composition. By warming up together by exploring music visualization first, and then movement auralization, you will get to know each other well and be ready to make informed choices about when to follow each other and when to strike out on your own. Be playful, have fun, and allow the entire process to reveal new and wonderful possibilities.

Movement Studies

1. Work with a musician and create a movement study that has influenced the accompanying music or sound score. Make sure that your movement is the inspiration for the music composition. Use your movement to help create an interesting sound score. Think about variations in the elements of movement to encourage variation in the music as well. The music must follow your movement precisely. As you create, make sure you remember what you have created and be able to perform it together repeated times without varying your final work. When you show your work, show it once as it was created, with the accompaniment created for you. Show it a second time in silence. Show it a third time accompanied by someone else's music. (If the movement or accompaniment is longer, simply move in silence or wait in stillness until both movement and sound are complete.) Discuss the relationship between the sound or silence and the movement and how it affects the performance. Evaluate which relationship works best.

2. Work with a musician and create a work that alternates back and forth between music visualization and movement auralization. When you are ready to show it, use the same process as in the previous movement study. Note whether it is possible to tell the difference between the two.

For both of these movement studies, it will be optimal to work with a musician. Student musicians are usually plentiful in academic situations, but experienced professionals who are willing to improvise and work with you are also wonderful resources and can be very challenging. Remember that a musician might be a trained choir member or opera singer as well as an instrumentalist. If you work with professional musicians, you must not allow yourself to be intimidated by the professionalism of the musicians, because that might keep you from really taking over the control of the work. If no musician is available, then you must work with a dancer who can vocalize a sound score for you. If you select someone who has been through the explorations with you, you could return the favor by vocalizing for that person's work as well. It is just as important to memorize the sound score as it is to memorize your movement study. Both you and your musician or vocalist should be able to perform multiple times consistently.

Assessment

Use these assessment tools in evaluating your progress toward understanding movement auralization.

Class Critique

- Describe the relationships between movement and music. Is it possible to tell that the music was created from the movement? Is the sound score interesting? Do both the movement and the music have variation to create interest?
- What happened when the movement was performed in silence? Was the movement strong enough to stand on its own?
- What happened when you tried other music with the work?

Rubric

Following is a sample rubric that you may use in evaluating the first movement study on music auralization. If you prefer, design your own rubric to include the criteria you believe to be important in your understanding of movement auralization.

Rubric for Movement Auralization

Criteria	Strong evidence (4 points)	Some evidence (3 points)	Little evidence (2 points)	No evidence (1 point)
Logical relationship between movement and music				
Interesting variation of movement and music				
Movement strong enough to stand on its own				
Total: (maximum 12 points)				

Documentation

Record your work on video. Make sure that your recording has good sound quality. Label these recordings as "Movement Auralization" and include the completed rubric as an evaluation of your work. You may want to add comments that list any challenges you faced, with suggestions of how you might overcome them in the future. Also include comments from the class critique.

 ## Essential Question

How does the relationship between sound or music and movement affect the overall intent of the dance as perceived by the audience?

Warm-Up

1. Find some avant-garde music or sound that includes a great deal of space or silence between sounds. Scores by John Cage or Brian Eno (see the Music Resources section) work well. If you have musicians, ask them to create music that is sparse with a lot of space between sounds. Lie comfortably on the floor with your eyes closed and listen to the music. Begin to react to the music by moving after you hear the sounds. Your movement should be a response to the sound, as if you were answering a question or commenting on a statement. Start small. You do not have to mirror the music. React in any way you like, but do not move until a set of sounds has been completed. Develop your reactions to more full-body movement.

2. Repeat the previous exercise in a group of three or four dancers. Begin at a low level with everyone in contact with each other in a relaxed position. Establish this as a unit, and do not lose the closeness of the group in intent. React to the sounds as if they were some outside entity to be dealt with. The group, or unit, must work together to react or communicate with the sound. Not every dancer must react to every sound. Explore different ways of reacting. If the sounds are strong, try reacting with weak movements. If the sounds are elongated and sustained, try answering with sharp, abrupt movements.

   REFLECTIVE QUESTIONS   What reactions to sound did you discover by waiting and listening and then responding? • What choices of movement were possible that might not have been possible had you reacted immediately to the music or sound? • What was the overall effect of working this way?

Improvisations

1. In a group, create movement that is slow and sustained. Accompany this with strong dynamic music (see Strong Dynamics in the Music Resources section). This music may be provided by musicians, dancers who vocalize, or appropriate recorded music selections. Make sure you have an opportunity to watch another group as this improvisation takes place.

2. Repeat the previous improvisation with two more opposing qualities, such as fast and strong movement with music that is adagio (see Adagio in the Music Resources section).

   REFLECTIVE QUESTION   What is the overall effect created by movement that is accompanied by music or sound that opposes the quality of the movement?

3. Music as partner: For this improvisation, you will need musicians or dancers who will vocalize, because the music or sound must be improvised. As the dancer, begin by creating a movement that makes a statement in conversation with the musician or vocalist. After the movement is complete, the music or sound responds in some way. The response should follow the rules of a conversation—usually agreement, disagreement, or a development of the same thought. After the response, the musician may make a statement to which you (the dancer) respond in the same manner. Take time with this to make choices that are logical and make sense, as a conversation makes sense. Remember that in a conversation people do not usually talk at the same time. When they do, they are

no longer listening to each other, and the actual communication stops. Keep the communication going in this improvisation. In the end, allow the conversation to come to a logical conclusion.

REFLECTIVE QUESTION   What relationships developed between the dance and the accompaniment in this partnership? What worked well, and what were your challenges?

4. For this improvisation, the musician or vocalist will create music or sound according to what they see the dancer perform. However, it is no longer necessary to mirror the movement. In fact, the goal is to reflect your internal landscape—what you (as the dancer) are feeling. This may be quite different from the way you are moving. For example, if you establish a fearful mood, you may take time to slowly contract into a small shape with the head erect and watching. Rather than the music or sound following this slow sustained movement, the accompaniment might become fast and agitated to reflect your controlled energy. In this improvisation, the musician may not always perceive your emotion as the dancer as you feel it, but that is okay. Continue the improvisation regardless and allow the work to develop according to the musicians' perception. You may wish to manipulate the music somewhat with movement that has more clarity of meaning, but the ultimate decision for the music or sound should remain with the musician or vocalist.

REFLECTIVE QUESTION   How does what we see when we listen to music affect our interpretation of what we hear?

5. Reverse the roles in the previous improvisation. Begin with music or sound and you, as the dancer, reflect the meaning of the music through movement. Again, go beyond the actual timing and quality of the music or sound. Try to find something beyond the music or sound that you can reflect through movement. This is the most difficult, because you will be tempted to use music visualization. Begin slowly, moving in a sustained way and allowing the music to establish itself. Try reacting to changes in the music with a delay in your reaction. Try opposing the timing and quality of the music. Try taking one idea from the music and repeat it over and over as the music goes on to something else. Explore many relationships with the music. Do not be restricted by what you think won't work. This improvisation could take place with recorded music, because it is you, the dancer, who improvises.

REFLECTIVE QUESTION   How does what we hear when we watch a dance affect our interpretation of the movement?

6. If you are lucky enough to have musicians in your class, the ultimate conversation between music and dance is to create the work together, with neither leading as in the previous two improvisations, but alternating the lead and making choices for yourselves based on your combined individual artistry. With a musician as partner, improvise together, alternating the lead, working together, going off on your own, reacting to each other. Your choices become completely free in how you work together. The only rule is that you must work together. There must be some relationship between you two. You can do this with a partner in your class and have your partner vocalize. Since your partner is trained as a dancer and not necessarily as a musician, this will limit the result somewhat, unless you and your partner have had a lot of experience in this type of work.

REFLECTIVE QUESTION   What do you believe to be the optimal relationship between music or sound score and dance? Explain your preference.

Discussion of Key Concept

If you are a dancer who knows music well, understands its structure, hears the individual instruments, and reacts easily to its texture and tone, you have an advantage over those who do not. With this knowledge, you may make informed choices about your relationship to the music. You may decide when to go along with the music, when to stop and allow the music to progress on its own, when to oppose the music, and when to anticipate the music yet to come because you can hear and make sense of the structure of the music. Ultimately, it is an advantage to understand and have the ability to hear music in all its nuances, but you must also have the courage to make your own statements without becoming a slave to the intricacies that you hear.

As a student choreographer, I selected Respighi's suite *The Birds* to create a piece of choreography, because I love the music and its structure. I went to the Audubon Society in Washington, DC, researched the birds, and discovered the habits of each species reflected in the music. I found these habits reflected impeccably in the music and decided to do the same with the movement I created. I was lucky enough to have been assigned as Antony Tudor's assistant for his choreography at the time, and he became a mentor in my work. He never attended one of my rehearsals, but he kept asking me, "What on earth are you going to do with all those horrid 'cuckoos'?" He was referring to the sound of the flute as it mimicked the call of the cuckoo bird. That should have been a warning, but I thought I knew what I was doing. I had a particular movement motif that I used every time that sound repeated in the music. After my work was presented in performance, many musicians came up to me and complimented me on my work. They were amazed at how much I had heard in the music and appreciated my knowledge of the music content and structure. Tudor, on the other hand, was honest and blunt. "What made you think you had to be so faithful to Respighi's work? He's been dead for years." Knowing that Tudor was an incredible musician, I listened closely to what he had to say. He spoke of the music he had selected for his classic work, *Jardin aux Lilas*. He said he got to the point where the music got so powerful that he was stumped and did not know what to do. So he decided to do nothing at all. Somewhat by accident, it turned out to be the most brilliant thing he ever did, because the music became the internal feelings of the dancers, not a dictation of the dancers' movements. This was the beginning of my awareness that music and movement should be separate entities working together to create a new and unique effect that cannot be created by either alone.

Whether knowledge of music comes from formal training, experience in listening, or simply the natural ability to feel it, understanding the entity with which you are creating a conversation is absolutely necessary in order to establish a communication that works. Besides the fact that you will not have the tools at your service to set up the communication well, it is possible to create a faux pas in your conversation with music if you do not understand it. We say every idea is correct and nothing is wrong, but there are ways of working with music that could be offensive to the musical ear. Ignoring the structure in a complex fugue is one example. Ignoring the cultural origins of a piece of music is another example. If you wish to go against the fugue, you must know its structure in order to not clash with its intent. Knowing the cultural origin of music will allow you to make an informed choice about the culture itself—whether to go with the sound or not. But knowing the audience will be expecting it, and if you do not go with it, there must be a reason. Requiring a composer to fit everything he creates for you in 8-count phrases might be another example. All of these things may occur and be successful with knowledge of music and intent, but if they come from ignorance, they usually don't work.

When you work with a musician who composes music for your choreography, you will also want to be able to speak the correct music terms when referring to the music in order to gain the respect of the musician and create an easier working relationship. Every choreographer should receive training in the structure of music from at least one music theory course and the content of music from at least one music appreciation course. Many times I have witnessed dancers and choreographers with little knowledge of music become frustrated with and critical of musicians during a collaboration because the musician is not able to understand their wishes. The choreographers believe the musicians to be incompetent when in fact it is their own lack of musicality and knowledge of music structure that poses the problem. Since dance and music are so closely related, both dancers and musicians should become familiar with and understand each other's work, especially if there is any plan to collaborate in a creative endeavor.

As you begin to choreograph and select your music, it is important to know as much as possible about the classic pieces of choreography that may already be related and well known for a specific piece of music. For example, it's just not a very good idea to rechoreograph the music to *Swan Lake* unless you are going to do a parody. The music and the choreography are well known and audiences come to expect a particular dance when they hear a particular part of Tchaikovsky's music. The same may be true for many modern works. Whereas you certainly have the right to use music that has been used before (if you have secured the copyright), you may not wish to be compared with the work of another choreographer. You will want your audience to come to your work with a fresh point of view and no preconceptions.

When selecting music, you also need to be aware of the power of the music and the number of dancers you have in your work. Full orchestral works, similar to those used for many classical ballets, are not appropriate for small groups of dancers. A Petipa ballet may have as many as 50 dancers on the stage at one time to balance the power of orchestral music. A group of 5 dancers simply cannot compete with that kind of music. The same is true with heavy rock music. It is difficult to have a conversation when one voice completely overpowers the other.

Finally, an important consideration when choosing music for your work is that of music with text. Many beginning choreographers start out using familiar popular music that speaks to the choreographer with text in a message that is easily related to because it belongs to the time of the choreographer. There is nothing wrong with selecting this music because it is possible to find an effective relationship between the dance and that music. However, I do not recommend this until you realize that your relationship with the music and the words must be a conversation, not a direct reflection of the music and the words. Words to music add another layer of complexity to be dealt with, and it is wise to first become proficient at dealing with the two layers of movement and music or sound before adding the third layer of text. The next section in this chapter helps you in developing a meaningful relationship between your movement creations and text.

What additional personal discoveries have you made that will help you in selecting music and sound scores for your work, and how will your work be affected by these new discoveries? Take a moment to record your thoughts.

Movement Studies

1. Find some music that expresses some emotional content that you would like to reflect in your choreography. Create a movement study that has extreme changes in dynamics and a great deal of stillness. Connect your choreography to the music in a way that is not predictable (i.e., do not always use high dynamics with high dynamics, stillness with silence, and so on). Explore opportunities to go against the music, and think of the music as an internal landscape for the dancers.

2. Work with a composer and discuss the structure of the piece you will create. Discuss details, such as mood, narrative (if there is to be one), number of dancers, number of instruments and which instruments, timing (including length of piece), and how it will begin, and how it will end. After you have come to an agreement on your plan, separate your efforts and create your work independently. After you have each finished, come back and rehearse the piece together. Look at the work carefully as is before making any changes. Make changes only if something really does not work. Otherwise, allow the two works to remain intact and perform them together.

3. Select music that you enjoy and that you think will be appropriate for your choreography. Create a work that explores music visualization, movement auralization, and a conversation with the music that includes reacting to the music after the music has completed a statement, anticipating something in the music before it happens, and going against the music completely. Be ready to explain where each of these relationships occurs in your choreography.

Note: Unless you are working with a composer, it will not be possible to explore movement auralization because that would require the music to be created from your movement. Simply eliminate that from your choices in this case.

Assessment

Use these assessment tools in evaluating your progress toward understanding the ultimate conversation between music and movement.

Class Critique

- Describe the relationships between movement and music. Can you identify moments when the movement is created to reflect the music, when the music is a reaction to the movement, and when the music is used to tell something about the inner landscape of the dancers?

- Identify any predictable moments and make suggestions for change. (Note: When music and movement start at exactly the same time, it is difficult to get a clear beginning. It is also very predictable to start and stop with the music. Are there other choices?)

Rubric

Following is a sample rubric that you may use in evaluating the first movement study on the ultimate conversation between music and movement. If you prefer, design your own rubric to include the criteria you believe to be important in your understanding of an ultimate conversation with music.

Rubric for the Ultimate Conversation

Criteria	Strong evidence (4 points)	Some evidence (3 points)	Little evidence (2 points)	No evidence (1 point)
Movement maintains its own identity				
Lack of predictability				
Music contributes to the emotional narrative without mirroring it				
Total: (maximum 12 points)				

Documentation

Record your work on video. Make sure that your recording has good sound quality. Label these recordings as "Ultimate Conversation" and include the completed rubric as an evaluation of your work. You may want to add comments that list any challenges you faced, with suggestions of how you might overcome them in the future. Also include comments from the class critique. Remember to include a discussion of your collaboration with a musician or dancer as vocalist.

 ## Essential Question

What role might text play in the creation of a choreographic work?

Warm-Up

1. Begin lying on the floor in a comfortable position. Focus on your breathing and the rise and fall of your chest. Allow your arms to extend the rise and fall of your breathing by moving to your breath rhythm. Now continue to add the torso to the movement, making it rise from the floor. Find various ways to move within the rhythm established by your breathing. Take your movement into a middle level, then eventually into a high level. Allow yourself to explore all levels while keeping your timing to match the breath rhythm you have established. As you are moving in this way, listen to the following words and include a reaction to them in your movement after hearing each one. Maintain the breath rhythm while interpreting the text through movement: rise . . . fall . . . expand . . . slump . . . surge . . . sticky . . . alive . . . moon . . . gather . . . mountain . . . paradise . . . circle . . . thought . . . bird . . . strange . . . true . . . neglect . . . stars . . . dazzle . . . soldier . . . strive . . . gold . . . abuse . . . cocoon . . . praise . . . leaf . . . question . . . answer . . . . Find a final stillness.

   REFLECTIVE QUESTIONS What relationships are possible between text and movement? • What kind of text lends itself most easily to interpretations through movement? What kind of text does not?

2. Sing the song "Row, Row, Row Your Boat." Quickly improvise movement to go with the song. Keep repeating the song and explore new movement to go with each phrase: 1) Row, row, row your boat 2) Gently down the stream. 3) Merrily, merrily, merrily ,merrily, 4) Life is but a dream.

   REFLECTIVE QUESTION What affected your movement choices more—the rhythm of the song, the melody of the song, or the words in the song? Why?

Improvisations

The Road Not Taken
Robert Frost

Two roads diverged in a yellow wood,
And sorry I could not travel both
And be one traveler, long I stood
And looked down one as far as I could
To where it bent in the undergrowth;
Then took the other, as just as fair,
And having perhaps the better claim
Because it was grassy and wanted wear;
Though as for that, the passing there
Had worn them really about the same,

And both that morning equally lay
In leaves no step had trodden black.
Oh, I kept the first for another day!
Yet knowing how way leads on to way,
I doubted if I should ever come back.
I shall be telling this with a sigh
Somewhere ages and ages hence:
Two roads diverged in a yellow wood, and I—
I took the one less traveled by,
And that has made all the difference.

Frost, Robert. *Mountain Interval*. New York: Holt, 1920.

1. Begin with the first line of the Robert Frost Poem "The Road Not Taken": "Two roads diverged in a yellow wood." (Or you may select another poem that interests you.) Speak the line out loud with your group. Listen to the rhythm of the words and the natural accents placed within the phrase. (See a possible translation of the rhythm for this first line translated to music notation in figure 7.3.) Now clap the rhythm as you say the words. Decide on where the claps should be louder (accents). Explore movement that is created with the rhythm you have discovered. You may wish to have a partner clap the rhythms for you, or play a drum as you improvise movement.

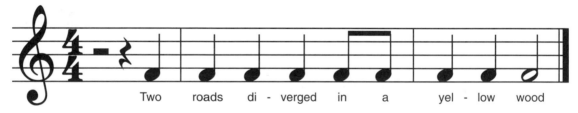

Figure 7.3 Rhythmic structure of the first line of "The Road Not Taken."

2. Now change the accents in the poetry. Place the accents in unlikely places and try reading it with these new accents. Explore movement that is created with this new rhythm. Make sure you reflect the accents in your movement.

   REFLECTIVE QUESTIONS How is the sound of spoken word similar to and different from sounds produced in music? How do these similarities and differences affect the way you partner with these sounds when creating movement?

3. Use the literal meaning of the words in this poem to explore movement that expresses that meaning (see figure 7.4). Explore many ways of expressing the meaning of this first line as you interpret it.

   REFLECTIVE QUESTIONS Which words were you able to translate literally to movement? Which ones did you choose to ignore? Why?

4. Improvise a dance that reflects the deepest meaning of the entire poem. Ask yourself what the message is behind the poem. Translate something from that message into your

Figure 7.4 Which dancers depict each phrase? 1. Two roads diverged in a yellow wood. 2. And sorry I could not travel both. 3. And be one traveler, long I stood.

movement. If you are not familiar with the poem, read and study it before trying this improvisation. You must reflect on the intent of the poet to do this.

5. Choose only a few key words from the entire poem that you consider key words to your movement interpretations. Speak these words in appropriate places as you improvise your movement. You may wish to speak them with different emphasis. You may also vary the timing with some words close together, others far apart. Try to make the sounds of the words part of your improvisation.

REFLECTIVE QUESTIONS What part of the poem lends itself well to movement? • What might you add to the poem that is not there in the reading when you create movement for it? • Why would you want to partner movement with this text?

Discussion of Key Concept

Text within a music composition adds another layer of information that must be dealt with in the creation of a choreographic work. It must not be ignored, nor should it be approached in a trivial manner. One solution is to have the dancers act out the words (mime the words with specific gestures). For example, in **liturgical dance**, particular gestures are often assigned to specific words in a song; when those words are repeated in the song, so are the gestures. This is an attempt to emphasize the words and to create an even more emphatic statement than the song will make on its own. It indicates that the dancer has taken ownership of the music and the words and has been guided by the spirituality of the message. When this type of dance is performed with commitment and intent, the result can be powerful.

But even liturgical dance may benefit from a more sophisticated relationship between words and movement, because each may enhance the other, again in conversation, rather than literal translation. Like the movement motif assigned to the cuckoo in Respighi's music, this solution to text may become predictable and insulting to a sophisticated audience and does not extend the opportunity to say something new. A sophisticated choreographer will look for something that has not already been said by the music or the words, something that needs to be stated with movement. Like the relationships you explored earlier with music, you should also explore your relationships with text. But with text you must consider the quality of the sound as well as the literal meaning of the words. Choices must be made about whether the movement is in agreement with the words, in opposition to the words, adding depth to the meaning, or continuing a conversation set up by the words. Or you may just want to play with the sounds the words make.

All of the explorations designed to help you discover your relationship to music may be repeated to help you discover a relationship to text. You should explore using poetry, narrative, songs with words, and compositions that include text. Remember in your explorations that the text may be manipulated, just as the music was manipulated by musicians. If you get someone to read the text, or if a dancer speaks as he or she dances, the sounds may be manipulated the same way you manipulate movement by changing volume, timing, energy, or quality. If using text becomes important to you in your work, you should engage in vocal lessons available in music and drama departments and use dancers who are trained in this way. A weak delivery of text in a choreographic work might destroy your intent.

A particular challenge concerning music with text is that unless everyone in the audience already knows the words, they are going to miss a lot of them, because it is impossible to concentrate on music, movement, and words and be able to absorb all the information in one performance. A good way to drive this home was offered at a workshop led by L. Tarin Chaplin (coauthor of *The Intimate Act of Choreography*) at an American College Dance Festival. She asked each participant to think of a story to tell. She then arranged the group into groups of partners and had each group tell their stories to each other. Instead of having them take turns talking to each other, she had them tell their stories simultaneously so that each person had to talk and listen at the same time. After they were finished, she asked them to repeat what they could remember from the other person's story. She compared this challenge to that of an audience member trying to watch movement and listen to text at the same time. Her point was that something would be lost in the telling. Dancing and music and text all at once would be like three people talking at once. Each time you add a layer, you add more information. And since the human brain can absorb only so much at once, the choreographer must understand that not all the information will be related to the audience. The choreographer must then make choices and decide these things: What is most important? How do I draw attention to something so it will not be missed? Is it important that the audience understand everything? Will it work if they do not? Can I create something new, or am I only re-creating something that has already been done? Will any of these layers cause my audience to react in a way that goes against the intent of my choreography? Which layer will be most prominent and take the attention of my audience?

In dealing with text, you must not assume that the text is unimportant and can be ignored. I have seen this done often with lyrics that are in a foreign language. If you assume that no one will understand the lyrics in your audience and choreograph to your interpretation of the music without thought to the intent of the composer, you run the risk of making a mistake. You may be interpreting music to be light and happy when the lyrics tell you that the piece is really about the death of children. It is very possible that someone in the audience will be familiar with the music or at least familiar with the language and will know the meaning of the work. They will be confused, offended by your treatment of the subject, or at the very least chagrined by your ignorance. In the selection of accompaniment for your work, make sure you are informed of the intent of the composer and get a translation of the lyrics if they are not in a language you understand. Then you can make an informed choice about how to approach the relationship of your own work to that of the composer. You do not have to use the composer's intent, but you should know what it is and how your work relates to it.

Choreographing for musical theater requires a different relationship to music and text. In this case, the dance may not be considered first and foremost in the mind of the director. Of course, there should be exceptions, as in *West Side Story*. If you are choreographing musical theater for an amateur company, you will have to pay attention to choreographing in a way that supports the performers in their ability to project the music to the audience. If they are not wearing microphones, then the positioning of your cast members as they dance and sing at the same time must be such that they may keep their faces toward the audience so that the sound will be projected forward. You will also have to take care not to require too much energy in the dance so that they will have enough breath to do the singing. And finally, you must realize that your work is a collaboration. It will be important to communicate often with the music director and the stage director to make sure you are working in a way that meets with their approval. You can save yourself many hours of wasted rehearsal this way, because I have seen many scenes get cut by a director on first showing. Communicate well and rehearse well before the directors see your work.

Professional musical theater is another story. Today's Broadway performers are often "triple threats." They are great singers, actors, and dancers. And today, in professional theater, everyone holds or is wearing a microphone. You only have to see the increase in number of dance musicals to realize this is the case. If you think that as a musical theater choreographer you no longer have to pay attention to all the choreographic concepts you have explored in this text, you are wrong. You do not want to mirror the text in musical theater any more than you do in choreography for a dance concert. I have seen this done, and it is predictable and trite and mediocre at best. If you want to be a choreographer who is noticed, you must find surprises that work. It is true that the text must not be ignored, and it is your job as the choreographer to enhance the message in the lyrics rather than to detract from it. And you must take into consideration that the primary purpose of musical theater is to entertain. As with any of your work, you must take into consideration your audience. It will probably not be appropriate to be esoteric. But you must create interest in your work with variations in energy, space, and time if you want to be rehired. Just as these rules apply to every dance technique, they apply to musical theater.

Movement Studies

1. Locate a piece of music with lyrics that you enjoy and that you think will translate well as a dance. Create a dance by selecting a few important words in the text to reflect. Find a unique way to draw attention to these words without creating literal gestures to perform each time the words come up in the music.

2. Find a poem that you think will translate well to movement. Explore timing, rhythms, sound, and meaning in the poem and improvise movement material using these elements as inspiration. Select your favorite material and decide on a way to coordinate that material with the poem in a dance. Try developing a unique partnership by mixing up sequence, changing emphasis, and exploring depth of meaning. You may perform the poem with the dance, or have it narrated, or even have it taped. You may choose to use music as well, but make sure the music does not detract from the poem, which should be your primary emphasis.

3. Create a dance using a selection of single words as text. You may use music as well if you like, but it is not required. You may want to use words that create literal meaning to your dance, or you may choose to be more abstract, using sound, texture, and timing to inspire your work.

Assessment

Use these assessment tools in evaluating your progress toward understanding the use of text in your work.

Class Critique

- Identify the relationships you noticed between text and movement. Evaluate those relationships. Are they typical and trite? Or are they unique and interesting? Why?
- How are the elements of energy, space, and time used to enhance this partnership with text?
- Do you understand the intent of the choreographer?
- Does the text make the work more confusing or more clear?
- Are there any surprising relationships to the text that add interest to the work?

Rubric

Following is a sample rubric that you may use in evaluating any of the movement studies on the use of text. If you prefer, design your own rubric to include the criteria you believe to be important in your understanding of the optimal relationship between text and movement.

Rubric for Text

Criteria	Strong evidence (4 points)	Some evidence (3 points)	Little evidence (2 points)	No evidence (1 point)
Interesting and effective relationship between movement and text				
Lack of predictability				
Variations in energy, space, and time to create interest				
Clear intent				
Total: (maximum 16 points)				

Documentation

Record your work on video. Make sure the sound quality is adequate for you to be able to hear the text in the work. Include an explanation of your creative process. What decisions did you make about your relationship to the text? What do you think worked well? What do you need to do to make this more effective in the future? Apply comments you have received to make these evaluations of your work. Save this work in your digital portfolio.

Drawing Conclusions

Breaking the Rules

- Find some music with a strong beat, and create your movement to go completely against the beat. Your movement should have a beat that exists independently of the music. This will be hard to perform, but it's worth a try.

- Find a piece of music with lyrics or text, and create movement that stays literal to the text and always ties a particular piece of movement to a particular word or words in the text.

- Find a poem that has no emotion and no action in it. Create a dance that coordinates with the poem.

REFLECTIVE QUESTIONS   What is the effect of movement that is counterpoint (against the beat) to the music? Is this something you might want to use as a choreographer? When does it work? When doesn't it work? • What is the effect of literally translating text to movement? Is this something you want to use in your choreography? Why or why not? • How is it possible to work with text that has no emotion and no action? • What do you use in the words that will relate to movement? Does this work? Why or why not?

Drawing Conclusions

Critical Thinking Essay

Choose one of the movement studies you completed in this chapter to illustrate your opinion of how movement should relate to sound (music, sound score, or text). Explain how your opinion about this relationship has developed or changed since you completed these explorations. An outline follows to help you use the critical thinking model for your essay.

I. Introduction: Make a statement that includes your opinion of what the relationship between movement and sound should be.

II. Discussion

    A. Analysis: Describe the movement study, focusing on the choices you made concerning your relationships between movement and sound.

    B. Reflection: Discuss the purpose behind these choices (why you made them and what effect you expected from your choices).

    C. Integration: Relate these choices to past experience such as performances you have danced in that were choreographed by others, works that you have seen your peers choreograph, or works by professional companies.

III. Conclusion: Evaluate your choices for movement as it relates to the sound in this particular movement study, and summarize your opinion about its success. Draw conclusions about what you should do in the future as you work with music, sound, and text.

Working With Music and Sound Scores

Many choreographers work with music and sound scores without ever reading a score or creating a visual score as they work. Most dancers have an innate sense of music and know what and how they want to partner with their accompaniment without the need to see the sound score visually. A choreographer who works organically may actually create movement first and find accompaniment for the movement later. But choreographers who choose to work with an accompaniment that has been precomposed or recorded and like to plan the partnership will find a visual score helpful. Student choreographers who are required to create visual maps of their accompaniment are forced to analyze the sound and are able to make informed choices about the partnership they create for their choreography.

There are various ways to visualize a sound score. The most obvious is to secure the musical score of the work. This may or may not be available. If it is available, it is the best possible visualization of the accompaniment because every detail will be written in the score. However, it is necessary to have enough knowledge of music theory in order to read the score, which is considerable. And honestly, in a musical score, there is a lot more information than is needed for the choreographer, which can get in the way, especially when the choreographer has chosen to count the music in a different way than is written. There are any number of ways to create your own visualization of your accompaniment in a much simpler format and with somewhat less knowledge of music theory. After trying these two methods, which I have found helpful in my work, you may create your own that is designed to your specific needs. Mapping the counts is helpful when working with music that has clear musical structure that may be followed using counts by the dancers. This method also maps the phrasing of the music. Graphing the sound is more helpful when counts are not obvious and you plan to cue your dancers by particular sounds in the music or sound score.

Mapping the Counts

1. The first step in mapping the counts is to simply listen to the music over and over until you become very familiar with it. (See Samples for Mapping the Counts in the Music Resources section.) Listen for any structure in the music. Does it have a melody? Is the melody carried by different instruments? Which instruments take your focus, and which are in the background? Are there any repeats in the music? If so, where are they? How does the piece begin? How does it end? Does the timing change throughout the piece, or does it stay the same throughout? Can you hear a meter in the work? Is it a waltz or a march? Or some other familiar dance form? Once you have become very familiar with the music, you are ready for the second step: finding a basic count.

2. Listen to the music again, this time counting where it seems natural to count. You may find yourself tapping your foot or nodding your head. As you are counting, begin to notice if the counts seem to group themselves in even numbers. As dancers, we are apt to count the 8s or the 4s. That is fine, because much of music has been composed in a way that you can do this. Groupings will make themselves evident in a phrase of music. Once you have established where the counts are, determine how many counts exist in a single phrase of music. You are not attempting to count every beat in each measure as you would in music notation. You are looking for dancers' counts. Ask yourself how you would count the music as you teach the movement to your dancers. The music may be a waltz in 3/4, but you will probably count only the first beat of each measure. If you are able to detect the meter, you may wish to write a note at the beginning that gives the meter by saying 3/4, or waltz. If you are very knowledgeable about the music, you may even wish to note some thing like "Each count equals one measure of 3/4" if this helps you.

3. Begin at the beginning. On a piece of lined notebook paper, place the number of counts, one phrase on each line, down the left side of the paper. For example, what you perceive to be the introduction in the music might consist of four phrases of 4 counts each. Write the word introduction beside the first number 4, and place a straight line under the last 4, where you perceive an end to the introduction in the music (see figure

7.5). Now count each phrase of music after the introduction in the same way. Suppose you perceive an 8-count phrase, two 4-count phrases, and a 12-count phrase. Continue to write one number for each phrase on each line on your paper. Under the line that marked your introduction, you will place the numbers 8, 4, 4, 12 each on the next four lines, leaving space to the right to write notes. Here you may perceive an end of one idea and the beginning of something new. Place another line under the 12 to note a change in the music here. Continue this way until you come to the end of the music. Use a double line at the end. This may take quite some time. You will need to stop and start

over many times to make sure you have the correct number of counts for the phrasing as you hear it. The way you hear the phrasing may be different from someone else's interpretation of the same music. That is okay, as long as you understand how you are counting the music and that you hear it the same way each time you listen to it.

If you are having trouble with a phrase because the counts seem to overlap or get chopped off before the next phrase, you may be choosing a unit for your counts that is too big. In other words, you may need to count faster in order to make the counts fit in a phrase. For example, suppose in the previous example, the phrase that has 12 counts was really almost 13 counts but did not allow you to actually count to 13, but it was longer than 12. That would mean you would need to count twice as fast, counting two counts for every one. Then the phrase might actually be 25 counts. You would then need to go back and count everything twice as fast. Your intro would be four 8s and the first section of music would be 16, 8, 8, 25. The 25-count phrase is difficult to manage, so you may wish to see if it easily breaks up into 10, 10, 5 or 8, 8, 9 (see figure 7.6 on page 164).

4. Once you have mapped out all your counts, which is the hardest process and takes the most time, you should go back and write some notes to the right of each phrase that will help you visualize the score. Include notes such as "First melody begins here . . . melody continues . . . new melody starts . . . loud trumpet sound . . . first melody repeats softer this time . . . energy builds . . . gets faster . . . slows down . . . sounds agitated . . . very sad . . . slow drum beat underscore here . . . flute playing high above melody here." See a sample of a final score using this method in figure 7.7 on page 164.

Graphing a Sound Score

For music that does not have obvious counts, or sound scores that use sound rather than music notes, you will need another method to develop a visual map of the accompaniment. This method is simpler yet less precise than the previous method. It may be used in place of the mapping the counts method even for music with audible counts if you

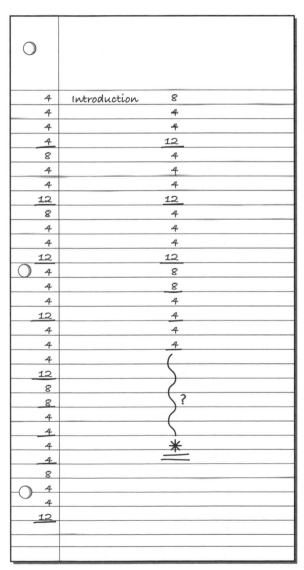

Figure 7.5 Step 3, mapping the counts: handwritten music score for dance.

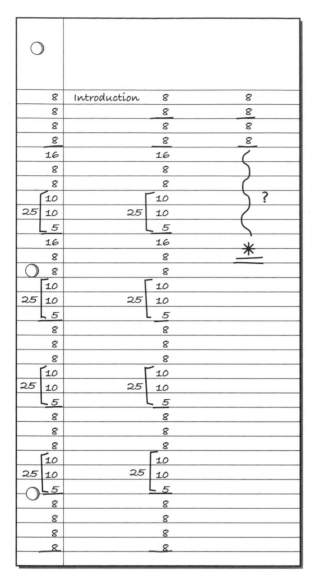

Figure 7.6 Step 3, mapping the counts: alternative score for figure 7.5, counted twice as fast to accommodate the 25-count phrase.

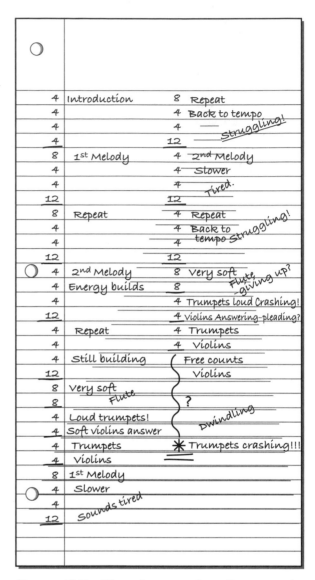

Figure 7.7 Step 4, mapping the counts: dancer's music score with descriptions added (final score).

want only an overall view of the score without specifics of timing. It is possible to add more specifics in timing by placing a notation for the number of seconds on the graph. This, of course, works only for recorded music or music that is played exactly the same each time it is performed. If the sound score is played live and changes timing, it will be more important to note the sequence, basic structure, sound quality, and sound cues within the work.

1. This is the same as in mapping the counts. Listen to the music repeatedly until you become very familiar with it. (See Samples

for Graphing the Sound Score in the Music Resources section.) Ask yourself these questions: Is there a structure I can follow? What happens at the beginning? What happens at the end? Is the sound or music continuous, or are there long pauses without sound? Is there a change in the energy? Do I recognize what is making the sound? Are there any instruments? Are there environmental sounds? Are the sounds electronic? Is there voice? What is the quality of the sounds? How long do the sounds last? Do they change in pitch, loudness, and softness? Is the sound manipulated? If so, how? What do I recognize? What will my audience recognize with only one hearing? If there are words, what language are they in? Will my audience hear the words? All the words? Which words? What part of the sound score stands out? What part of it is in the background?

2. This time your notation will read from left to right instead of top to bottom. The best option for paper is a roll of paper rather than separate sheets, although you can tape sheets together to make this work. Establish a scale at the left of the page with low pitch at the very bottom and high pitch at the very top of the page. Listen to the sound score again and draw a line, as you might see on a cardiograph, where the line goes up to the top of the page for very high sounds and down to the bottom of the page for low sounds or no sound at all (see figure 7.8). Or you may want to leave a space on the graph when there is no sound. Try to keep the timing proportional so that the times you are indicating stay consistent throughout the graph. If there is a great deal of space between sounds, you may wish to condense your graph so that you are not using huge amounts of paper to indicate very little. If you can have your paper ready so that you do not have to stop writing while you are listening, you can do the entire piece in one sitting. I would recommend doing it two or three times until you have something you think most accurately represents the sound and timing that you are recording.

3. Listen to the sound score again and mark the graph with specifics about what the sounds are (see figure 7.9 on page 166). You may choose particular symbols for this, such as XXX for three claps or ∿∿ for waves crashing. You may want to actually describe the sounds or indicate quality. You may want to note a structure by placing segment lines along the graph. This form of graphing is much more free form and is left to each person to decide how to best create a visual map that can be used for the choreography.

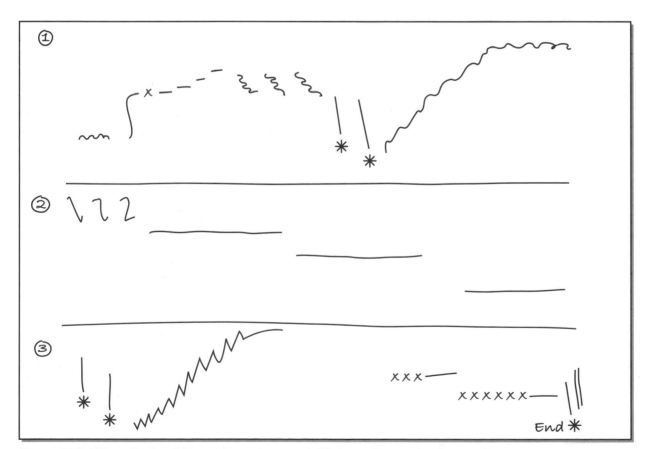

Figure 7.8 Step 2, graphing a sound score: initial cardiograph of sound.

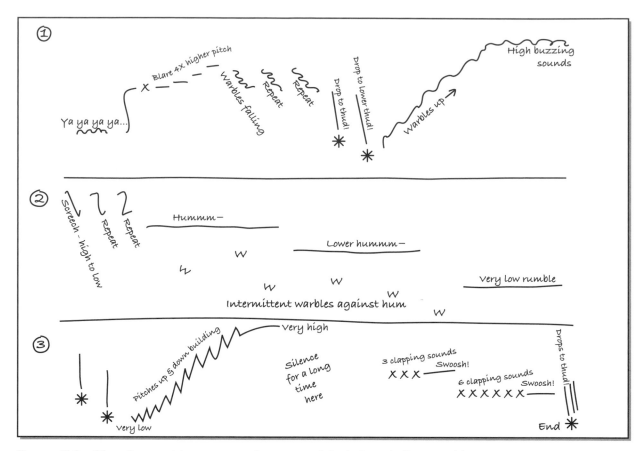

Figure 7.9 Step 3, graphing a sound score: added descriptive markings.

Use and Manipulation of Copyrighted Music

All recorded music is copyrighted, whether you obtain it by buying it in a retail store or whether you download it from the Internet. For the most part, if you have bought it initially, copyrighted music may be used for educational purposes without permission as long as you do not make multiple copies and as long as there is no monetary gain such as admission charges or class fees. This is known as fair use. So you are usually safe using it in a choreography class at a college or university, as long as no public performance is planned. You will have to be careful to keep your video recordings private because you could be in violation of copyright laws if you post your video on the Internet. You may be tempted to post a dance that you are particularly proud of on YouTube, but that is precisely where you may get caught for public use of copyrighted

material. This is not the case with profit-making dance studios. And every time you are using music in a public performance, you must obtain permission to use it, regardless of whether you charge admission for the performance. The publisher of the music usually owns the copyright. You may contact the publisher directly by using the information on the recording. Describe the intended use of the work to the publisher, including dates of intended performance, anticipated audience size, and purpose of performance (e.g., capstone project, choreographer's showcase). It has been my experience that when you make it clear that it will be used for educational, nonprofit purposes, the publishers are willing to allow use for no charge or for a very nominal fee. If you are at a college or university, check with your music department. Sometimes educational institutions purchase blanket copyrights from music publishers. Make sure that these permissions cover the recording you intend to use. Some composers are more protected than others.

For example, it is very difficult to get permission to use Stravinsky's music. Some popular music is easy to obtain the rights to because the publishers enjoy your promotion of the work.

Because music is highly protected, it is advantageous to work with a composer who is willing to allow you to use his or her composition. But you should never assume that once the music has been composed for you that it belongs to you, unless you have come to that agreement with the composer. You may want to put your agreement in writing to protect future performances. A gentleman's verbal agreement is fine, as long as you remain collegial. If you think there is any chance that the relationship could change, and the choreography with the music composition is important to you to preserve, your best procedure is to have the agreement in writing.

If you have a question about whether you have the right to use a piece of music or a sound score that you have selected and you cannot find an answer, the best option is to not use it and find something else that you may use without fear of violating copyright laws. I encourage students to find other students who want to collaborate on compositions. The collaboration can be tricky, but the rewards are well worth the effort.

When obtaining permission to use a piece of music or sound score, you also must determine if you have the right to mix, cut, or alter the work. With today's technology, it is easy to mix, cut, and alter music. The question is whether it is ethical. If you think of the music composition as someone's creation, just as your own choreography will be your original creation, then ask yourself if it is okay to take that composition and cut it up, rearrange it, combine it with other work, and then present it as a new work.

Copyrights may apply, so you'd better check before you use the new music score in a public performance. But regardless of copyright, you must take into consideration your audience and their sense of musical justice. For example, Samuel Barber's *Adagio for Strings* is an incredible work of art. It has a long pause after a dramatic build before it resolves itself into a conclusion. It has been a popular selection for choreography, and one student choreographer whom I observed chose to cut the music at the pause before the resolution. My sensibility cringed at the loss of the musical resolution—so much that regardless of how wonderful the choreography was, and I have no memory of it, I cannot condone the butchering of the music, nor can I even attempt to justify the choreography. I left the theater in anger at the senseless treatment of what I deemed to be a masterful piece of music. My reaction was just one in perhaps a couple hundred, but I believe a choreographer must ask, "Do I want to risk that kind of a reaction to my work? Do I care? Am I even aware that this may happen?" Other pieces of music may be cut and edited without this sense of loss because the music may have already resolved itself for one statement before striking out into something new, or it may have no resolution and is continuous in its statement and may be faded as if the musicians had disappeared off into the distance. Again, it is important to understand music structure and acquire a musical sensibility in order to do this editing without being offensive to your audience.

Chapter 8

Transitions

Initial Inquiries

"Preparation, fourth, pirouette, finish!"

Is this truly the best choreographic transition for a pirouette? • Is it possible to begin and end a pirouette any other way?

Here is another example: Complete a series of piqué turns from upstage left to downstage right, and finish with a flourish in arabesque croisé. Execute a demi-fouetté to change your direction and walk to the upstage right corner and prepare the left leg to repeat the turns coming back on the opposite diagonal.

Does that walk honestly fit the intent of your choreography? • Is there any other way to get from downstage right to upstage right?

Classroom technique can be the biggest roadblock to effective transitions in your choreography. It is important to remember the difference between technique learned in class and choreography for the stage. For those of you who have trained many years in technique classes, this will be a hard lesson to learn, because what you have repeated several times will feel natural to you. You have practiced long and hard. So you will not always be able to depend on your kinesthetic sense to develop transitions in your choreography that will be interesting, logical, and driven by the intent you have chosen for your work.

This chapter provides you with explorations in a few types of transitions that will help you begin to think carefully about these moments in your work. There are an infinite number of transitions available to you, so after your explorations and movement studies and efforts to create successful work without transitions, you should feel free to express your own ideas in the critical thinking essay assigned.

 ## Essential Question

What are the elements that constitute a good transition in choreography?

Warm-Up

1. While standing in self-space, create a movement sequence as follows: Perform isolated movements with your right arm for 4 counts, perform isolated movements with your left leg for 4 counts, and perform full-body movement for 8 counts. You may do anything you like, but use the movement to begin to warm up your body as well as to establish a logical sequence. Repeat the sequence beginning with the left arm, progressing to the right leg, and then again using full-body movement. Focus on creating smooth, logical transitions from one part of this sequence to the next.

2. Repeat the previous sequence changing levels each time you change to the next part of the sequence. For example, isolate the right arm in a high level, isolate the left leg in a low level, and move to the middle level for full-body movement.

   REFLECTIVE QUESTIONS What transitions were required in order to accomplish this sequence? How did that change as you performed the sequence in different levels?

Improvisations

1. Create an interesting shape in any level. As you perform this shape, focus on how the shape feels. Where is the energy in the shape? What part of the body feels like it needs to move? Where is your weight? Focus on a body part that may lead you into movement. How will it lead you? Will it release its energy? Or will it use more energy to take you to a new place? What is the most logical way to leave the shape you are in? On your instructor's cue of "Go," move to a new shape in the most logical way and then find a stillness in a new shape. *Go!* Repeat this, starting from the new shape. Continue to explore ways to go from one shape to another with a great deal of focus on how you get there in the most natural way possible.

   REFLECTIVE QUESTIONS What makes a transition feel logical and natural? If any of your transitions did not feel natural, can you explain what happened and why it did not work?

2. Repeat the previous improvisation, evaluating each shape and a natural direction to lead to a new shape. But instead of following the natural direction of movement, do exactly the opposite from what seemed natural. In other words, if you feel as if you should fall forward, try jumping backward instead. If you feel as if your right arm should lead you out to the right, try leading with your left foot out to the left. Think about how you will accomplish this task of going against the natural flow or weight of your position before you try it. Do your best to make it work. *Go!* Repeat this many times, exploring ways to go against the obvious, finding new and different ways to move from one shape to the next.

   REFLECTIVE QUESTIONS What is the difference between these transitions and the ones you created in the first improvisation? • What is required to make these transitions work? Is it even possible? Why would you choose one over the other?

3. Preparation: Create an 8-count phrase of movement that has a beginning, middle, and end. Practice it a few times until you are sure you remember it. You may use any technique you like, but try to follow all the rules of craft that you have learned so far, and

perform the phrase with intent. When you finish this phrase, walk to another spot in the room (this is not part of the performance) that is a long way away from where you finished performing your first phrase. Create another 8-count phrase beginning in this new spot. Do not think about how the phrases might fit together. You should create two entirely separate phrases of movement. You must also begin your new phrase in a new level. For example, if your first phrase finished at a low level, this new phrase must begin at a high level.

4. Creating transitions: Go to the place where you created your first phrase of movement. You will now perform both movement phrases. You must create a transition that gets you to the new space and level for the second phrase. Try the following methods for developing a transition. Make sure the transitions become part of the choreography. Practice them a few times until you have created something that ties the two phrases together in a logical way. (Hint: Create an intent for each transition.)

- Create a transition that gets you there as fast as possible, in a direct route.
- Create a transition that takes a very long time to get to the new space and level and meanders throughout the performance space before arriving at the new space.
- Extend the last part of the first phrase and vary that movement so that you finish the first phrase in exactly the right space and level to begin the second phrase.
- Combine material from your first and second phrase to create a new transitional phrase.
- Paying a great deal of attention to performance, perform the first phrase as if it were an entity of its own, completing its intent. Pause while holding on to a performance quality. Then, with a new intent, such as determined, nonchalant, hurried, or carefree, walk to the new space, as you would walk in a performance. Pause for a moment, then settle into the new level and begin the second phrase.

REFLECTIVE QUESTIONS How do different transitions affect the intent of a work? When might you choose one over another? • When is a transition a transitional phrase, and when does a transitional phrase become an important phrase of the work and no longer a transition?

Discussion of Key Concept

Creating good transitions is one of the most difficult skills to develop. Yet if you simply watch for logical intent throughout a piece of choreography, and fix any place in your work that does not have intent, all the transitions will work well. (Yes, easier said than done.) You must develop an eye for intent and lack thereof. And once you have developed the ability to detect when the intent is lacking, you have to develop an eye for what is needed in order to add the intent back into the work. The problem with transitions is that often the intent of getting from one place to the next becomes more important than the intent of the work. It becomes a simple abstract problem: "How do I get from A to B?" But before you ask yourself how, you need to ask yourself why. What is the motivation for your work? And if you cannot answer the question why, then something may be missing in the logical sequence of your work.

People who work organically rarely have problems with transitions, because organic form could be considered one large transition that becomes the entire work. Working **organically** means that you start with a small idea and you develop that idea slowly from that kernel or seed. Every creation of new movement relates back to that seed movement and is connected in idea, form, and content. Someone who works organically never creates the end before the middle. In fact, if you create organically, you must create each movement growing out of the last, and the ending simply comes when you feel it is logical. You explore and find the ending. You do not know where the piece will end up as you begin it. Every new movement is a transition that grows out of the previous creation. (Organic form is explored fully in chapter 13.)

However, creating in sections, planning ahead, improvising, and moving forward with an idea without necessarily knowing how something will materialize are very good ways to create. This method allows you to brainstorm many solutions to movement problems and to choose what works best. It allows you to move forward when you hit a mental block. And it opens up opportunities for using formulas to develop your movement, which is discussed in chapter 9. When you are using this method, you must become proficient in developing good transitions.

As the word connotes, a **transition** is a place where you change from one idea, phrase, position, or place in the performance space to another. Transitions are needed for everything: to go from a beginning pose into movement for the first time, to get onstage from offstage, to connect one movement to another, to connect one movement phrase to another, to change from dancing alone to dancing with a partner, and to change from self-supporting to being supported by someone else or being lifted by someone else.

Let's first talk about transitions that take dancers on and off the stage. A common fault in creating transitions before, during, and at the end of a work is simply to take dancers on and off the stage as an indication of the beginning and ending of a section of movement. However, you need to ask these questions: "Why am I taking this dancer offstage? Where is she going? And why am I bringing my dancers on from offstage? Where have they been?" Bringing dancers onstage and taking them off arbitrarily does not usually work unless there is a reason. Again, there must be intent. Also, if the work is very short, taking dancers on and off is like adding chapters to a story that is only three pages long. If you are working in a proscenium theater, where dancers may enter and exit the wings and not be seen until they reemerge, the exit offstage or entrance from offstage has substantial meaning (see figure 8.1). This must not be ignored. For example, a dancer may enter the stage slowly and reluctantly, with a strong focus offstage. This may symbolize that something is offstage that is important to that dancer, and the dancer for some reason is being forced to leave it. For the rest of the performance, the audience knows that in that direction offstage, something important exists. If you as a choreographer now ignore what you have set up, the audience will become confused and wonder what happened to the idea that was never realized or resolved from the beginning of your work.

You have explored a few ways to create transitions both organically (as in improvisations 1 and 2) and in an abstract way (as in improvisation 3). In improvisations 1 and 2 you were identifying a seed of intent within a shape and using that to propel you to the next shape. In improvisation 3 you explored the actual craft of building transitions by creating movement for a transition. There is no set rule about how you should create transitions or what transitions work and which transitions will not work. Every transition will require you to take into consideration the intent of the entire work and the intent of the transition itself. Looking for something that seems logical might be a good guide. But even illogical transitions work if there is a reason—such as to jar the audience or to create an element of surprise. These transitions are created in an illogical way but with intent. Yet who is to say

Figure 8.1 Strong focus onstage will give a reason to enter, or a reason to exit, as a reaction to the focal point.

what is logical and what is not? The rule for you should be that it has to make sense for you. If you have created it without thinking about the intent, it may or may not work. Sometimes surprises happen. But if you think about the intent and know that it exists, you will almost always come up with something that works.

There may be times when it seems absolutely impossible to create a transition that works. In this case you need to look carefully at the parts that need a transition. Perhaps the problem is not with the transition but with the material that you are trying to connect. It may be that you have not completed a statement before attempting to leave it. Or it may be that not all of your material belongs together. You may have more than one fully developed idea, the blending of which is illogical. You may have been inconsistent with your movement development and need to rethink the pieces you are trying to connect. You may have material for five separate pieces of choreography; if that's the case, you will need to look at what you are doing and choose one direction to take and re-create the rest of the material to go with the chosen direction.

It is often difficult for you as the choreographer to see problems with transitions. You are teaching your movement to other dancers, and the problem of communicating that movement accurately to your dancers becomes consuming. It is easy to think that the reason something is not working is that the dancers have not yet fully accomplished the task you have requested of them. And as you watch the rehearsal, you become so involved in helping them perform your movement that you forget to watch the choreography itself to see if you have given them something that can be easily performed, especially when it concerns transitions. So you need to practice watching the choreography itself, as you imagine it should be. Ask yourself as you watch your dancers, "If they were performing the movement as I requested it, would it work?" Usually when a dancer is struggling with a particular spot in the choreography, it is because the transition is not logical for the dancer. Either the dancer does not understand the motivation behind the transition or there is no logical transition in the choreography. It becomes your job as a choreographer to find out where the problem lies and fix it for your dancer. If you are certain the intent exists, but your dancer does not understand it, you may spend time working with the dancer to help him with it. But if rehearsal time is limited, you may wish to create a new transition that your dancer is able to understand easily. This is a difficult judgment call for you as the choreographer. The work is yours and you do not want to have to change your work and your intent because a dancer is having difficulty with it. You may even demoralize a dancer by changing everything as soon as your dancer has a little difficulty with it. The dancer may want to go away and work on it, accepting the challenge. Every dancer has a unique sensibility for movement, and it is rare to find a dancer who is able to completely match your unique movement sensibilities. In dance, you must use the instruments that are available to you—your dancers. Each one is special and has something to offer your work. If you are attuned to your dancers and have a good feel for their capabilities and strengths, then you may use that in your work. If you are attuned only to your own strengths and want everyone else to match your movement capabilities, then you might as well just create solos for yourself and forget choreographing for other dancers. You do not need them to do what you are already capable of doing alone.

So as you rehearse your choreography, practice watching for problem spots (see figure 8.2). If you are having a difficult time identifying the trouble spots, invite someone else to come in and help you. This could be another student or someone you respect as a choreographer. Ask that person to point out any part of the choreography that is not working. Then focus on those spots. Tweak the movement by trying some of the improvisations in this chapter. You might even ask your dancers to tell you where they feel they should naturally move next. Have them do something that works for them and see if it works for you. The ultimate decision is yours because you are the choreographer, but there is nothing wrong with seeking ideas from your dancers and from outsiders. If you do this with respect and acknowledge your dancers and friends for their participation, they will enjoy being a part of the creation.

Figure 8.2 Partnering may present challenging transitions. Take time to rehearse. Fix any awkward moments.

Movement Studies

1. Decide on an intent for your choreography and create five separate short movement phrases that express the intent you selected. After creating the five movement phrases, label them from 1 to 5 and place the numbers in a bowl. Place the movement phrases in the sequence that you draw out of the bowl by chance. Use the ideas for transitions that you explored during the previous improvisations to connect your five movement phrases in the order that you selected by chance. Find transitions that work for your intent, but try the extraordinary, rather than what you would normally choose, to see if it works. Expand your vocabulary by trying something new. Remember that your beginning and ending are also transitions.

2. Repeat the previous movement study in a different sequence.

3. Select what you deem to be the best sequence for your work. Create a third variation of these five movement phrases connected by transitions. Show all three of your variations of this movement study and discuss the similarities and differences in intent created in each variation.

Assessment

Use these assessment tools in evaluating your progress toward understanding transitions as a key concept in choreography.

Class Critique

- Identify the transitions in the work. Discuss the process that was used in creating these transitions. Identify any moments in the work that need better transitions (look within the original movement phrases as well to evaluate the smaller transitions there).

- As a choreographer, discuss your challenges in creating transitions that were drawn out of a bowl rather than planning the order for yourself. What happened as a result of this requirement?

- Evaluate what each choreographer deemed as the best choice for the sequence of his or her work. Do you agree? Why or why not?

Rubric

Following is a sample rubric that may be used in evaluating the third and last movement study on transitions. You may complete this for your peers and have them complete one for you. If you wish, you may change the criteria to be more in line with what you believe to be important content for this movement study.

Rubric for Exploring Transitions

Criteria	Strong evidence (4 points)	Some evidence (3 points)	Little evidence (2 points)	No evidence (1 point)
Application of various types of transitions				
Transitions create logical sequence of movement phrases				
Expanded movement vocabulary				
Clear intent in transitions				
Beginning, middle, and end				
Total points: (maximum 20 points)				

Documentation

Record all three variations on video and label them "Chance," "Exploration," and "Personal Choice." Include comments from your journal that evaluate your success at sequence by chance as opposed to the sequence you chose. Decide which was most successful for you and comment on why. Include this document along with the videos and the rubric in your digital portfolio.

Drawing Conclusions

Breaking the Rules

Create five phrases of movement that are unrelated. Try creating phrases from various techniques, such as jazz, ballet, and tap. Perform the phrases together with no transitions. Try different sequences of the five movement phrases until you find what works the best. Find music to accompany the work. Show your work to the rest of your class or to a group of your peers.

REFLECTIVE QUESTIONS As you observed works created by your peers, which pieces created by your group worked for you? Which did not? Why? • Is it possible to make choreography work without transitions? What effect does it create? When might you want to use this effect?

Drawing Conclusions

Critical Thinking Essay

Write an essay on the process of developing successful transitions in choreography. Discuss the methods you have explored, and add any ideas you think will work but are not mentioned here. Support your ideas with experience. An outline is provided to help you get started. Remember that the order of your essay is up to you.

I. Introduction: Make a statement about the importance of transitions in choreography.

II. Discussion

    A. Using intent to design transition

        i. Analysis: Explain the process for developing transitions including specific techniques that may be used.

        ii. Reflection: Explain the effects that may be obtained through the use of each method.

        iii. Integration: Discuss your experience and how it relates to these methods of developing transitions.

    B. Making the transition very quick and direct (with analysis, reflection, and integration).

    C. Drawing out the transition to make it very long (with analysis, reflection, and integration).

    D. Expanding or combining material from the original movement phrases (with analysis, reflection, and integration).

    E. Personal discovery (with analysis, reflection, and integration).

III. Conclusion (evaluate): Draw your own conclusions about the need for transitions and how that need might change depending on the intent of the work.

Chapter 9

Formulas

Initial Inquiries

What is it that makes all the movement in a piece of choreography look like it belongs together? • Why is it important to recognize movement that we have seen before? Or is it? • How much repeated material is too much, and how much is just right? • What can you do to keep going when you think you are stuck with choreographer's block? • How is it possible to keep finding new material when your own experience seems limited? • What tricks of the trade will help you keep going as a choreographer and give you the confidence that it is always possible to create something more that will work?

*W*hen I was a fairly young, emerging choreographer, Phyllis Lamhut (who began dancing with Alwin Nikolais and became lead dancer in the Murray Louis Dance Company) said to me, "Diana! You are a master of formulas!" I took this as both a compliment and an admonishment. And I think I was correct. I was very good at manipulating a small amount of movement. It gave me the confidence to go on, even though I considered my own movement vocabulary to be somewhat limited. I believe she wanted me to expand my movement vocabulary without being so dependent on formulas. That is why I have placed this chapter quite far along in this text—to allow you to explore and build your personal movement vocabulary before you discover these wonderful formulas that you may indulge in endlessly. But now you are ready, and just as a puzzle gives you pieces to play with and put together with satisfaction, these formulas help you to place movement together in a way that is both interesting and satisfying.

The formulas you will explore may be grouped into two types: those that use repeated material and those that develop material. Each of these is explored in depth with improvisations, movement studies, and opportunities to break the rules. The end of the chapter gives you an opportunity to explore a method introduced by Merce Cunningham called choreography by chance. Even though this seems like choreography without formulas, his process is a formula in itself. However, there are no rules to follow with this formula, so there will be no assessment, only reflection to help you keep track of your discoveries. You will summarize your experiences in a critical thinking essay.

 ## Essential Question

Why is it important to understand the effects of repeated material?

Warm-Up

1. Create a swinging movement that travels the distance of one step across the floor. You may do this any way you like, using only a few body parts or using a full-body swing. Your traveling may move in any direction as long as there is some progression through space in a straight line. After creating this one swinging movement that travels, begin at one side of the room and perform the movement repeatedly until you have traveled all the way across the room. Try this again with a different swinging movement. Explore movements that you think might work when they are repeated like this, and progress across the stage space.

2. For safety purposes, you should be able to complete this exercise with plenty of space and no obstructions, such as furniture or exercise equipment. Also, if at any time you become nauseated, stop and do not complete this exercise. Begin spinning in self-space without spotting. Start slowly and try to establish a balance. As you become accustomed to a particular speed, try increasing it. If you begin to lose your balance, slow down or stop if necessary and start again. Continue to spin faster until you have accomplished a moderate speed and are able to remain in self-space and balanced. Now, very gradually begin to travel around the room while spinning. Do not attempt to spot. You will have to feel your way around the space, because you will not be able to use your eyes to focus on anything. You may use them to detect light and shadow, which will help orient you in the space. If you ever feel unbalanced and unsafe, stop and rest a minute and then start over. Try watching others as they attempt this exercise.

   REFLECTIVE QUESTIONS What is the effect created by repeated movement? What kinesthetic effect is created and what is the visual effect created? How would you use this in choreography?

Improvisations

1. Create a 4-count movement phrase that is bold and interesting. Think of variation to supply interest. Four counts is not very long, but there is enough time to create two contrasting movements that follow each other or one movement that includes contrasting elements within it. Practice your phrase until you know it well. Then get into groups of three or four dancers. Teach each other your movement phrases so that everyone in the group knows all the movement phrases and can perform them in sequence. Decide on the best sequence as a group. To do this, you should think not only about how easy it would be to go from one phrase to the next but how the movements look together to give the most interest and variation of movement. Add or change material if you need to in order to create interest and transitions that work, but keep the timing consistent to 4 counts per movement phrase. Practice the sequence together until everyone knows the sequence and can perform it accurately without following each other.

   REFLECTIVE QUESTIONS What did you have to do to make the four phrases fit together logically? • What elements did you consider when you decided on an order that worked for the group?

2. Using the groups from the previous improvisation, and performing the same material, practice performing the material in a canon. Select one person to begin the sequence. The second person should begin the first phrase after the first 4 counts while the first

person goes on to the second phrase. The third person begins the first phrase after 8 counts while the second person is beginning the second phrase and the first person is beginning the third phrase. The last dancer begins the first phrase after 12 counts while the third dancer is beginning the second phrase, the second dancer is beginning the third phrase, and the first dancer is completing the sequence with the fourth phrase. All dancers should continue the sequence in their own time until all the last dancers have completed the sequence twice. If you have trouble keeping the sequence in the correct timing, simply stop and start over until you think you have it right.

3. Once you have practiced the previous improvisation enough to be completely accurate with the sequence and timing, play around a little with the spacing. As a group, make some decisions about what you think works best. Should someone begin facing back while everyone else faces front? What facing directions work best? Do you want everyone to stand in a line to begin, or should you place yourselves around the stage space? Should you be close together or far apart? Try lots of ways of performing the same material. Select one that the group likes the best and show it to the rest of the class.

   REFLECTIVE QUESTIONS   What makes a canon of movement interesting to watch? What parts of the canon were more interesting than others? Why? • As you made choices about spacing and facing directions, what were your considerations? How did you decide what worked best?

4. Create a slow 5-count phrase that begins in a high level, somehow progresses to a low level, and ends in a high level. Make sure the phrase may be repeated easily without the need to create extra transitional material. Keep it simple! As you create this movement phrase, also focus on line and shape. After you create your phrase, add one powerful accent to your movement somewhere in the phrase. Begin performing your movement phrase in the center of the performance space with the rest of the class watching. Keep repeating your phrase until someone else feels they can join you. One at a time, add a dancer to the performance. Make sure that each time a dancer is added the performance is really in unison before the next dancer begins. Continue adding dancers until at least five dancers are performing together. Each dancer should be careful to perform the movement exactly as you are performing it, with the same focus of the eyes, same facing direction, same energy, and the same timing, lines, and shapes. After the last dancer has been added, perform three more times together and then stop together in a committed stillness to find a conclusion to the work. Repeat this with different dancers so that everyone has a chance to observe. If there is a time when dancers are having trouble following the original material, start again and find a movement phrase with simpler movements. Finally, take one of the movement phrases that was simple enough for the entire group to do well, and perform the phrase repeatedly as a group. Pull one person out at a time to observe the effect created by a very large group performing together.

   REFLECTIVE QUESTIONS   What happens to the effect of a movement phrase when it is performed by more than one person? • What is the difference in the effect created by a large group performing and only one person performing? What are some of the problems inherent with requiring an entire group to perform the same movement phrase?

5. Create a strong 4-count movement that you think will bear repetition well. Now, leaving that 4-count movement, improvise slow and sustained movement that floats through space. When you hear a cue (from a drum, a clap, or any agreed-on cue), transition to and perform your 4-count movement and then immediately return to the slow, sustained floating improvisation. Do this several times, noting the kinesthetic effect as you perform and the visual effect as you observe others. Change the material that you use in the improvisation by working with other effort actions, such as wring or glide.

What is the effect created by a short contrasting movement repeatedly interrupting a continuous quality of movement? • What quality of movement works best as a contrast to the 4-count movement you selected? Why?

Discussion of Key Concept

Repeated material provides a means of connecting material within a work and adding continuity, which can hold a piece together. An audience will look for strong elements that repeat in some way so they may recognize them and relate them to the work as a whole. Repeating material without manipulating it can be extremely effective or extremely boring, and there are no rules to follow that will guide you regarding when there is enough repetition.

Minimalism is a label given to an artistic form that uses a very simple motif or phrase and repeats it over and over, creating an almost hypnotic effect that can be quite powerful. *Bolero*, composed in 1928 by Maurice Ravel (1975-1937), is an example of a music **motif** that is repeated for about 15 minutes (depending on how it is performed) without once changing material, only changing the instruments performing it. Created as an experiment, *Bolero* has become a masterpiece of music literature and Ravel's most famous work. More recently, composer Philip Glass (1937-) has employed this technique in a more modern style and with minimal development.

A 19th-century example of minimalism was created by Marius Petipa in "Kingdom of the Shades," a scene from the ballet *La Bayadère*. It begins with a series of arabesques and a cambré back, performed first by one dancer and followed by another and another until the entire company, an average of 32 dancers, fills the stage. The audience knows after the first 90 seconds how the work will continue, but for some reason the predictability is no longer an issue; the momentum builds and mesmerizes the audience, and the effect is breathtaking.

Laura Dean (1945-), a postmodern choreographer, uses spinning to create a minimalist effect. Her dancers spin for 10 minutes or more, changing their traveling patterns or perhaps an arm position, but the spinning is repeated continually throughout her works and has become a signature for her as a choreographer. Laura Dean may have received her inspiration from the Turkish Whirling Dervishes, who have taken a practice that was originally performed as a means of approaching nirvana and transformed it into entertainment that has traveled the globe with performances that have captured thousands who are willing to watch their continual spinning with no embellishment or variation.

There is no doubt that repetition may create momentum and a hypnotic effect that captures an audience. Part of the requisite for success must be the exactness and simplicity of the performance. The minute one dancer creates a slightly different line or rhythmic structure, the effect is lost.

Repetition of movement phrases performed in canon, or a round, provides an automatic variation that includes familiar material and often produces harmonic material that pleases the eye. A canon in music occurs when a simple melody is sung by more than one voice entering at different times, but all voices sing the same melody. "Row, Row, Row Your Boat" is the most familiar childhood song that teaches the use of canon. In music, it is extremely important to consider the relationships of pitch that occur when one section of the music is sung or played against another. In dance, these relationships are not as critical because the equivalent of dissonance rarely occurs in dance. Taking a simple phrase of movement and placing it in canon will provide very interesting combinations of movement, without the choreographer having to think much about it. This is particularly true if the original material is simple yet carries with it good variations of space, rhythmic structure, and energy. However, if a choreographer considers how the material will fit together in a round and thinks about the opportunities for correlation of line, syncopation of accent, and variations in level, canons may be created that are incredibly effective (see figure 9.1 on page 184).

Figure 9.1 A change in level provides interest for this canon.

Figure 9.2 Ripples are canons timed very close together, creating a wavelike effect.

The problem with canons is that they tend to be overused, and if they are not surprising in their structure, they can be just as predictable and uninteresting as repetitious movement. One solution to this problem is to set a canon that the audience thinks will be predictable and then altering the structure to leave the canon just when the audience was about to think they have seen this before. Canons that are placed very close in timing so that the dancers are only one or two counts apart in their movement create something we call a ripple effect (see figure 9.2). This effect has been used very successfully by the Rockettes, a precision dance company that performs at Radio City Music Hall in New York City. **Ripples** create wavelike movement across the stage and may add a surge of energy to the choreography. However, if the choreography does not lend itself to interesting ripple effects, and the timing of a canon is placed too close together, it can look as if the dancers are simply trying to be in unison but are missing the timing. When the audience is unsure about whether the movement is supposed to be unison or canon, the confusion is detrimental to the work.

Another form of repetition may occur in choreography when an important recognizable movement or movement phrase is repeated throughout a work. It is not repeated immediately but returns here and there at selected moments in the piece after new material has been introduced. This may be a method of referring back to an original idea or theme. It may be symbolic or completely abstract, but if the movement itself is simple and strong, it will be recognized by the audience. Beethoven's (1770-1827) famous *Fifth Symphony* uses his four-note music motif repeated throughout the first movement. The motif is composed of three notes of the same pitch followed by a note one third lower and repeated again lower still in a minor key (see figure 9.3). The rhythmic structure is short-short-short-long.

Figure 9.3   Motif from Beethoven's *Fifth Symphony.*

This motif has taken on the symbolic meaning of fate knocking at the door. If you would like to repeat a statement in your choreography, this can be done easily by using a simple movement motif.

Movement Studies

1. Create a movement study that employs repetition and canon. Add elements of surprise here and there to keep your work from being too predictable.

2. Create a study using a short movement motif that keeps reappearing within new material in your work.

3. Create a canon that does not work. Be ready to discuss the elements necessary to create an effective canon, and why your movement study is not effective.

Assessment

Use these assessment tools in evaluating your progress toward understanding repeated material as a key concept in choreography.

Class Critique

- Identify repeated material and label it according to minimalism, canon, or motif.
- Evaluate the consistency of the repetitions to determine whether the repetitions are accurate.
- Evaluate the effectiveness of the repeated material.
- What suggestions can you make to increase the effectiveness of the material?
- If something becomes predictable, make suggestions to add more surprise to the movement choices.

Rubric

Following is a sample rubric that you may use in evaluating the first movement study on repeated material. You may complete this rubric for your peers and have them complete one for you. If you wish, you may change the criteria to be more in line with what you believe to be important content for this movement study.

Rubric for Repeated Material

Criteria	Strong evidence (4 points)	Some evidence (3 points)	Little evidence (2 points)	No evidence (1 point)
Interesting movement motifs				
Clear use of minimalism, canon, motif, and unison				
Elements of surprise				
Clear intent				
Beginning, middle, and end				
Total points: (maximum 20 points)				

Documentation

Record your work on video. Make sure you film the video from an angle that allows you to see all parts of the repeated material, particularly if you are recording canons. Include comments from your journal that evaluate your success at making repeated material interesting. Decide what was most successful for you and comment on why. Include this document along with the videos and the rubric in your digital portfolio.

Drawing Conclusions

Breaking the Rules

Warning: This is very difficult, but don't give up on that account! Create a dance that includes no repetition. This will rule out walking and running because these both require a repetition of steps. It will rule out symmetrical design because symmetry is repetition of shape. There may be no unison movement because that is repetition of movement by more than one dancer. You might find it interesting to try this movement study in a particular technique, such as modern or jazz, creating a work that never repeats a single step, arm movement, or position. Good luck!

REFLECTIVE QUESTIONS   What were your challenges in creating this piece? Does it work? How do you unify a piece if you are not allowed to repeat any material?

 Essential Question

Why is it important to understand how to manipulate movement?

Warm-Up

1. Standing in the center of the performance space, close your eyes, and take a few moments to relax and focus on your breathing. Feel your joints loosen and release toward the floor. Gently release your knees and feel the floor under your feet. Slowly and gently circle your right shoulder forward. Repeat this action. Now repeat it on the left. And again. Now circle the shoulders in the other direction, one at a time as before. Now circle both shoulders at a time. Circle your head slowly and gently to the right. Repeat. Then to the left and repeat. Then circle both shoulders forward while circling the head to the right. Circle both shoulders backward while circling the head to the left. Circle the right arm forward. Repeat. Circle the left arm forward and repeat. Circle both arms forward. Repeat the sequence, circling the arms backward. Pause and focus one more time on your breathing. Think about what part of your body needs to move. Use the circling action established to move that part of your body to loosen it up. Find a circular movement. It could be anywhere, in any body part, as long as you are creating circles in space. Make the circles larger. Make them smaller. Change the direction of the circles. Continue to find new ways to create circles any way you like with any body part. If you want to travel through space, that is okay too, but make sure you open your eyes to watch for other dancers. Some of your circles may be pathways. How many ways can you explore circles through movement? Try changing your dynamics, your speed, the level you are performing in, and so on, but never lose the integrity of your circle motif.

   REFLECTIVE QUESTIONS   How did changing the body part affect the circular movement? • What challenges did you have while changing the energy, space, and time of the circular movement? • Were you able to maintain the integrity of the circle? If not, did it matter?

2. Create a short, simple movement that is soft and free flowing. Perform it several times. Then do the same movement, but change the energy to bound and the quality to sharp. Explore various ways to change the energy and quality to the extreme opposite of the original movement. Then return to the original movement. Explore ways to accomplish the original movement while traveling through general space. Explore various pathways and directions of travel. Continue to perform the original movement while exploring ways to move through the space. You may change levels to add interest, but maintain the integrity of the original movement.

   REFLECTIVE QUESTIONS   How is a simple movement affected by changes in energy and quality and traveling through space?

Improvisations

1. Stand with other dancers in a circle and assign one person to begin. That person begins by creating a literal gesture with specific meaning—something such as waving good-bye or shaking your finger in a "shame on you" gesture. The next person in the circle must analyze everything about that gesture and perform it again by changing something. You may change level, tempo, rhythm, spatial elements, energy, or body part. Continue until you have made it all the way around the circle and each person has selected something different to change.

REFLECTIVE QUESTION   How is the intent of the gesture affected by the variations of movement?

2. Now in a space on your own, create a gesture with your right hand. It may be any gesture you like, either one that has literal meaning or one you create that is very abstract, but make sure it is small and definite and that you know it well enough to repeat it in its exact form many times. Practice the gesture over and over while you focus on every detail about the gesture. What pathway does it follow through space? Is it direct (creating straight pathways) or indirect (creating curved pathways)? What is the shape of the gesture? What positive shapes are made by your right arm while you perform the gesture? What level are you performing the movement in? What kind of energy does it take to perform the gesture? Is it free flowing or is it bound? Or does it change? Is it strong, or is it light? What is the timing of the gesture? How fast or how slow is it? Does it change tempo? What are the meter and rhythm of the movement? If you had to count it to help someone else perform it for you, how would you count the movement? Think about the quality of the movement. If you had to describe that quality for someone in order to help him perform it, what words would you use? Remember this information as you begin to manipulate this gesture in the next few exercises. You may wish to record this information in your journal.

REFLECTIVE QUESTION   Why is it important to analyze a small movement in such detail? How might you use this information as a choreographer?

3. Take the gesture you created in the previous improvisation and make the gesture bigger. Keep everything else about the gesture the same if you can. The timing may have to change in order to accomplish a larger movement, but try to hold on to the rhythm, meter, shape, pathways, and energy created in the original gesture. Make the movement as big as you can. Now make the movement smaller than the original. Make the movement as small as you can. Go back to performing the original movement. Now perform the movement in a different level. Change the level again. Go back to the original gesture, walk to a different place in the room, and perform the gesture again. Go to another place and perform the gesture. Try another place. Go very close to someone else in the space and perform your gesture. Find someone else to get very close to and perform the gesture again. Now get as far away as you can from everyone and perform the gesture. Find another space that is far away and perform the gesture again. Come back to your original spot in the performance space and perform your gesture one more time.

REFLECTIVE QUESTION   How did variations in size, level, and stage space affect the intent of your gesture?

4. Using the same gesture from the previous improvisation, alter the direction of the gesture. If it was moving forward, do that same thing moving backward or sideways. Then alter the pathway and focus of the gesture. Where the gesture is direct, change it to indirect. Where it is indirect, change it to direct. Practice this a few times to make sure you get it right.

REFLECTIVE QUESTION   How did variations in direction affect the intent of your gesture?

5. Alter the timing of the gesture. Slow it down and speed it up. Change the meter. If it seemed to be performed in duple meter, change it to triple. If it was triple, change it to duple. Add stillness in at least one place during the gesture. Change the rhythm. Put new accents in the movement. Try repeating the gesture multiple times.

REFLECTIVE QUESTION   How did variations in timing affect the intent of your gesture?

6. Alter the energy of the gesture. Where it was strong, make it light. If it was light, make it strong. If the energy is controlled and bound, perform the gesture freely. If the gesture is free, control it more and bind the movement. Change the quality of the gesture. If it is sharp, perform it smoothly. If it was performed serenely, try performing it with anger.

   REFLECTIVE QUESTION   How did variations in energy and quality affect the intent of your gesture?

7. Change the body part that is performing the gesture. Explore variations in other body parts, two or more body parts at a time, and full-body movement. Be careful to maintain the integrity of the movement.

   REFLECTIVE QUESTION   How did variations in body parts affect the intent of your gesture?

8. Try performing the gesture on the opposite side (flip symmetry) or upside down (turn symmetry). (See Symmetry and Asymmetry in chapter 4, page 69.)

   REFLECTIVE QUESTION   How does the use of symmetry affect variations of movement?

9. Try performing the gesture backward by performing the ending first and finishing at the beginning. Perform the gesture in pieces. Break it apart and perform the parts separately, or perform only one or two parts and leave the rest out.

   REFLECTIVE QUESTION   How does changing sequence affect the intent of movement?

10. Change the shape of the rest of your body while performing the gesture. Add another movement with a different body part while you are doing the gesture, keeping the gesture as the focal point.

    REFLECTIVE QUESTION   How does it affect the intent of a movement to add or change the movement of other body parts?

11. Decorate your gesture by placing extra detail in it, making it more complex. You might take your arm through many pathways in order to complete the gesture, or finish the gesture with a flourish. Add tiny movements around the simple gesture to decorate it. The focus remains on the original gesture.

    REFLECTIVE QUESTION   How does it affect the intent of a movement to add decorative details to it?

12. Take the gesture and add another movement to it, such as a turn, a fall, or a slide. Here the focus may travel from the gesture to the new movement. They are not performed together, but one after the other.

    REFLECTIVE QUESTION

    How is a movement affected by adding another movement after it?

13. Finally, take your gesture and explore variations of movement by combining all of the possibilities explored in these improvisations. Make sure every movement you explore has its roots in the original gesture.

    REFLECTIVE QUESTION   What is the effect when all movement is created from a single idea?

Discussion of Key Concept

There are two ways to create **developed material**. One is to use an organic approach, where every movement grows out of an idea that existed in the previous movement. (Organic form is explored fully in chapter 13.) The second way is to take all of the elements you learned from part I and use these elements to manipulate material from your original idea, motif, or theme.

Motif and development is an effective formula, which you explored during the previous improvisations. It is the act of taking a very simple, short movement, such as a gesture, and manipulating it. This formula may be used to create a unified piece of choreography that fits together naturally, because it is made up of material that is continuously related. It also provides a great deal of interest for audience members who may be on the edge of their seats wondering what you are about to do next. Or they may not be aware of the formula you are using consciously, but the material makes sense together because you have created it from a single idea and it is engaging. We look for the familiar in order to make sense of the world. An audience will do the same with your work. By using all of the elements of dance that you explored in part II to develop the movement from a simple movement motif you have at your fingertips, an infinite number of variations to be explored. No longer do you need to struggle with what to do next. Take what you have and go further with it by manipulating what you have.

You can use motif and development to expand material you have selected (see figure 9.4). Or if you are struggling to find a transition between two sections of your work, you may use this formula to create a transition using the material you have created before and after the transition you need. Or you may create an entire work based on one simple movement motif using this formula. Formulas are tools you may use to mold and shape a small amount of material so that creating a work becomes easy once you get started on your original idea. The trick becomes finding a motif that is simple enough to allow many manipulations but also interesting enough to withstand multiple manipulations. Usually a simple movement that has contrast within it will manipulate well. The manipulations may become more interesting than the motif, and that is okay because you want to draw the interest of your audience as the work

Figure 9.4 Variations on a circle motif.

progresses. But if you are having trouble developing interesting manipulations, you may need to go back to the motif and redesign it. You may not have given yourself enough to work with and you may need to add or change the original movement motif.

Theme and variation is similar to motif and development in that you begin with original material and manipulate it. The difference is that a theme is a larger statement than a movement motif. A motif is a single movement. A **theme** is a movement phrase or may even be several phrases placed together to create a whole. Variations are created on the theme by manipulating the movement within the phrases the same way that you manipulate a motif. Theme and variation may become an overall form used to create an entire choreographic work, just as theme and variation has been used as a form to create music compositions (an example is Tchaikovsky's *Theme and Variations*). This is discussed further in chapter 13.

One critique that I often hear about choreography is that the movement was not developed enough. Choreographers have many wonderful ideas and they may string them together, one after the other, without exploring the possibilities of each idea and without creating meaningful or logical relationships between ideas. Those choreographers are often told they have enough material for 10 dances. If you hear this critique, go back and pick one or two ideas and develop those ideas and save the rest of your material for another piece.

However, sometimes, in creating dances it is necessary to string together steps. Dances are often arranged for recitals, where it is important to show that students have learned a number of steps throughout the year, all or most of which need to be showcased in one dance. Competition dances will be arranged to show off the tricks that dancers are able to perform or that judges will look for in their evaluations. This is particularly true for competing ice skaters. Sequencing steps in order to show off the talents of a dancer is an art in itself because the one who arranges these dances must find smooth transitions between what often seem to be unrelated ideas. With attention to variation in the elements, even this arranging of a sequence of required steps can be made more interesting. But when the focus is on the development of the movement itself rather than the talents of the dancer, true choreography is born. Developing each idea as it is presented in a work is an important skill, one that separates the choreographer from the one who arranges dances.

A list of all the ways that a movement may be manipulated and developed is in table 9.1 on page 192. Most of these ideas are taken directly from the elements of movement in part II, such as elements of energy, space, and time. Some come from musical ideas that may be adapted to choreography, such as instrumentation. You may think of more ways to develop your motif and add those methods to this list. As you practice developing movement, you will no longer need this list, because variations will present themselves to you without requiring you to think about a formula. But the list is always available to you when you get stuck.

Movement Studies

1. Motif and development: Create a movement study using only manipulations from the material in one small gesture or movement motif. Every movement in the study must be a development of that motif. The original motif must exist somewhere in the work, but it does not have to be at the beginning. Even transitional material must relate back to the original movement. Be ready to support each movement choice with an explanation of how it relates to the movement motif.

2. Theme and variation (abbreviated): Create one movement phrase that has contrasting elements of energy, space, and time. Call this phrase the theme. Using at least one of the methods to manipulate movement (see table 9.1), create a second movement phrase by manipulating part or all of the material in the original movement phrase. Call this variation 1. Create four variations total, using this method, using different methods of manipulation to provide interest to and development of the original movement phrase. Perform the theme and the four variations in order. Provide transitional material when

Table 9.1 Ways to Develop Movement or a Motif

Choreographic element	Suggestions for development
Energy	• Dynamics: If it is strong, make it light; if it is light, make it strong. • Energy flow: If it is bound, make it free; if it is free, make it bound.
Space	• Variations in level: Change the level. • Augmentation: Make it bigger; make it as big as you can. • Diminution: Make it smaller; make it as small as you can. • Change the body part (instrumentation): Perform a hand gesture with the foot, hip, or elbow. • Stage space: Take the motif to a different place in the performance space; change the relationship to props, scenery, and other dancers. • Shape: Change curved to straight, symmetry to asymmetry. • Direction: Alter direction of travel, movement, facing direction. • Change focus: If it is direct, make it indirect; if it is indirect, make it direct. • Inversion: Turn it upside down or do it on the other side.
Time	• Tempo: Make it faster or slower. • Meter: Change a duple meter to a triple. • Rhythm: If it is sustained, make it sudden or change sudden to sustained; add stillness; change the accent.
Quality and form	• Quality: Make something soft sharp; make something heavy light; make something steady shaky. • Repetition: Keep it the same, but do it several times. • Retrograde: Reverse the order of performance (begin at the end and end with the beginning). • Fragmentation: Break it into parts and perform the parts separately, or perform only one or two parts and leave the rest out. • Vary the background: Change the body shape; add another movement with the other body parts; add another person moving around you while doing the movement. • Embellishment or ornamentation: Add detail to the movement, such as shaking the arm while moving forward; add loops or zigzags to a straight path. • Additive: Add a turn or a leap or movement in another body part performed at the same time. • Combination: Combine any of these elements.

needed. Make sure the entire work has a beginning, middle, and end. (Note: You will have an opportunity to explore theme and variation as a form for a complete work in chapter 13. This movement study is based on only one movement phrase, whereas theme and variation typically involves a theme that includes a number of phrases that create their own beginning, middle, and end within a section of choreography. This theme is then varied in a formal way, and each variation is a complete section of the choreography.)

Assessment

Use these assessment tools in evaluating your progress toward understanding developed material as a key concept in choreography.

Class Critique

• Identify the original gesture, motif, or theme in each work.

- Identify the manipulations that you noted from table 9.1.
- Evaluate any movement that you could not identify as a manipulation of the original material by asking the choreographers to defend their process. If you think the defense was inadequate, make a suggestion to clarify the manipulation. However, ask yourself whether you believe it is important for the audience to know the thought process of the choreographer in these manipulations. Decide what works for you and what does not.

Rubric

Following is a sample rubric that you may use in evaluating both movement studies on developed material. You may complete this rubric for your peers and have them complete one for you. If you wish, you may change the criteria to be more in line with what you believe to be important content for these movement studies.

Rubric for Developed Material

Criteria	Strong evidence (4 points)	Some evidence (3 points)	Little evidence (2 points)	No evidence (1 point)
Clear development of motif or theme				
Choreographer is able to support process				
All movement relates to original material				
Clear intent				
Beginning, middle, and end				
Total points: (maximum 20 points)				

Documentation

Record your work on video. Include a document with the recording that describes the variations according to a manipulation found in table 9.1. Include journal entries, class critique, and a rubric with your recording and place it in your digital portfolio.

Drawing Conclusions

Breaking the Rules

Create a dance that includes no manipulation of movement. Either every movement must be repeated precisely as it was presented originally, or you must find completely new movement that has no relationship to the rest of the movement in the work. Again, you may not walk or run because the second step or run is a symmetrical variation of the original step.

REFLECTIVE QUESTIONS What were your challenges in creating this work? Did your solution to the problem work for you? Why? Why not? How does working this way stretch your limitations? Or does it?

 Essential Question

Why would a choreographer decide to combine movement haphazardly by chance?

Warm-Up

1. Create four short repetitious movements that do not connect to each other. Each one should be created to accomplish a specific goal for a proper warm-up as follows: raise body temperature, loosen joints, strengthen, and stretch. Assign each movement 8 counts and perform them in the order listed previously (raise body temperature, loosen joints, strengthen, and stretch). Find ways to transition easily from one movement to the next without losing any counts so that the final performance is exactly 32 counts.

2. Write the numbers 1 through 4 on separate pieces of paper and place them in a bowl or box. Mix them up and draw them out, keeping a record of the order you have drawn these four numbers (e.g., 4-2-3-1). Do the warm-up again in this new order (e.g., stretch, loosen, strengthen, and raise body temperature). Again, fix your transitions so that the movements follow each other easily in this new order. Repeat this process with a new order.

REFLECTIVE QUESTIONS How does the order of these four movements affect the aesthetics of the entire sequence? How does it affect the efficiency of the warm-up?

Improvisations

1. Create an interesting shape. Call that shape 1. Create another shape; call that shape 2. Create a third shape; call that shape 3. Now arrange yourselves in groups of at least three dancers in each group and preferably five dancers. Stand close together and face any direction you like. Maintain that facing direction while everyone in the group performs shape 1. You may make small spacing adjustments only. If you think you need to be farther away, you may move slightly. If you want to be closer, you may move slightly. Now, everyone change to shape 2. And then to shape 3. Rehearse this sequence as a group, making some decisions together such as timing and amounts of energy used to move from one shape to the next.

2. Keeping the same shapes and the same groups, change the order of the shapes and perform the new sequence (e.g., 3-2-1). Change the order again and perform it one last time. (e.g., 2-1-3 or 2-3-1). You may wish to draw these orders out of a box or bowl.

3. Keeping the same groups, have each person in the group perform his or her shapes in a different order. Try this many different ways.

REFLECTIVE QUESTIONS How do the relationships between the dancers affect the intent of the shapes performed? • Do all the combinations of shapes work? Which combinations work better than others? Why?

4. In a group of five or six dancers, create a short movement phrase that all of you are able to perform in unison. Practice the phrase until you are all very familiar with it. Make sure that you are each able to perform the phrase accurately alone as well as with the group. Put three slips of paper in a box or bowl. The papers should have the words 1: very fast or presto, 2: very slow or largo, 3: medium tempo or moderato. Each dancer in the group selects a paper, reads it, and replaces it in the box or bowl. Now the group performs the movement phrase simultaneously as indicated by the paper. Obviously those who perform the movement very fast will finish before those who perform it very

slowly. To create a piece where each dancer starts and finishes at the same time, each person who performs must repeat the phrase until the entire group has performed the phrase at least once. Try to be aware of each other to accomplish a logical and coordinated ending to the improvisation.

REFLECTIVE QUESTIONS As you observed different groups, which performances worked the best, and why? • How did the changing in the tempo of the movement affect the intent of the work?

5. Write the eight effort actions on pieces of paper and place them in a box or bowl. (Effort actions are glide, flick, float, dab, press, punch, slash, and wring.) Select three pieces of paper, one at a time, and record your selections in order either by memory or by writing them down. Create a movement phrase that includes these three effort actions in the order you selected. Now place pieces of paper with stage directions in a bowl (USR, USL, CSR, and so on; if you need a list of stage directions, see figure 4.26 on page 86). Select two pieces of paper out of this bowl. The first selection will be your position on the stage, and the second selection will be your facing direction. Now rehearse your movement phrase beginning in the stage space you selected and facing the direction you selected. Finally, find a way to assign dancers in groups by chance. If you have enough dancers to create six groups, you might have everyone roll a die and have each dancer work with the group that corresponds to the number on the die. Or you may draw numbers from a bowl. Perform your movement phrase with your group in the stage space and facing direction you selected. You might have to adjust slightly if your spacing places you in someone else's path or if two of you start in the same place. Try to stay as true as possible to your selections. Finally, if you like, play various pieces of music as you perform the phrases. Allow the selection of music to be random rather than selected for intent.

REFLECTIVE QUESTIONS What was the effect of the combined phrases performed as a unified dance by each group? • Were there any surprises that worked extremely well? What made these surprises work? • What did not work? Why? • How might you use this method in your choreography? • What are some ways to control or increase opportunities for success with this method of combining movement?

Discussion of Key Concept

Choreography by chance is a method that was introduced by Merce Cunningham (1919-2009), who was a lead dancer in the Martha Graham Company and became a revolutionary force in avant-garde dance) and has been used frequently ever since because of its ability to provide fresh new material that is unhampered by preconceived ideas, formulas, or rules that dictate what is right and what is wrong. Often when things are unplanned, surprising things happen that might never exist otherwise. Some people choreograph by chance and present that chance performance as a finished production, as Cunningham has done for many years with much success. Others use chance to begin the choreographic process and then make choices about the results. Some results are kept and some are discarded. So although the original movement was created by chance, the selection of which movement to perform is planned and controlled by the choreographer.

However chance is used in the choreographic process, it may be important to consider how to set up the rules of chance in order to come out with a successful result. As always, contrast provides interest, so if movement is created with contrast, it will often be successfully combined with other movements. Bursts of energy from different movement phrases may coincide to add dynamics or follow closely to provide a syncopated rhythm. When choreographing by chance, you may wish to think of what will actually be the common element that holds the work together. In improvisation 4, the movement phrase was the same, so the material holds the piece together, but the timing is altered to provide interest and variation without conscious decision making. In improvisation 5, contrast is built into the work by forcing dancers to use three different effort actions. The relationships of the different efforts performed should provide interest through contrast. The common element in the dance is the use of effort actions. Placing everything else by chance, including the music, creates opportunities for surprise relationships to develop between dancers, movement phrases, and music.

It can be a lot of fun to think of structures or parameters that may be used to create choreography by chance. Merce Cunningham argues that all of life is made up of chance encounters and that dance should reflect life. You may or may not agree with this philosophy, but it is fun to play with the idea, and you learn a great deal in the process, even if you never choose to use this method as you choreograph your final works for the stage. You will find things that happen by surprise that you want to actually use as you plan your choreography. Write these surprises down so you don't forget them. As you set up your structure for chance dance, think of all the elements of dance you explored in part II and all the ways to manipulate movement you explored in this chapter as listed in table 9.1 on page 192.

What is your impression of this process of choreographing by chance? Is this a process you think will work for you? What have you noticed about how this process works for you, and how might you structure your process to optimize your success?

Movement Studies

1. Create a dance by creating your own parameters that include variations in energy, space, or time; using the roll of a die; or drawing from a bowl to make decisions for you.

2. Create a dance with three or more people. Each person must create a solo for himself or herself that takes a particular amount of time (e.g., 2 minutes, or 32 bars of 4 counts each). Do not use music to coordinate the timing. After the solos are completed, perform them all together at the same time. Use chance drawing to decide where to place everyone in the performance space. Try waiting until the showing of this work to put it together for the first time. If the timing is not exactly coordinated, it is okay. Finally, try placing randomly selected music behind the choreography.

3. Create a dance using a solo, a duet, and a trio. Create each of these parts separately without thought to common intent. Try to coordinate timing. Perform all these dances together as one dance using chance to decide who starts where. Play around with the timing as well, and perhaps have them start in a random sequence so that the timing is not coordinated. Try random music selections.

   Note: For all of these movement studies, be ready to explain the structure and process you used in creating the choreography.

   REFLECTIVE QUESTIONS What moments in the choreography by chance worked particularly well for you? Why? • What moments did not work at all? Why? • As you listened to your peers discuss how they structured their choreography by chance, did some structures seem to work better than others? Why? • Is it okay to create a dance like this and produce it for a live, paying audience without making a decision about what works and what does not? Support your answer.

Assessment

Choreography by chance is the ultimate exercise in breaking the rules. For that reason, assessment is not possible. There is no goal to accomplish but simply a process to explore. There is an expectation that you will make new discoveries, but for that reason, reflection becomes the primary culminating activity for these movement studies, not class critique or a graded rubric.

You will certainly want to document your movement studies by recording them, and include with that documentation any reflection that took place. And finally, you must respond to the essential question.

Essential Question

Why would a choreographer decide to combine movement haphazardly by chance?

Drawing Conclusions

Critical Thinking Essay

Write an essay that answers the three essential questions in this chapter:

1. Why is it important to understand the effects of repeated material?

2. Why is it important to understand how to manipulate movement?

3. Why would a choreographer decide to combine movement haphazardly by chance?

An outline is provided to help you get started, although you may decide to write your essay in any order, as long as you include each part of the critical thinking model.

   I. Introduction: Summarize the tools used in this chapter to create movement and make a value judgment about their usefulness to you as a choreographer.

  II. Discussion

     A. Analysis: Describe your experience working with each of these tools.

     B. Reflection: Discuss some of the results you were able to achieve with these tools.

     C. Integration: Relate these results to previous experience.

 III. Conclusion: Evaluate these tools answering the three essential questions presented previously. Make sure you have supported your responses to these questions with your analysis, reflection, and integration.

Chapter 10

Solos,
Duets,
Trios, and
Groups

Initial Inquiries

What is easier: choreographing for 1 dancer or choreographing for 20? • Why is it that most solos are very short and group dances are usually much longer? • Why is it that choreography involving many dancers can be extremely powerful? • Why do duets keep us on the edge of our seats? • Why is it that trios often leave us with beautiful pictures in our minds? • What is it about changing the number of dancers we use in our choreography that changes the dynamics of our work?

Everything you have discovered up to this point will help you explore the possibilities that are inherent in working with various numbers of dancers. Whether you are working with only one dancer or with many dancers, the basic choreographic concepts remain the same. The possibility for relationships governs your use of these concepts. One dancer may relate to something imaginary from within or without, or to an environment, or to symbolic space. Two dancers may do all of these things and relate to each other. With three dancers the relationships increase. With each new dancer, more opportunities arise. In this chapter you will explore working with solos, duets, trios, and groups, discovering your strengths as a choreographer. Some choreographers love creating solos and are very good at it. Others are masters at manipulating large groups of dancers in intricate patterns. After your explorations, movement studies, assessments, and trials at breaking the rules, perhaps you will discover your mastery.

Essential Question

How do you make movement important enough to be worthy of a solo?

Warm-Up

1. Stand in the performance space with your eyes closed or with an internal focus. Release the knees and ankles, and relax all of your joints as much as possible. Begin to rock back and forth shifting your weight from one foot to the other and allow your body to be loose and free. Move all the joints in your body in order to loosen them. Loosen your shoulders, hips, spine, wrists, and fingers. Now begin to carve the space in the room around you. You may begin to travel around the room. Open your eyes, but maintain an internal focus. Try to find different ways to carve the space around you by focusing on different body parts. Change your level, your focus, your timing, and your energy. Use full-body movement, and then try a very small movement with only one body part. Try to find as much variation as possible in your movement. Take your time. Explore one way of moving fully and then find something contrasting to explore.

2. Make a still shape. Now explore ways to begin moving from that shape. Try bursting into sudden action from the stillness so that others do not see any anticipation of the movement while you are being still. Now explore beginning your movement very slowly—so slowly that the audience does not realize when the movement actually begins. This will take some time to perfect. Keep going back to your stillness and try to get even slower with your beginning. Finally, explore a more normal beginning, where there is some anticipation to let us know you are about to move before you actually begin moving, and do so at an average tempo.

   REFLECTIVE QUESTIONS   How do you make individual movements important? What qualities within a movement will draw an observer's attention? Why are some movements missed by an audience?

Improvisations

1. Improvise with two other dancers, creating movement phrases that focus on line and design. Do not use unison, but create lines and shapes that are available to you as you work together. Continue to explore the possibilities of creating line and shape with three dancers working together. Now the two other dancers step away to observe while you continue to move through the same movements you discovered while improvising with the other two dancers. You may do this three times, each taking turns dancing alone while the others watch. Remember to start together, focusing on design.

   REFLECTIVE QUESTIONS   What happens to the design of the work when two of the three dancers are removed? How is it possible to continue a focus on design with only one dancer?

2. Again, improvise with two other dancers, designing a few phrases that are based on action and reaction with the use of contrasting energies. You should react to movement created by others in the trio, and they should react to you. Again, perform the phrases together as a trio, and then remove two dancers to form three separate solos. Observe each other.

   REFLECTIVE QUESTIONS   What happens to the dynamics of the movement phrases when two of the three dancers are removed? How is it possible to create extremes in dynamics with only one dancer?

3. Introspective movement: Sit on the floor and develop an internal focus. Begin by focusing on your breathing and how your breathing changes the shape of your torso. Be aware of every subtle change that occurs in your body as you breathe. Now begin small movements with the fingers of your left hand. Focus on every change you make. Think about how the joints are moving, what new surfaces your fingers are touching, and what new space you are moving in. Do not allow any movement to occur without being fully aware of what is happening. What new shapes are you making and what kind of energy are you using? Add wrist movement to this. Maintain a high sense of focus on the part of your body that is moving, using either your eyes or your kinesthetic sense, or both. Continue to explore more movement this way. You should keep your movements small until you have mastered a complete sense of focus on what you are doing. You may try larger movements as this is mastered. Larger movements may elicit responses from you, almost as if you are surprised your body was capable of the movement. In this exercise, you should move as if you have never experienced movement in your body before and you are feeling everything for the first time. Do this in groups so that you have an opportunity to observe others in this improvisation.

   REFLECTIVE QUESTIONS   What are your observations about movement that is created by a performer this way? Where is the focus of the audience?

4. Using your knowledge of movement created by an outside force (review energy in chapter 3 and negative space in chapter 4), explore movement that is controlled by an imaginary source outside your body. Concentrate on making that source of movement visible to your audience. Explore ways the source may change in its energy, location, and frequency of influence on your movement. Make sure it is very clear to your audience exactly where the source is, how strong it is, what quality it has, and how fast it acts on you. Play around with this idea. Stay very focused. Do not allow any movement to occur that is not a reaction to this outside force.

   REFLECTIVE QUESTIONS   What are your observations about movement that is created by a performer this way? Where is the focus of the audience?

5. Decide on a narrative that may be performed through movement. Keep it simple. It may be a sequence of emotions that you have gone through recently. It may be actions that you took to accomplish a task. You might think about something happening in a book you are reading. Try to make sure the sequence of events lends itself to being expressed through movement. Now explore ways to express the narrative you have decided on by moving through the sequence you have selected. You may want to try focusing on different aspects of the narrative. First you might focus on the actions that took place and develop those actions into choreography. Then you might focus on the emotional sequence. You also might focus on outside observers' reactions to the narrative. Whatever you decide on, explore ways to get through the sequence with your movement. Try to make all your movements important and related to the events that occurred. Improvise as you think through the individual events to create your movement.

   REFLECTIVE QUESTIONS   What are your observations about movement that is created by a performer this way? What is necessary for creating interest in movement that is created this way?

6. Get with a partner. Each of you should think for a minute and decide on some movement that you are particularly good at that you like to show off. You might want to think of two or three things that you like to do and are comfortable doing. Now put these movements together with some transitions so that they feel like they all belong together. Show your tricks to your partner. Make suggestions to each other about how

to put these movements together. You may want to fix transitions or add a little more material between the flashy moments. Or you may want to change sequence. You will also want to help your partner fix anything that is keeping these flashy moments from looking really great. Find ways to help each other look wonderful.

REFLECTIVE QUESTIONS   What are your observations about movement that is created particularly for someone's strengths? What do you need to do to make these movements look interesting for an audience? • What transitions work, and which ones do not? • What do you need to think about when you sequence movement this way?

Discussion of Key Concept

Capturing the elusive solo is one of the most difficult things to accomplish as a choreographer. On the one hand, it is easy to think of movement for only one dancer because you may have less material to compose. However, it is much more difficult to provide variety of movement with only one dancer available to you. You will undoubtedly have noted from your improvisations that creating line and design with three dancers offers opportunities for three-dimensional design, whereas having only one dancer as your instrument is extremely limiting in the area of three-dimensional shape and design. There are no opportunities for complementary lines and negative space between bodies. You do not have the option of providing variation in level and stage space. It is also difficult to set up relationships and energy transfer without an actual person to develop a relationship with. So it is imperative to develop focus and intent in a solo.

A few ideas may help you to hold an audience's interest in a solo. You may use movement that is so unique, interesting, or noticeably tricky that it amazes the onlooker. You may create a strong internal or external focus that captures the attention of your audience. Or you may develop a particular reason for moving. This last idea usually requires some form of narrative—if not literal, then at least a sequence of change that captures the audience and leaves them wanting to know what will happen next. Whatever the method used, it is easy to fall into the trap of self-indulgence. What feels good to the dancer as a solo may not come across to an audience. So I recommend that if you are creating a solo for yourself, have someone observe it during various stages of the process to give you honest feedback so that you will know whether it is working.

Because you have less opportunity to emphasize line, design, pattern, energy, and intent, it will be important to exaggerate your use of these elements. If your solo is abstract, then your intent will have to be under the first category of developing interesting movement that amazes your audience. You may be aware that your body, or that of a dancer you are creating the solo for, has some unusual abilities that you would like to showcase. In classical ballet you might build an entire solo on turns for someone who is able to perform multiple turns easily. In her performance of *Grand Pas Classique*, Cynthia Gregory (1945-), principal dancer with American Ballet Theatre, was able to tease her audience with balances on pointe that seemed to last impossibly long. This always elicited a standing ovation. Danish choreographer Jiri Kylián (1947-) could create the most incredible movement pretzels through modern technique that always made audiences wonder, "How did he do that?" You would want to see it more and more to try to figure out how it is done. However, a masterful choreographer will use a movement like that only once to tease the audience and keep them guessing. And remember that an element of surprise will draw the focus of the audience.

Marius Petipa placed **tour de force**, or tricks, in the solos of his ballets to show off the ability of the dancers. The problem with this method, of course, is that if the dancer comes up short and is unable to perform the feat with ease and precision, it can be painful for the dancer and the audience alike. So the solo must fit the dancer. If you need to change the turns to the left instead of to the right, or remove a split leap and add a large pas de chat, remember that it is okay to do that. It is a solo, and the dancer does not have to coordinate with anyone else on the stage. If you watch carefully in a Petipa ballet, you can always tell if a soloist is a left or right turner, because the choreography will be changed to suit his or her strengths.

If your solo has narrative intent, then it will be important to ensure that every movement and every transition is based on that intent, and you will have to be careful that you do not create movement simply for the sake of movement. This is always true, of course, but even more so in a solo, because in a solo the entire focus is on one dancer and the audience does not have the opportunity to look around for a more interesting movement on the stage. A solo dancer must have incredible focus. There can never be a moment when the dancer drops out of the picture or loses concentration. Each time a soloist does this, the audience also loses concentration. This does not mean that the dancer may never make a mistake. The best dancers make lots of mistakes. But they never lose focus, and every mistake looks to the audience as if it was meant to be part of the choreography.

As a choreographer of a solo, you need to make sure that your dancer is comfortable enough with the movement to remain focused for the entire length of the solo. If there is a point in the solo that is not working, or if the soloist is unable to maintain focus throughout, it is time to rethink the choreography. It is possible to create a great solo for any dancer. But it is extremely important for the choreographer to get to know the dancer, to work with the dancer in a way that helps him or her to feel comfortable with the choreography, and to make sure the dancer understands every aspect of the solo in order to perform it. It is fine to be challenging with a solo as long as the dancer is capable of meeting the challenge.

So often choreographers create solos for themselves without thinking about the dancers who will eventually perform the solos. The choreographer becomes frustrated when the dancer does not perform the solo precisely the way it was intended to be. It may be that the choreographer has a compact body that is strong and moves quickly in short spurts with lots of energy, and the dancer in the solo may be long and lanky and move beautifully in slow adagio with extended lines but is very awkward trying to move quickly. So body type as well as training and talent may be limiting factors in a choreographic work. I encourage you as a choreographer to look for the strengths in the dancers who are working with you rather than to work only with what you might explore in your own body. You may discover that your dancer is capable of doing something you would never consider on your own, which will expand your movement choices. You may wish to set up some structured improvisations and watch your dancer move for a while before deciding what choreography you will ask the dancer to perform, particularly if you are considering a solo.

Movement Studies

1. Create a solo for yourself or for someone else that has a very strong internal focus, as was explored in improvisation 3. Make sure you or your soloist is aware of the importance of every movement, no matter how small. Pay particular attention to the importance of your beginning and your ending.

2. Create a solo for a dancer other than yourself. Design the solo to show off the specific abilities of the dancer you are working with. Make sure you do not lose the intent of the movement as you focus on the tricks to be performed. Also pay attention to the need for setting the flashy moments so that the audience is surprised when they occur.

3. Create a solo that focuses on a particular narrative, either literal or abstract. Your intent needs to develop in a sequence that the audience can follow.

Assessment

Use these assessment tools in evaluating your progress toward understanding how to create successful solos.

Class Critique

- Talk about your favorite parts in the solos. Try to reflect on why these moments are particularly strong. Make suggestions for places where you think a weak point might be improved.

- Teach the revision to the soloist and observe the change. Try a few alternatives until the group comes to a consensus on the best choices.

- Reflect on why some choices worked and others did not.

Rubric

Following is a sample rubric that you may use in evaluating the first movement study on solos. You may complete this for your peers and have them complete one for you. If you wish, you may change the criteria to be more in line with what you believe to be important content for this movement study.

Rubric for Solos

Criteria	Strong evidence (4 points)	Some evidence (3 points)	Little evidence (2 points)	No evidence (1 point)
Awareness of every movement				
Interesting solo material				
Strong beginning, middle, and end				
Total points: (maximum 12 points)				

Documentation

Record your work on video. Do not be tempted to move the camera to follow the dancer. You will want a record of the stage space used. Write an artist's statement to go along with your video. An **artist's statement** explains the intent of the work and the process used in creating it. Include comments from class critique and the rubric used in evaluating your work, and add these documents along with the video to your digital portfolio.

Drawing Conclusions

Breaking the Rules

Create a solo without a focus on making every movement interesting. Keep it extremely simple with little variation, focus, or dynamics. Also do not focus on any design elements.

REFLECTIVE QUESTIONS Is it possible to create a solo that works with simple movement that is not exceptional in any way? What is required in order to sustain the attention of an audience on a solo?

 ## Essential Question

Why is a kinesthetic sense important especially for partner work in duets?

Warm-Up

1. While lying on the floor with your eyes closed, focus on your breathing. Think about how your breathing causes the shape of your body to change. Focus on the relationship that your body has with the floor. How does that relationship change as you breathe? Which surfaces of your body are touching the floor? Do those surfaces change with your breathing? Begin to explore finding new surfaces of your body that might make contact with the floor. Take it slowly and gently, but continue to explore ways to find contact with the floor with all the surfaces of your body. Keep changing. Continue this exploration until you have explored all body surfaces and then come to a sitting position and rest until everyone has finished.

   REFLECTIVE QUESTION Why do you think this heightened awareness of your sense of touch will be important for partner work?

2. Still with your eyes closed, from a sitting position, explore ways to take yourself gradually into an off-balance position, catch yourself, and allow yourself to lower gently to the floor. Return to a sitting position and repeat this another way. Keep exploring different ways of taking yourself off balance and lowering to the floor, very slowly and gently. Add kneeling or other positions that begin at a middle level. Eventually explore changing from a high level to a low level, but never suddenly. You may need to open your eyes here, but maintain an internal focus. During your explorations, always find a moment of being off balance that is caught gently and then lowers gradually to the floor.

   REFLECTIVE QUESTION Why is it important for a dancer to be aware of balance and imbalance?

Improvisations

1. From a standing position, allow your feet to be a comfortable distance apart, relax your knees slightly, and feel as if your feet have roots that are holding you to the ground. Begin shifting your weight gently side to side between your feet. Feel your hip joints loosen as you shift your weight and allow your upper body to sway slightly with the weight shifts. Keeping this gentle rocking motion, allow yourself to actually slide one foot out and take a step away from your center of gravity, still with the knees released and the hips loose and the feet grounded. Explore ways of traveling like this, sliding the feet along the surface of the floor, swaying the hips, and gently releasing the knees and the upper body so that you remain grounded and in control after each weight shift. Now add your right arm to this exploration, navigating the space around you. Feel the flow of air around your arm. Change energies. Explore the space above and below, through, around, and behind you. As you travel through space, allow your arm to lead you to different places in the performance space and to different levels. Now change arms and lead with the left.

2. Stand with a partner. Your partner will be passive and you will be active. Hold your partner's hand and gently guide the hand in an exploration of the space with that arm the same way you explored the space on your own in the previous improvisation. Begin slowly and gently. Both of you must remember to keep your base of support grounded yet loose and flexible. Your partner should not be a dead weight. Your partner should allow

you to be the leader through an exploration of space but should not make any choices about where to move. Your partner needs to remain receptive to change. While you are the leader, focus on the needs of the other person. Make sure that you do things that are easy and comfortable at first. Be gentle but definite. You must communicate your choices through your contact with your partner, never by talking. Both you and your partner must focus on the communication that takes place through movement and touch. You are the leader and your partner is the follower, but both of you are responsible for making it work. As you get comfortable with the movement, you may add changes in tempo, energy, and space (traveling, changing levels, and so on). Change hands. After exploring fully with both hands, change roles by trading places with your partner, exploring the opposite relationship of leader and follower. You may wish to do this twice.

REFLECTIVE QUESTIONS   What are the challenges in working with a partner this way? What makes it work? What makes it difficult?

3. Try repeating the previous improvisation with the follower keeping the eyes closed. Start slowly. As leader, you must ensure that you are leading safely; as the follower you must pay more attention to your kinesthetic sense and react to the feel of the hand that is leading you. Remember that the leader must watch out for others in the room and for the boundaries in the room and pay attention to the space that your partner is using as well as the space you are using.

REFLECTIVE QUESTIONS   What new challenges did you experience with the eyes closed? What is required in order to make this work?

4. Listening with your kinesthetic sense: Stand back to back, with your full back in contact with your partner. Release your knees and feel your feet rooted to the ground. You will want to lean slightly back into your partner to get a full sense of what your partner is doing at all times. You will each be reading information through your back. With good contact between you, begin shifting your weight from one foot to the other. You will need to coordinate your movement in order to avoid losing contact with each other. The only communication you have available to you is the contact you have between you, so you must use your kinesthetic sense. Remain in contact at all times. No one is the leader. You must move together, and you must begin shifting your weight from one foot to the other to set up a slow, gentle rocking motion together. Once you have established this coordination, find ways to actually take steps together. This is much harder, but if you simply extend a shift of weight together, you may both take steps together. Steps side to side are easier than forward and back, but try them all. Take your time and "listen" with your back. If you lose contact with each other, simply stop and return to standing back to back and begin rocking again until you set up a connection between you.

REFLECTIVE QUESTIONS   What is meant by "listening with your back"? Why is this important? What kind of adjustments did you need to make in order for it to work?

5. After you are comfortable with the previous improvisation, you are ready for a little weight sharing. Again, stand back to back with your partner leaning slightly to gain full contact. Try bending your knees, sharing weight with your partner by leaning against your partner. Allow your feet to separate a little until you are each in a sitting position (sitting in the air, holding each other up by leaning against each other with your backs). Return to a standing position, but keep your rooted base with all your joints loose and flexible. Lean back a little on your partner while your partner bends forward slightly to take your weight. Then your partner gently lifts you back up by straightening up and leaning gently on you as you bend forward slightly to take your partner's weight. This

movement should be very subtle in the beginning, with very little weight exchange. The first few times you move back and forth this way, concentrate on the communication it takes to do it smoothly and with the weight being shared between you without ever losing contact with each other. The person leaning back should never lift himself up but should allow himself to be lifted back up by the partner. In the moment between, when no weight is shared, the backs must still remain in contact. Once you have mastered this with very small amounts of weight being shared, begin to take a little more risk and lean back farther on your partner each time you go back and forth, giving your partner more and more of your weight. If you are comfortable with this, you may progress as far as actually allowing your feet to leave the floor as you are supported on the back of your partner. If you get this far, you may wish to add support to each other by holding hands or supporting with other body parts to keep from rolling off the back of your partner. Remember to keep your knees bent, especially as you support your partner on your back. Also, keep your back rounded as you lean forward. (Arching your back while you are supporting someone may cause you to lose contact with your partner and does not provide the support you need for your own back.) After you have found the largest amount of weight sharing you feel comfortable with, gradually decrease the amount of weight you share until your back-and-forth movement comes to a stillness as you stand straight once again, back to back.

REFLECTIVE QUESTIONS   What is required in order to feel comfortable giving your partner control of your weight? How do you make sure you are comfortable taking the weight of your partner?

6. Stand facing your partner and hold both hands. Pull away from each other. Bend your knees and sit backward until you are balancing each other with an equal amount of weight sharing (if you let go of your hands you would both fall backward to the floor). Pull yourselves up and do this again. Try this while holding only one hand. Now, after pulling yourselves up, try leaning into each other in a way that allows both of you to depend on the other person to hold yourselves up. It should be some kind of position that you could not do on your own, where you are both leaning into each other and you are both supporting the other person to keep that person from falling. Continue to alternate between pulling away from each other and leaning into each other. Try to keep your transitions smooth with a focus on that transition point when you are responsible for your own weight; move toward giving up responsibility for your own weight while taking responsibility for the weight of your partner. Do not talk and plan. Simply pull away, pull each other up, and lean into each other. Grab a body part (it does not have to be hand to hand as you begin exploring) and pull away; pull each other up and lean in. You may stay simple, or if you are comfortable with simple and want to get more ambitious and daring, go ahead. Try different shapes, facing directions, levels, and body parts. Just be careful to take care of yourself and your partner. Never make a sudden move that cannot be understood and reacted to by your partner. Focus on each other and where your weight is at all times.

REFLECTIVE QUESTIONS   What new challenges did you have with this improvisation? What worked? What did not? How did you adjust to make things work?

7. Group and partner improvisation: Divide into two groups so that one may observe while the other dances. The active group spreads out in the performance space; find your own individual space that does not invade anyone else's space. Begin this improvisation as the first improvisation, finding a rooted base and swaying gently. Progress to finding ways to travel through the space and explore the space around you with your arms. While you are traveling through space, you may find an opportunity to come into contact with someone else in the performance space. If you mutually agree (don't talk; all communication must

occur through movement alone), you may take the hand of another person and begin to lead that person through the space by the arm. From here you may choose to return to individual movement, or you may progress to weight sharing back to back, or you may choose to pull away and lean in together. Once the group has begun moving, you may connect with any partner, and you may move in any way that has been explored through the previous improvisations, and you may break away and move on your own, or you may even find a concentrated stillness. As you work together, care for each other. If you are leading, take the responsibility of leading your partner in safety. If you are giving your weight to someone, do so gradually and gently so that the other person may react and support you. Always be ready to catch yourself if something does not work. At the end of the exploration, simply find a stillness. That stillness may be by yourself or with a partner in any of the weight-sharing positions you have been exploring (see figure 10.1).

REFLECTIVE QUESTIONS   How did you communicate with other dancers in this improvisation? • How did you know what you should do to react to others? • What was the overall effect of this improvisation? • How might you use the effect of this improvisation in your choreography? • Why do you think these skills that you have practiced today are important for partner work, even if you create a duet with no contact?

Discussion of Key Concept

Communication and trust are the most important skills to develop in any relationship; duets in choreography are no exception. For this reason, this exploration of partner work begins with **contact improvisation**, a technique that employs physical contact and shared responsibilities for movement choices. To be successful, this partner work must employ communication that takes place completely through movement. In order for any duet to be successful, there must be a connection between two dancers that transcends verbal language. That connection must be real, comfortable, and complete, whether it is in a classical pas de deux, a Fred Astaire and Ginger Rogers ballroom number, or a modern abstract duet. The connection between the dancers must exist whether or not there is an actual physical connection. By practicing concrete physical connections first, you will understand immediately what is meant by a connection with a

Figure 10.1   Weight sharing.

Figure 10.2 Connections between partners in dance transcend verbal language.

partner that transcends verbal language (see figure 10.2).

Contact improvisation began in the early 1970s. Its invention is credited to Steve Paxton (a gymnast-turned-dancer who was part of the Judson Church group of the postmodern dance movement). Contact improvisation broke the mold of partnering that was originally established in the romantic period of ballet and had not been significantly altered even with the early modern dancers, where men traditionally lifted women to show them off. Contact improvisation established a practice of men lifting men, women lifting women, and even women lifting men, which also paralleled the social and political climate of the time. Contact improvisation includes **lifts** and falls, supports, and **weight sharing**. Advanced explorations require strength, flexibility, and mats for safety. But more than anything else, the technique requires communication between dancers that is without boundaries and completely focused. Every decision and choice of movement must be made together. The practice of always taking care of yourself and taking care of your partner is essential in this work. Explorations must progress gradually, always working in the comfort zone of both dancers, and never going beyond what each is capable of doing safely. This requires you to know your own capabilities well, to communicate those abilities to your partner, and to focus on the capabilities of your partner as well. (If you are interested in learning more about contact improvisation, a good resource is *Contact Quarterly*, a biannual magazine. You can access information on this publication at www.contactquarterly.com/cq/contactq.html.)

There is no way to describe with words how to communicate with a partner in a way that will be successful for the performance. It is something beyond words, just as movement intent is beyond words. A partnership requires shared intent, or at least a knowledge of intent that is shared or not shared but coexists. Some partnerships are based on extremely elaborate and difficult technique. The technique must be mastered before the intent can be established and perfected. But without the intent, the performance will be less than optimal and possibly dangerous if difficult lifts and supports are involved.

As you work with lifts, supports, and shared weight in your choreography, work gradually, and always be aware of the comfort of your dancers. Dancers will want to be challenged, but they must not be frightened. The previous improvisations have guided you through very basic weight-sharing and support exercises (see figure 10.3). If you want to explore further, you should consider using mats in case anyone falls, and you may wish to employ the use of spotters if you are attempting lifts. Be aware of vulnerable areas in the body, in particular the lower back and the neck. The neck area should never carry additional weight, and the lower back must be supported by the abdominal muscles when supporting the weight of another dancer. Anyone with weak core muscles should not be asked to do difficult lifts until that area has been strengthened. Advanced work in contact improvisations does require good core muscle tone and strong balanced muscle groups throughout the body.

Movement Studies

1. Create a duet based only on the movements introduced in the improvisations in this exploration of contact improvisations. Begin by using improvisation to explore possibilities, but set the choreography so that it may be performed more than once. Pay attention to variation in your choreographic elements to create an interesting work. How will you begin? How will you end?

2. Using the same process, create a group work that includes many duets using the contact improvisation techniques covered in this exploration. Again, you may use improvisation to begin the process, but as the choreographer, you must make choices about what is working and what is not, where you need to add, and where you need to subtract. Pay attention to contrasting elements of movement. Be conscious of a good beginning, middle, and end.

Assessment

Use these assessment tools in evaluating your progress toward understanding how to establish communication and trust in duets using contact improvisation.

Figure 10.3 Weight sharing is accomplished when you become dependent on your partner for support.

Class Critique

- Identify your favorite moments in each of the works. Explain why they are successful.
- Notice moments that do not seem to be working; make suggestions to fix them.
- Describe the overall effect of the works.
- Evaluate the success of each duet (especially those within the group work) in establishing communication and trust. Which ones worked the best and why?

Rubric

Following is a sample rubric that you may use in evaluating either of the movement studies on establishing communication and trust in duets. You may complete this for your peers and have them complete one for you. If you wish, you may change the criteria to be more in line with what you believe to be important content for this movement study.

Rubric for Communication and Trust in Duets

Criteria	Strong evidence (4 points)	Some evidence (3 points)	Little evidence (2 points)	No evidence (1 point)
Clear communication and strong trust between partners				
Safe and successful weight-sharing technique				
Good movement contrast and intent				
Strong beginning, middle, and end				
Total points: (maximum 16 points)				

Documentation

Record your work on video. Keep the camera fixed in one spot that covers the entire performance space. Watch the video carefully and evaluate the work for communication and trust in the partner work. Take notes that indicate where it works the best and where it may need to be fixed; indicate why. Include a rubric with your work and comments as you add this to your portfolio.

Drawing Conclusions

Breaking the Rules

Create a duet that shows no communication or trust.

REFLECTIVE QUESTIONS Is a duet that has no communication or trust really a duet? Why would you create this kind of choreography for two dancers?

 Essential Question

How can the elements of energy, space, and time help to create a successful duet?

Warm-Up

1. Begin sitting while facing a partner. Focus on how your body feels at the moment. Are you stiff? Tired? Agitated? Lethargic? Performing for your partner, create a small movement that communicates your feeling. Your partner must answer your movement with another movement. Answer your partner again with another movement. Keep going back and forth this way, first one person moving and then the other. You begin with the way you are feeling but you may progress to anything you like. Gradually increase the size of your movements. Allow your dynamics to build. The only structure you must follow is that your answer must relate to the statement made by your partner. You decide how. You may be literal or abstract. You may stay in place or move around the performance space. Have fun. Play with it.

   REFLECTIVE QUESTIONS   How were you able to craft a response to your partner? What did you observe, and what kinds of decisions did you make for your responses?

2. Level chase: Begin by facing your partner, both standing. Create a shape in any level; your partner responds by creating a shape in a different level. Then you change to a shape at a different level from your partner. Keep going in this way, always creating a shape at a level that is different from the level of your partner. Focus on your transitions, creating intent. What is your reason for moving to the next shape? Begin with the intent of getting out of the level imposed by your partner, as in a game of tag. You may progress to any intent that feels logical to you and your partner.

   REFLECTIVE QUESTIONS   What intent, if any, materialized from this abstract idea? How did it feel kinesthetically?

Improvisations

1. Under and over: Improvise movement with your partner that is based on moving under and over each other. Find variations in time and energy, but keep your focus on movements and stillness that are under and over each other. Again, once you have established the abstract intent of moving into shapes that are under and over each other, allow the intent to progress to any logical reason for movement that materializes in the improvisation. Go with that intent and see where it takes you.

   REFLECTIVE QUESTIONS   What relationships between the two of you materialize as you work this way? How might you use this in the future?

2. Line and design: Improvise with a partner using a focus on line and design. You may use a mirror for this improvisation, and you may take time to brainstorm some interesting lines and shapes that you may make together. After you have created a shape or design that you really like, work on ways to transition in and out of the shape. Then move on to another. Keep going by adding more shapes that are focused on spatial design. Each time you create something new, go back to the beginning and work on transitions in and out of the shapes in sequence. Allow an intent to surface, and use it. If you like, show a few of these to others in your group and comment on them.

REFLECTIVE QUESTIONS When you work with a partner, what opportunities for variation in line and design are different from the opportunities you have when working with a solo or a larger group? What intent materialized, and why?

3. Work with a partner, but place yourself far away, across the performance space. Improvise movement that relates to each other. You may even relate by not relating (showing isolation). Remember that in order to show isolation, you must be isolated from something or someone. How does the audience know from whom you are isolated? Explore reasons for being apart. Also, continue to think about interesting line and design. Try a focus on energy. You may need to exaggerate to make this work.

REFLECTIVE QUESTIONS As a dancer, what were your challenges in creating relationships that are far removed spatially? • As an observer, what did you notice about these duets that were set far apart? • Which ones seemed like duets and which ones seemed like two solos? Why? How does distance affect the intent created in a partnership?

4. Action and reaction: Improvise with a partner using movement that causes your partner to react in some way. It may be as simple as a conversation, as in the first warm-up. Or you may use negative space and energy to simulate a battlelike dance. There are many other options. Explore.

REFLECTIVE QUESTIONS What relationships materialized between partners in this structure of action and reaction? How did energy play a part?

5. Create movement with a partner in unison. Try to follow each other exactly. Explore various stage placements with your unison movement, such as side by side, facing each other, far away, and very close.

REFLECTIVE QUESTIONS Why would you want two dancers to move exactly the same way at exactly the same time? When would this unison work be appropriate? When would it not?

6. Now try a **canon**. One person begins by moving for 4 counts. You repeat those 4 counts while your partner performs a new movement to 4 more counts. Continue this way, always having to learn the new movement while performing the previous movement. Keep a strong focus on your partner. This takes a great deal of concentration. Start simple so that it's easy for your partner. Progress to more complex movements. Change leaders.

REFLECTIVE QUESTIONS What intent is created with this kind of canon improvisation? What challenges occurred and how did you resolve them?

7. Dance with a partner in different meters. You dance in a meter of 4 while your partner dances in a meter of 7. You may want to have someone keep the pulse with a drum. Explore ways to relate to each other but hold true to your meter. If you get lost, stop and start again. You may wish to play with your rhythms once you get comfortable with the basic pulse and meter. Change meters, exploring relationships created by contrasting meters.

REFLECTIVE QUESTIONS How does the timing affect the relationship between two dancers? How is this different from the unison dancing in improvisation 5? Why might you use this in your choreography?

Discussion of Key Concept

What are some of the reasons that you might decide to create a duet? Perhaps you know two dancers who move beautifully together and seem to complement each other in performance. Perhaps you know two people who look a lot alike and you think that the visual effect created by those two dancers would be pleasing to the audience. You may have a story you want to tell about two characters. Or perhaps you simply have two friends who are willing to dance for you and you have been thrown into the structure of a duet without much thought to intent. Whatever the reason, you may use your knowledge of the elements of energy, space, and time to create the effect you are looking for.

A duet provides the opportunity to focus on a particular relationship. It is practically impossible to place two people on stage without the audience immediately drawing conclusions about a relationship between the two. Even if you pay no attention to a relationship between them as you choreograph your work, the audience will form their own ideas about the relationship between the two dancers. So you will have to decide whether you want this relationship to be determined by your audience or whether you want to manipulate the relationship yourself. Even when you decide to manipulate that relationship, however, each member of the audience will bring to it his or her own experience in the interpretation of that relationship. Try to leave yourself open to the idea that your interpretation may be quite different from that of the audience. The depth of feeling may remain intact, but how each person reads each character may be quite different. And even when the relationship you have selected is completely abstract, with an eye to the elements of movement rather than to narrative, the audience may create its own narrative. So strong is the need for human beings to create meaning from what they observe.

The opportunities for creating and manipulating narrative increase as you add dancers. Drama is based on conflict. So if you want to create a narrative drama, you will find it easier to create that conflict between two dancers than to create conflict in a solo. With a soloist the conflict must be either internal or external. An internal conflict would include a strong internal focus. External would have to include a strong focus from an imaginary source outside the dancer. With two dancers, you may play the conflict between the dancers as well. Conflict is most often obtained through a use of contrasting energies, but it may also be reinforced with shape, spacing, and timing. You undoubtedly noted from your improvisation in contrasting meters that timing may set up surprises that may be used effectively in narrative. In narrative it is important to explore what intent is desired and then review your notes about each dance element and how it communicates. Since you are communicating a relationship, you need to establish the correct relationship for your intent with all the elements of movement. You must not ignore the effect of one element while establishing another. The relationship should be clear and not confused by conflicting movement choices.

For an abstract intent, two dancers provide more opportunities for variations in line and design. If you think of a soloist as a point, two dancers create two points that allow the audience to draw lines between those points. So your design goes from one dimension to two. Of course each dancer may create three-dimensional design within the shape of his or her own body, but the overall effect from a distance may still be somewhat flat, even with two dancers, because two points connected create lines, not shapes. However, if you pay attention to stage space, placing dancers on the diagonal rather than side by side or in front and in back of each other, you may approach more three-dimensionality. A use of contrasting levels will also enhance this idea. This does not mean that you must always work toward three-dimensional design as you create. If you want a picture to be flat, it is easy to create that effect with two dancers. You may want to think of what a flat design suggests rather than a three-dimensional one. A flat design may indicate equality between the dancers. It can be balanced and comfortable, whereas three-dimensional design may enhance a feeling of energy and conflict.

One last thing you will need to consider as you create duets is gender (see figure 10.4 on page 216). If you place a man and a woman onstage, before you have them move at all, the audience will be thinking about some kind of intimate love or hate relationship. It is difficult to create movement for this heterosexual duet that does not enter an intimate realm, at least in the minds of your audience. So if you do not want to go there, it will be important to establish what you do want the audience to read from the relationship right away. And always be aware that without much thought on your part, it will end up as an intimate relationship.

Same-sex partnerships are more readily interpreted as platonic relationships, but if two men are caring for each other in your duet, most of your audience might read the couple as homosexual. Two women can perform intimate movement easily without giving the impression of a sexual relationship; it can be interpreted as a close friendship or a mother–daughter relationship. This is a reality in our culture, although these realities evolve. And these interpretations will change according to your audience. An experienced dance audience will not always read contact improvisation between two men as a homosexual relationship unless you add that in your intent, but a conservative, inexperienced audience probably will. It is important to know your audience because it will affect the interpretation of your work.

Figure 10.4 Male–female relationships may be created without romantic intent, but it is difficult.

Movement Studies

1. Create a duet using contrasting elements as your theme. You may want to select one or more elements to focus on, such as contrasting energy or level and shape. Be sure to craft your work with logical transitions and developed material. Do not think about narrative. After the work is presented, discuss how the audience reads the abstract work. Has it stayed abstract for them, or did the audience create meaning that was unintended in the creation?

2. Create a duet that depicts an emotional narrative. With a beginning, middle, and end, take your audience on a journey with these two people. Ask yourself these questions before you begin: "Who are these people? What is their relationship before the dance begins?" As you progress, decide how that relationship changes and why. Use the elements of movement to communicate these ideas: "What will be the deciding moments in the work that cause change in that relationship? What will that relationship be when the work is finished?"

Assessment

Use these assessment tools in evaluating your progress toward understanding how to use the elements of movement to establish relationships in duets.

Class Critique

- Identify the relationships you see in the work. Identify the elements of movement that were used to establish these relationships. Can you make any suggestions to clarify the relationships that seem to be intended?

- How did the choreographer create transitions that logically changed relationships?

- What was the difference between the abstract relationships and the narrative ones? Which seemed most effective? Why?

Rubric

Following is a sample rubric that you may use in evaluating either of the movement studies on using the elements of movement to establish relationships in duets. You may complete this rubric for your peers and have them complete one for you. If you wish, you may change the criteria to be more in line with what you believe to be important content for this movement study.

Rubric for Elements of Movement in Duets

Criteria	Strong evidence (4 points)	Some evidence (3 points)	Little evidence (2 points)	No evidence (1 point)
Use of elements to communicate ideas				
Clear established relationships				
Good movement contrast and intent				
Strong beginning, middle, and end				
Total points: (maximum 16 points)				

Documentation

Record your work on video. Explain some of the relationships you established in the work through still shots in a slide show. Discuss your successes and challenges. Create a list of next steps for yourself as you progress as a choreographer. Include all of these documents along with a rubric and your recorded work in your digital portfolio.

Drawing Conclusions

Breaking the Rules

Create a duet with no contrasting elements of movement. Find ways to create a relationship without this tool.

REFLECTIVE QUESTIONS   What kind of relationship is created without contrast? How might you use this in your work?

 Essential Question

How is a trio different from a duet, solo, or group work?

Warm-Up

1. Stand in groups of three. Space yourselves in the shape of a triangle with everyone facing the same direction. The person at the top, or front, of the triangle is the leader. As the front person, begin a warm-up exercise that everyone can follow. As you progress, turn to face a new direction. The person who becomes the front person then takes over as the leader. That person may want to continue the same movements or add on to what you were doing, or that person may change to something completely new. As the new leader changes facing direction, the lead will go to whoever is at the front of the triangle. Try to keep your movements simple enough to follow and keep your transitions from one leader to the next very smooth. The new leader must pick up immediately without pausing to plan.

2. Again in groups of three, one person in the group makes a statement with movement. The other two reply to the statement with a movement statement of their own. Then another person makes a statement that is followed by movement from the other two. Keep rotating the movement phrases. One person, then two. Next person, other two. Last person, then the other two. Notice the replies are created by a duet. The duets should try to work together in their reaction to the statements made.

REFLECTIVE QUESTIONS What are the challenges of connecting your intent with two other dancers as opposed to just one? What relationships begin to develop?

Improvisations

1. In groups of three, do an improvisation with a focus on contrasting levels. Make sure that at least one person is at a different level from the others at all times. You may all three be at different levels. Try movement that is close together and movement that is far apart.

REFLECTIVE QUESTIONS What opportunities in design are available in a dance with three that are not available in a duet? How does this affect your movement choices?

2. In groups of three, decide on a point in space and attach a symbolic meaning to it. (See chapter 4 for discussions on negative space.) It might be a strong hot light down stage left, or it could be an imaginary creature that moves menacingly through the space that all of you must react to. Find ways to work together to create intent that includes the symbolic space. You will have to discuss and create an idea together before you begin. Try showing these to each other to see if you have made your symbolic space clear.

REFLECTIVE QUESTIONS How does symbolic space help to create relationships between dancers? What relationships developed in your trio? How did they change as you worked?

3. Using the mirror, create many shapes with three dancers together that are interesting in design. Once you have selected a few shapes, find logical ways of transitioning from one shape to the next. Again, show your work and observe any intent that materializes out of the work. Comment on the relationships that happen with the dancers, paying particular attention to transitions and how they affect the relationships of the shapes.

REFLECTIVE QUESTIONS How is this improvisation different from the same improvisation done with only two dancers in the previous exploration?

4. In your group of three, explore duet versus solo. However, as you work, make sure all three dancers are related in some way, but two dancers are definitely working together while one works alone. It could be that two are working against one, or one is trying to stay away from the others. Then try changing roles. Explore transitions that move logically from duet to solo and back again.

   REFLECTIVE QUESTIONS What are the dynamics created in these relationships? How is it different from the dynamics of a duet?

5. Still in your group of three, space yourselves far apart, and explore three solos that belong together. Remain in your isolated spot, but find ways to make sense of these three solos being performed together. Remember to create interest with contrasting elements of movement.

   REFLECTIVE QUESTIONS What creates a duet, and what creates a solo? What is required, other than the obvious placement in stage space, for the audience to read solo or duet when all three dancers are in the performance space? • Is it possible to have the duet far apart while the soloist is close to one of the dancers in the duet? • Is it possible to create three solos when all three dancers are close together? How? What intent is created?

6. Explore opportunities for weight sharing between three dancers. Not all three have to be sharing weight at the same time, but it would be interesting to find moments when this is possible. Be careful not to plan. Try starting with all three dancers back to back. Slowly take turns giving each other your weight and receiving it. Remember that you may also hold a body part and pull away. Or you may lead each other through the space with your hands. Is it possible to do this with all three of you working together at the same time?

   REFLECTIVE QUESTIONS What were your challenges in working this way with three dancers? What adjustments did you have to make, and how was this different from working with only one other dancer? • What kind of intent is created by three dancers during weight-sharing movements?

Discussion of Key Concept

A trio may be three dancers working together, a solo and a duet, or three solos. Often this configuration will change in a choreographic work. But whatever the configuration, it is important to note that when three people are on stage together, they are part of a trio. Each person has some relationship to the other two. Even choreography for a trio that is created with no related material between dancers, just as in the duet, will read as if the dancers are related to each other. The audience will search for the relationships and create them on their own. As you create, you may wish to leave these relationships up to chance and allow your audience to conjecture. Or you may manipulate the relationships. Regardless, as the choreographer, you should be aware of all possibilities, stand back and observe your choreography after it is created, and see if the relationships are as you intended or if a relationship has materialized that you did not intend.

Three-dimensional design becomes automatic with three or more dancers, because the audience will create lines between the three points in the performance space. You no longer have to work hard to create depth, but if you do take notice of these increased opportunities, you may increase the quality of your work. Place your dancers out of line with each other in the performance space, use a few levels, be aware of line and shape, and you have a rich possibility of depth within the space you are creating (see figure 10.5 on page 220). On the other hand, if you want something to look flat, you have to work at it. Russian dancer Vaslav Nijinsky's (1890-1950) *L'Apres Midi d'un Faune*, choreographed in the early 20th century, is an exceptional example of movement for groups of dancers that gives the illusion of a flat painting. History

Figure 10.5 Trios allow for depth of design.

tells us the dancers had great difficulty accomplishing the task. The dancers were restricted to movement in one plane while performing in front of a two-dimensional painting by Bakst. The effect was to transport the audience into the painting itself. (Complete versions of *L'Apres Midi d'un Faune* are on YouTube.)

Any kind of weight sharing or partnering in a trio will create the eternal triangle. Even when the partnerships are rotated, or when all three are participating in a weight-sharing moment at the same time, there will almost always be one person with unequal status. There may be moments where all three share the weight equally, but even at these times, the one dancer in the middle may seem to be the support figure for the other two. There will always be the apex to the triangle. This can be used to great advantage. A figure who can take on two others gives the allusion of great strength. In the reverse, a weaker figure at the apex may allude to victimization by the other two. Whereas a duet may depict intimacy, a trio may easily depict confrontation. Of course, there are exceptions, and duets may be confrontational, but they do not have the opportunity for as much strength in that confrontation as a trio may have. Likewise, a trio may not be as intimate as a duet because there is never as much privacy afforded the dancers.

Movement Studies

1. Create a trio that depicts the eternal triangle (one against two). The relationships do not have to be love relationships, and they do not have to stay constant but may change throughout.
2. Create a trio based solely on line and design with contrasting elements of timing and energy to create interest.
3. Create a trio that is two-dimensional.
4. Create a trio where all three dancers are isolated from each other. Make sure the dancers belong in the same work and that you are not simply creating three solos.

Assessment

Use these assessment tools in evaluating your progress toward understanding how to create effective trios.

Class Critique

Identify the relationships that develop in each of the trios and reflect on the devices used to create these relationships. Ask yourself if the work needs to be a trio or if it would work just as well as a duet or solo. What makes it work as a trio?

Rubric

Following is a sample rubric that you may use in evaluating any of the movement studies on exploring trios. You may complete this rubric for your peers and have them complete one for you. If you wish, you may change the criteria to be more in line with what you believe to be important content for this movement study.

Rubric for Trios

Criteria	Strong evidence (4 points)	Some evidence (3 points)	Little evidence (2 points)	No evidence (1 point)
Clear relationships between all three dancers				
Works as a trio with all dancers necessary to the overall effect				
Strong beginning, middle, and end				
Total points: (maximum 12 points)				

Documentation

Record your trios on video. Include a narrative that explains your process. Describe any challenges you had in making these relationships important, especially for the trio built on three isolated characters. Identify the material you used to connect the dancers. Evaluate your success by commenting on class critique and rubric. Include the video, narration, description, and evaluation in your digital portfolio.

Drawing Conclusions

Breaking the Rules

Create a trio that is a dance for three people who are completely unrelated. Try some device that separates them, such as using different techniques for each, different styles of movement, or completely different intent.

REFLECTIVE QUESTIONS   Is it possible to have three people onstage at once and have them unrelated to each other? Does it work? Why or why not?

 *Essential Question*

How do large numbers of dancers work together to create a unified effect in choreography?

Warm-Up

1. Lie on the floor with your eyes closed. Focus on your breathing. Pay attention to the time you take to breathe in and how much time you take to exhale. Focus on the way your breathing changes the shape of your body. Begin to expand that shape by allowing your body to go with the flow of your breathing, creating new shapes. Grow into an expanded shape as you breathe in; release to a relaxed shape as you exhale. Begin to add levels to your exploration while opening your eyes but still using an internal focus. Continue to alternate between an expanded shape and a relaxed shape, paying attention to the rhythm of your breathing. Gradually begin to focus on others around you as you work. You may be in a position that is totally opposite from those around you. Or you may be quite similar in your rhythm pattern. At first simply take note of other rhythm patterns around you as you continue your own. Then, without stopping your exploration, begin to coordinate your rhythm with others around you. Do this gradually. All of you will need to adjust, but not all at once. Connect to the timing around you until the entire group is working together, not necessarily in movement but in the timing and rhythm of your movement. Once you feel the entire group is in sync, begin to slow down the rhythm gradually as a group until the entire group has come to a stillness together.

2. Everyone begin to walk around the room at your own pace. Do not follow anyone else. Find your own pathways through the space. Allow yourself to adopt a normal walking rhythm. Notice how the entire group has picked up the same rhythm and, even though you are not following each other in pathways, you are following each other in your rhythm. Now as a group gradually begin to speed up that rhythm. Do not allow any one person to lead, but each one of you should follow those around you. Increase your speed until you are walking very fast. Allow yourself to change to a gentle jogging motion and gradually to a run, trying to keep the same speed as everyone around you. Then gradually begin to slow down; make sure you all transition from the run to the walk at the same time. Slow down your walk until it is slower than a normal walking tempo; allow it to get very slow. Finally, everyone come to a stillness at the same time.

   REFLECTIVE QUESTIONS   How is it possible for a large group of dancers to work together without verbal communication? How does it feel when the group is working together well? What challenges limit the ability of groups of dancers to work together?

Improvisations

Subdivide your peers into two large groups. *Large* here is defined as about six or seven dancers, and more if possible. If the group of dancers working with you is small, use only one group, but have at least one person sit out to watch. Observing and directing will be important as you work on group explorations.

1. Pick a leader, and have the leader create an interesting but simple 8-count movement phrase that has variations in spatial elements, energy, and timing and travels through space somewhat. Everyone in the group then learns the phrase well enough to perform it without help from anyone else. Once everyone has learned the phrase, perform the phrase together starting from the same facing direction, close enough together that you look like you belong together. Keep repeating the phrase over and over. Once you get going, you may each make choices to face different directions. If someone near you

changes and you want to follow that person, go ahead. This may take you in different directions, so be careful to adjust your spacing so as not to run into anyone. Keep the choreography the same and stay together with the group in your timing. You may wish to use music or a drum or body sounds to keep together. Keep exploring different facing directions for a while, but eventually everyone return to face the same way (not necessarily the way you began). When everyone is back together again, come to the end of the phrase and create your ending.

REFLECTIVE QUESTIONS What is the overall effect created by unison movement with a large group? • What happens to that effect when facing directions and movement directions change but the unison movement is maintained?

2. Pick another leader. As the leader, you must choose an effort action and begin moving using that effort action. Everyone else in the group, as soon as they have recognized your effort action, joins you by creating their own movements using the same effort action. Work together as a group. Try to find a common intent. Once you have completed your intent, come to a conclusion and finish the exploration. Rotate leaders and change effort actions.

REFLECTIVE QUESTIONS What effect is created by a large group of dancers using a common element of movement, such as an effort action? How does this affect the relationships between the dancers in the group?

3. Design a wall. In a large group, focus on line and shape as you form a line that is horizontal across the performance space. Make an interesting design that is read as a unit. Place this wall upstage. You may want to face the mirror as you do this to help you see what the rest of the group is doing. Once you have established your wall, begin moving as a unit downstage. Make sure you hold on to the wall as a unit, but its line and shape may change as you move. Continue slowly until you reach the front and then find an ending. Repeat this in a vertical line traveling from stage left to stage right. Repeat it again in a mass moving from upstage right to downstage left. Continue to focus on line, shape, and design as you perform these improvisations.

REFLECTIVE QUESTIONS What effect is created by a large mass of dancers moving across the performance space together? How does this effect change depending on the shape of the group and the direction it is moving in?

4. Have a group of dancers create an environment for a single dancer to travel through. Place yourselves in the performance space in interesting groupings and shapes. Remember to use contrasting levels, and think about balance of the entire space as you do this. Pick positions that you can hold indefinitely. The single dancer is to move through the space, relating to the spaces and shapes that have been created. Try this once without having anyone in the group move or react. Try it again with the group reacting to the single dancer's encounters. However, make sure you hold on to the idea of the group being the environment and the single dancer as the active participant in the environment.

REFLECTIVE QUESTIONS What is necessary in order to establish a feeling of stability as an environment? What is necessary in order to establish dynamics as an active participant? How do these two responsibilities differ? When the environment is allowed to interact with the single dancer, how is it possible to maintain the feeling of the group as an environment?

5. Again in a group, you will create an improvisation based on a society. Choose a society that has distinct members and may be illustrated through movement. It might be a town with the bold leader, sad homeless man, two silly schoolgirls, a grumpy old man, and so

on. Each person selects a character to perform. Your society may be animals out in the wild. You might pick a lion pride or a herd of zebras or gazelles. But if you pick animals, make sure you have a good knowledge of the relationships of these animals. If anyone is unsure, go back to picking a group of people instead. You are undoubtedly more familiar with human behavior than animal behavior. Each person should have an idea of where they are coming from and what they plan to do. But as you begin moving, try to stay a little removed from the literal. In other words, if you are a sad homeless man, think about the shapes you might make and what kind of effort actions you might use rather than the literal actions you might engage in, such as pulling a blanket around you or digging through a trash can. Keep your movements in the realm of dance where you abstract the feelings of the characters and express those feelings through your movement. Allow your society to interact. Allow relationships to occur and intent to materialize. Allow the entire group to explore possibilities without one or two people making all the decisions.

REFLECTIVE QUESTIONS   What relationships occur in a group of diverse personalities? How is the entire group affected by relationships that materialize within a group?

6. Again, begin with a leader. The leader should choose to move in a way that illustrates personal style and personality. Move the way you like to move. Move in a way that seems most natural. One at a time, each member of the group should add to the movements of the leader. Keep the movements consistent with those of the leader, finding some way to relate your movements, but maintain your own style and personality. Everyone should look like they belong together even if the movements are not exactly the same, although you may follow exact movements if that is possible. The leader would have to establish repetitious movement in order for this to happen. Keep going until the entire group is moving, and then come to a conclusion as a group with everyone either coming to a stillness or exiting offstage.

   REFLECTIVE QUESTIONS   How is this improvisation different from the previous improvisation? How does this affect the intent of the group as a whole?

7. Pick a movement motif for your group to perform. Everyone perform the motif several times and then go on to explore different ways to develop the motif. While you are thinking of new developments, stop and go back to the original motif so that you never drop out of the improvisation, and repeat the motif once in a while. If you want to follow someone else's development, that is okay. You may also interact with others in the group, but every movement should be related to the initial motif.

   REFLECTIVE QUESTIONS   How does the use of a common motif affect the overall intent of the group? How might you use this in the future?

Discussion of Key Concept

Large groups of dancers create great power onstage. Even movement performed gently but together as a group has a powerful effect. Petipa, as he created the great classical ballets in the 19th century, knew the power of large groups and used them to perfection. Most of his work with groups was in unison, creating incredible visual effects that were both hypnotic and exhilarating to watch. In order for this to be effective, the selected dancers need to have similar build and be costumed alike so that each dancer is a mirror image of the others. These ballets are best performed by professional companies who preselect by body type and are willing to rehearse every subtle detail, from the shape of the wrist to the focus of the eye and the tilt of the head, so that every dancer is precisely alike in performance. People who try to imitate the structure of a Petipa classical ballet without these conditions fail to achieve the one effect that made these ballets so popular. So often, students of classical ballet who begin to choreograph imitate the formulas of the Petipa ballets without realizing the intent of the choreography and its requirements for success. While it is admirable to note and learn the structure of these classics, it is not advantageous to create an inferior copy. Today's choreographers do better to create their own style anew.

But today's choreographers do not have to shy away from unison dancing. Unison dancing in large groups can be very powerful. But it must be well rehearsed because one mistake will stick out. This is why the typical dance recital is so painful to watch. Every dancer's mistake is highlighted. You are asked to forgive the young dancers their indiscretions, because they are young students and don't know any better or do not yet have the strength and ability to hold that balance or shape that foot. But do we forgive the choreographer who fails to place these young dancers in situations that make them look their best? With all of the variations in elements of dance available to the choreographer, it is possible to make each dancer look successful in a performance, regardless of that dancer's training and background (see figure 10.6).

For those of you who are headed toward careers that require you to create dance recitals, my hope is that you will use what you learn in this text and not revert to old habits and traditional structures simply for the sake of tradition. In doing so, you will not only create dance recitals that are comfortable and actually enjoyable to watch, but you will also teach your audience to appreciate good choreography.

The alternative to unison dancing by large groups is powerful. Choreographers Jean George Noverre (1727-1810, whose 1803 book *Letters on Dancing and Ballets* became the first treatise for choreographers) and Michel Fokine (1880-1942, whose works *The Dying Swan*, *Le Spectre*

Figure 10.6 Combining dancers with varying levels of technique may be done effectively. The younger dancer on the floor is not yet strong enough to hold a correct arabesque line without the floor for support.

Figure 10.7 Groups without unison create a dynamic effect with common intent.

de la Rose, *Les Sylphides*, and *Petrouchka* are still part of the repertoires in ballet companies around the world) taught us the power of a mass of dancers, all with individual characters yet part of a common intent. They taught us that if we are attempting to depict real people on stage, then each person must be different because we are all unique individuals with separate personalities and different backgrounds. If you are creating a work about real people, you need to recognize the need for creating differences in your large groups. In this group, it is possible to go anywhere within the range of complete chaos, all the way to very similar movement that depicts an obvious common intent (see figure 10.7). Unison movement at the far end of this spectrum could depict a learned shared task, something such as hammering the spikes on a railroad, to show drudgery and lack of individual control. Yet even these tasks might vary in rhythm and strength depending on the individual. Unison movement often takes choreography into a realm of the **abstract**—without meaning. It transports the work into a focus on design or on supernatural and imaginary beings. A piece of choreography that is strong in its representation of humanistic qualities and narrative may lose its impact as soon as it enters into unison work. Unison can be restful, and it can make a statement about complete compliance among individuals, but it is important to use unison because of the statement it makes, not because of the ease it affords the dancers and choreographer in the setting of the work.

There is no doubt that in order for the audience to recognize a group as a group, there must be common elements that pull the group together. Just placing a large group of dancers on a stage does not automatically constitute a group of dancers. A common intent is the most obvious route to pulling a group together. But a more abstract method is to find an element of movement that is shared, or a formula that is used. Sometimes abstracting an intent will help to create variations in movement that you may not think of if you are considering only intent. For example, if you want a group to be menacing and angry, rather than trying to come up with movement that depicts these emotions, you might assign one or more effort actions to the emotions. In this case, you might select press (for menacing) and punch (for angry). As you create movement that stays within these effort actions, you may discover numerous movement choices that would not have been available to you while simply thinking of the emotional content. And the energy and effort created will be common elements that will hold your group together without trivializing the content of the work. You will be surprised at how easy this method is and how well it works for you.

Of course, any of the formulas you learned in chapter 10 will work to hold a group together, because they help you to create common material that holds the interest of the audience and allows the audience to relate diverse elements within your choreography.

A discussion of music, or sound, is appropriate here. If you have a large group of dancers, you have expanded your opportunities for music and sound choices. Before, with only a few dancers, you could not select very loud, full music or sound because it would compete with the visual effect you were able to create onstage. However, with large numbers of dancers, it is possible to compete with fully orchestrated works and loud electronically produced scores.

Finally, you should explore the use of large groups in combination with smaller groups or solos. A featured solo with a choral group as backdrop simulates the effect created by the Greek choruses of ancient times. The chorus may enhance the solo work, or it may react to the solo material or even foreshadow the solo material. The same may be employed as a backdrop for duets, trios, and even larger small groups (see figure 10.8). Or a large group may be used as a massive force that influences the soloist or small group in some way. Large groups are fun to use because they are incredibly powerful. But it takes a lot of time to create for and rehearse large groups. And many times you do not have the opportunity to work with large numbers of dancers. So when you do, take advantage of the opportunity and do not shy away from this work, because you will find it both captivating and rewarding as a choreographer.

What personal discoveries have you made concerning group work? How will you apply your discoveries to the group work you create in the future?

Figure 10.8 Groups working against each other using contrasting elements of energy and design.

Movement Studies

1. Create a work for a group of dancers (seven or more) where each dancer has a distinct personality but the group has a common intent.
2. Create a work for a group and a solo or a group and a duet. Decide on a relationship between the group and the featured dancers.
3. Create a work for a group that includes some unison work. Make sure the unison work is employed with intent. Your intent may be literal or abstract.
4. Pick a formula from chapter 9 to create a group work.

Assessment

Use these assessment tools in evaluating your progress toward understanding how to choreograph effectively for large groups.

Class Critique

- Identify moments when the entire group of dancers look unified in their intent and movement. Evaluate the process used in creating this unified effect. Identify moments where the unity of the group seems to deteriorate. Make suggestions to pull it back together.
- Discuss the effects created by different types of groups: those that work in unison and those that are unified by some other device such as common intent, common choreographic material, or related choreographic elements. How does each work, and when is it appropriate to use each?

Rubric

Following is a sample rubric that you may use in evaluating any of the movement studies on exploring groups. You may complete this rubric for your peers and have them complete one for you. If you wish, you may change the criteria to be more in line with what you believe to be important content for this movement study.

Rubric for Group Dynamic

Criteria	Strong evidence (4 points)	Some evidence (3 points)	Little evidence (2 points)	No evidence (1 point)
Group work effectively unified				
Movement appropriate for intent				
Variety of movement to hold interest				
Good beginning, middle, and end				

Total points: (maximum 16 points)

Documentation

Record your work on video. Place the camera far enough away so that you may get the entire group in the picture. You may need to place the camera on a diagonal if the studio you are working in is not deep enough to place the camera far away from the front of the performance space. If you do this, make sure you label the video so that it indicates where the camera is placed. Evaluate your work according to whether you were successful at creating an interesting unified effect with your group. Ask yourself whether this would work just as well as a trio or duet. Compare this work to your trios, duets, and solos. Place all these works together in your digital portfolio and include comments that draw conclusions about your work with different numbers of dancers.

Drawing Conclusions

Breaking the Rules

1. Create a work in unison that does not give the effect of a unified group.

2. Create a group dance that uses related material but does not create the effect of a unified group.

REFLECTIVE QUESTIONS   How is it possible to work with a large group onstage and still keep them all isolated? What devices are available to you to make this work?

Drawing Conclusions

Critical Thinking Essay

Write an essay that illustrates your preference as a choreographer for creating solos, duets, trios, or group work. You may decide on more than one as a preference or all, but you must support your opinion with explanations of your experience in working with each. An outline is provided to help you use the critical thinking model, but you may choose to organize your essay in any order you like.

I. Introduction: State your preference for working with solos, duets, trios, or groups.

II. Discussion
   A. Analysis: Describe your experience working with each of these numbers of dancers.
   B. Reflection: Discuss your challenges and how they were met. Discuss any difficulties that were unresolved. Also discuss successes that occurred especially as surprises.
   C. Integration: How did these experiences relate to your explorations of other key concepts?

III. Conclusion: Restate your preference with a summary of your experiences to support that preference.

Chapter **11**

Props

Initial Inquiries

What is a prop? • How is a prop used in theater? • How do dancers use props? • When does a costume become a prop? • What props work well for dance? Which ones do not? • What choreography have you seen that involved the use of props? • Are there any dance techniques that use props more than others? • Are particular types of props common for particular techniques? • Do props always add to a dance? • What is considered an effective use of a prop in dance?

Props can be a wonderful, or a disastrous, addition to any choreography. Before going any further, take some time to view dance that uses props. Some suggestions are the musical *Singin' in the Rain* with Gene Kelly and Debbie Reynolds (choreographed by Gene Kelly), many works by Alwin Nikolais and Bob Fosse, and Anna Sokolow's *Rooms* (1955), an examination of urban culture. The piece uses chairs as a symbol for small, confined spaces, and the work emphasizes isolation and fear.

This chapter has more improvisations than could possibly take place in one movement session.

Improvisations 1 to 5 include suggestions for a detailed exploration of a prop. It is recommended that you explore several props in this manner before progressing to the partner work and group work in improvisations 6 to 10. Improvisations 6 to 10 might also be repeated numerous times with various configurations of props. If you have an opportunity to explore many props that are the same, rather than different for a large group, this is also a choice you should explore. The warm-up offered here may be used each time you begin a new movement session. It allows you to begin to explore a particular prop before you start creating with it. All of these improvisations leave themselves open to adding more key concepts to the exploration, such as pathways, negative space, and rhythm. Use the table of contents in this text, or review table 9.1 on page 192 (Ways to Develop Movement or a Motif) if you would like to go further and want to remind yourself of all the key concepts available to you.

 *Essential Question*

Why does the inclusion of props in a dance both add to and limit opportunities for variation?

In preparation for this exploration, create a collection of props. Here are some suggestions:

- 3 yards (or meters) of medium-weight three-way stretch fabric
- 1 yard of soft silk or chiffon
- 2 yards of stretch fabric band (cut 2 yards of stretch fabric about 6 inches, or 15 cm, wide and stitch the ends together to create a giant rubber band)
- Plastic hula hoop
- 1 yard of plastic pipe
- Long lightweight fabric attached to the end of a stick
- Large umbrella
- Balls of various sizes, including exercise balls that will support the full weight of a dancer
- Cardboard boxes of various sizes, including large enough to climb inside
- Chair
- Stool
- Ladder
- Raincoat with hood

Warm-Up

1. Introduction: Choose a prop from the collection. Once you have chosen a prop, you should stay with it for the entire exploration. If you decide to change props, return to this warm-up first and repeat it with the new prop before moving on to more improvisations. You may repeat this entire exploration with any number of props and add your own ideas for improvisations to the list. You should do a thorough investigation with every prop before you decide to choreograph it into a dance.

   Place the prop on the floor to one side of you. You will do this warm-up without actually using the prop. Observe the prop in its current state. Analyze its shape. Is it a straight shape or a curved shape? Explore movement that reflects the lines in the shape you have observed. Create shapes of your own that complement the prop. Explore movement that creates lines in space reflective of the lines in the prop. Now analyze the prop again. Is it small or large? Add to your movement exploration by reflecting the size as well as the lines of the shape. Explore movement and stillness in self-space and general space. Return to your prop and look at it again. What is its texture? Is it hard? Smooth? Soft? Sleek? Rough? Explore movement that continues to reflect lines and shape and size, adding quality that reflects the texture of the prop. One more time, return to the prop. What kind of energy is suggested by your prop? Does it seem strong, or does it seem light? Would you think of it as bound? Or free? Add this energy to your exploration. Continue to explore movement that reflects every aspect of your prop. Find a logical ending to your exploration and hold a stillness until everyone in the group is still.

   REFLECTIVE QUESTIONS How did your choices for movement expand as you analyzed your prop? Why is it important for you to analyze your prop before creating movement with it?

Improvisations

1. Again, place your prop on the floor next to you. Starting from a standing position, review variations in size with full-body shapes. Make yourself as small as you possibly can, then as large as you possibly can. Continue going back and forth from small to large, changing levels and timing to create more interest. Continue to add elements in your exploration. While still using full-body shapes, change the effort you are using to go from small to large. Use a lot of energy. Use very little energy. Look for variations in curved and straight shapes and curved and straight pathways. Now begin to add your prop to your improvisation. Use the prop in some way to influence the size of your shape. Remember to think of your shape in relation to your prop. If you are in contact with the prop, such as holding it, the prop becomes part of your shape. If you are not in contact with it, think of creating shapes that relate to the prop and affect the feeling of size for your body shape. For instance, if you curl up underneath a ladder, you may seem smaller than you would if you were curled up on stage without the ladder. Play around with all the possibilities you can think of that influence an audience's perspective of size. Become as small as you can with your prop. Become as large as you can with the prop. Find a logical conclusion to your exploration and be still until everyone is finished.

   REFLECTIVE QUESTIONS How does using this prop affect the size of the shapes you create in your choreography? What are the extended opportunities? What are the limitations?

2. Begin this improvisation as before, dancing beside your prop. Once again, think of the lines and shape of your prop and begin exploring movement that reflects those lines in your body shape. Now add the prop to your exploration, using the lines in the shape of the prop to expand the overall effect of these lines. Explore shapes with the prop that emphasize these lines. Do the lines of your prop change as you begin to manipulate it? Find ways to keep them the same at first, then allow them to change and add to the design of your work with contrasting lines. Or add your own contrasting lines to the prop (see figure 11.1). Continue exploring the many possibilities available to you to enhance your own lines and that of the prop by working together. Think of the prop as you would another dancer, allowing it to have a life of its own.

   REFLECTIVE QUESTIONS How does using this prop affect the design of your choreography? What are the extended opportunities? What are the limitations?

3. Again, you will begin without your prop, focusing on its texture. What is the quality of the surface of the prop? Is there more than one surface with various textures? Explore movement on your own that reflects the textures of the prop by using movement qualities you think are similar to the texture. For example, something hard might be reflected as strong and sharp, especially if it has straight lines. Think about the lines, shape, size, and texture; begin using the prop to enhance these elements. You may use self-space or general space, but if you travel through the performance space, make

Figure 11.1 The straight lines of the legs contrast with the circular ball.

sure you are aware of others around you and move safely with your prop. After exploring ways in which the qualities of your prop may be enhanced with your movement, try contrasting your dance to that of the prop. Continue to use the prop by manipulating it; using it for support; finding ways to be inside, under, or through the prop; and even separating from it once in a while for effect but keeping a focus on the prop.

REFLECTIVE QUESTIONS   How does using this prop affect the quality of your choreography? What are the extended opportunities? What are the limitations?

4. This improvisation is the same as the previous improvisations, but the focus is on energy. What kind of energy does your prop suggest to you? Identify whether you think it is strong or light and if it is bound or free. Begin exploring movement on your own using the energy you selected, establishing it first with your movements alone. Then begin to use the prop in your work, first using the energy you started with and then contrasting that energy. Be careful once again as you use this energy with the prop. It is one thing to be strong in your own movements and accidentally run into someone else, but if you are swinging a hard prop with strong movement, you want to be sure that you have room to move freely in the space. You may wish to move into smaller groups to ensure safety.

REFLECTIVE QUESTIONS   How does using this prop affect the energy of your choreography? What are the extended opportunities? What are the limitations?

5. This time you will take a few minutes to look at your prop and think about something it might become rather than what it is. For example, a chair may become a tent. A balled-up piece of fabric could be a beehive. Choose anything at all. Nothing is too silly or common. Once you have decided on what it might be, create movement with it—or around it—that will establish some meaning for the prop. Try not to be literal with your movement. If it is a beehive, you need not let us know exactly what it is. But you might want us to understand how you feel about it and how you might treat it if you had to move it. Explore all the movement you can think of that works around this new object you have created. Once you have exhausted one idea, think of another and begin again. Do this several times until you think you have explored many ideas for this particular prop. Keep exploring ideas even after you think there is nothing else possible. People usually stop exploring props before they have exhausted all the possibilities.

REFLECTIVE QUESTIONS   How does changing the meaning of your prop affect your choreography? As you observe others, what seems to be effective? • How does the prop create opportunities for choreography? How does it create limitations? How do different props create different opportunities?

6. Select a partner and choose one prop to work with together. Again, begin by exploring possible designs, qualities, and energy. Progress to including explorations that create new meaning for your prop. See if you can do this without speaking to each other. When one person gets an idea, simply begin working with this idea. The other person will join you. Don't be afraid to join in before you understand everything about this new object. As you work with your partner, things will get clearer, or your partner may choose to change the idea to fit your movement. Once you have explored one idea this way, try another and keep going.

REFLECTIVE QUESTIONS   What additional possibilities arise when you add a dancer to an improvisation with a prop? What are the challenges? What are the rewards? • What were your observations as you watched others in this improvisation? How were the choreographic concepts you have been working with affected or used?

7. Again with your partner, each of you take a prop, but make sure you have chosen the same prop as your partner (e.g., both of you have a plastic pipe, or both of you have a stretch band). Work together to create interesting designs, qualities, and energy. Explore opportunities to work together and opportunities to work apart. Sometimes when you are working apart, your partner may get an idea of how to join you. Brainstorm together, without speaking, all the possibilities for working together and with your props. Have fun. Be playful. Enjoy!

   REFLECTIVE QUESTIONS   How does adding a prop change this improvisation? What do you think it would be like to have a large group using the same prop?

8. Repeat the previous improvisation using two different props, one for you and one for your partner. You do not have to keep the prop you start with. You may trade, put them together, or leave one alone for awhile (only remember that the prop is still there, so you must always have some intent that includes it). Work together to explore the opportunities these props bring to the improvisation. Again, play with it. Have fun.

   REFLECTIVE QUESTIONS   How does the added complexity of a different prop affect your improvisation? If you had a large group, would it work to have everyone with a different prop? What would be the challenges? What would you have to do to make that work?

9. As a group, set the performance space with a variety of props. Try to make their placement in the performance space interesting to look at. Think about size, shape, groupings, and balance of stage space. Also think about the pathways you are creating between the props. Find new opportunities for developing additional negative space. One at a time, begin to move through the performance space acknowledging the presence of the props without touching them or moving them in any way. By using the attributes of the prop to suggest movement, improvise as you did in the previous improvisations before you began working with the props. Think of ways to create a focus on the props. After each person has had a turn traveling through the space, discuss the importance of the props and how each dancer acknowledged that importance.

   REFLECTIVE QUESTIONS   What considerations were made by the group when placing the props in the performance space? How did your decisions affect the movement that was possible during the explorations? • What choices were made to acknowledge the props? Which choices were most effective, and why?

10. Leaving the props as they are placed from the previous exploration, have all the dancers sit around the performance space. Gradually dancers may enter the performance space as in the previous exploration, but this time you do not have to exit the space right away, and you may actually dance with one of the props. Use the previous improvisations as a guide to how you might use the prop you select. Before leaving the space, you must replace the prop in the space in an appropriate spot, not necessarily where it was before but certainly with the same consideration for balance of stage space and interesting visual effects. Picking up the prop and leaving it should be part of your dance. There may be more than one dancer in the space at a time. And you may actually explore more than one prop before leaving the performance space. As you are watching others dance, add to the movement when you think it needs something more. Leave the space if you believe the movement is getting too chaotic or unfocused. Try to create an interesting performance space together. Remember that variations in energy and timing will be as important as variations in space. Allow the uniqueness of the prop to enter into your movement choices.

Discussion of Key Concept

The use of props can be lots of fun and can open doors to innovative movement choices. Props provide an extension of body line and shape and add opportunities to enhance movement quality (see figure 11.2). A large flowing scarf expands the space of the dancer and creates a rippling effect when moved through space that cannot possibly be exhibited by the dancer alone. Visual effects when combined with lighting can be powerful. Loie Fuller explored these possibilities as early as the late 19th century with her "Fire Dance" that employed light projected through large silk scarves. Taking the time to discover all the nuances a prop has to offer will be rewarding, but it also takes patience and perseverance. Usually a few exciting ideas attract a choreographer to the prop, and these ideas become exhausted rather quickly. Movement choices may become predictable and repetitious. Sometimes the choices even become clichéd and trite. The challenge is to find new, unique, and surprising ways to employ the prop within the dance.

A prop has immediate limitations. Once you have established a relationship between dancer and prop, you can no longer think of the dancer alone; you must think of the dancer as related to the prop. Often the choreographer would like to give the dancer movements that are impossible because the dancer has to hold the prop. For example, in a simple soft-shoe (a relaxed, graceful dance done in soft-soled shoes and made popular in vaudeville), where both dancers use canes, if the choreographer wants the dancers to execute a lift, the man will need to find a way to put down his cane in order to free his hands for the lift. This has to be part of the choreography with a reason for letting go of the cane.

Once a prop is established to be a part of a work, it is difficult to let it go. If you place a prop in the performance space and leave it, the audience will keep an eye on the prop, holding an anticipation about what will happen to it next. Even if you take the prop offstage and

Figure 11.2 Scarves add shape to this performance.

return without it, the audience will worry about what happened to it and wonder about when it might return. If you decide to end your exploration of the prop at this point, your audience will be distracted from any new statements you try to make without the prop, because they will continually question where the prop is, why it is no longer with you, and when you will bring it back. So you will need to answer all these questions in your intent as you choreograph the release of a prop that you have established to be part of the work.

Too often choreographers begin with an idea of using a prop and work successfully for a while until the limitations of its use become burdensome. At that point the prop is discarded for no other reason than the choreographer seems to have exhausted all movement choices and needs to go on to something else. The use of props must follow the same rule that belongs to everything else in dance. There must be intent. The audience must see a reason for abandoning a prop in order for its abandonment not to become a distraction to the rest of the work. There must also be intent in the use of the prop to begin with (see figure 11.3). It is not enough to use a prop just because you want to play with it. The way you play with the prop must become essential to the dance. The dance must be married to the prop so that without the prop the dance would be impossible. The dancer must also be fully committed to and comfortable with the prop. If you are more focused on the success of a particular prop manipulation than you are on your own body shape and movement, the venture will be lost. So as you can see, adding a prop to choreography may create new opportunities for innovation, but it does not make it easier to create because it adds a complexity that must be treated carefully.

Movement Studies

1. Select a prop that will enhance a focus on shape and line. Create a movement study that will draw attention to the design you create. Select only one prop, but you may use as many of that one prop as you wish and as many dancers as you wish. Pay particular attention to intent during transitions.

2. Select a prop that will enhance your ability to focus on a movement quality (e.g., fabric band for elastic movement, soft scarves for floating movements, plastic pipe or sticks for sharp movement). Create a movement study that focuses on the movement quality inherent in the prop and that uses the prop to enhance the quality of your work.

Figure 11.3 This prop adds symbolism: a line connecting dancers through time.

Remember that contrast might also enhance a quality. Again, pay particular attention to intent during transitions.

3. Select a prop that has an obvious typical use, such as a hat or a chair. Explore ways to change the meaning of your prop. You may choose one new idea and stay with it, or allow the prop to change throughout the work. Make sure you have a good progression with logical transitions.

Assessment

Use these assessment tools in evaluating your progress toward understanding the use of props in choreography.

Class Critique

- Identify your favorite moments in the work. Analyze the techniques used in creating those moments. Reflect on why they worked especially well.

- Identify moments when you have a suggestion to make something more effective. Act on your suggestion by directing the dancers to make the changes you suggest, and view the work again. Have the entire group evaluate the changes and make new suggestions until there is a consensus from the group about what works best and why. Record the group comments and suggestions in your journal.

Rubric

Following is a sample rubric that you may use in evaluating the first movement study on props. You may complete this rubric for your peers and have them complete one for you. If you wish, you may change the criteria to be more in line with what you believe to be important content for this movement study.

Rubric for Exploring Props

Criteria	Strong evidence (4 points)	Some evidence (3 points)	Little evidence (2 points)	No evidence (1 point)
Good understanding of attributes of prop				
Design enhanced by prop				
Clear intent				
Strong transitions				
Beginning, middle, and end				
Total points: (maximum 20 points)				

Documentation

If you have an opportunity, record some of your improvisations as well as your movement studies on video. You may find that watching your explorations with a particular prop will help you select material for your movement studies. If you do not have time to do this, make sure you take time after your movement sessions to write notes about things that worked particularly well. The more information you collect about a particular prop, the more successful you will be at creating a work with it. As before, include a rubric, comments from class critique, and a written self-evaluation with a recording of your movement studies in your digital portfolio. Make sure you save your portfolio in multiple places. By this time, you should have a large collection of work, and you do not want to lose any of it.

Drawing Conclusions

Breaking the Rules

Select three or more props that have no relationship to each other; place them randomly in the performance space without thought to stage placement or balance of design. Perform a previous movement study (select any of the studies you have created that you can remember well) that was originally created without props, and perform it in the space with no acknowledgment of the props. This may mean that your dancers will actually run into or step on the props as they perform. If so, go with it, but make sure they do not hurt themselves or damage the props. Decide whether they need to acknowledge the prop at this point or whether they should continue to ignore the prop. Without planning any intent, allow the piece to find its own intent or relationship to the props. If it doesn't work, try again until it does.

REFLECTIVE QUESTIONS Why are props particularly interesting when used successfully in choreography? What creates success? What becomes problematic?

Drawing Conclusions

Critical Thinking Essay

Write an essay on the opportunities and challenges of working with props in a choreographic work. If possible, compare your experience with that of a well-known choreographer who uses props, such as Alwin Nikolais. An outline using the critical thinking model is provided to get you started.

I. Introduction: Make a statement about the use of props in dance that directs your reader to when they should be used and when they should not be used.

II. Discussion

    A. The challenges presented by the use of props.

        1. Describe (analyze) particular challenges.

        2. Reflect on why these challenges occur.

        3. Relate (integrate) these challenges to your experience and to that of a well-known choreographer.

    B. The opportunities available with use of props.

        1. Describe (analyze) particular opportunities.

        2. Reflect on why these opportunities occur.

        3. Relate (integrate) these opportunities to your experience and to that of a well-known choreographer.

III. Conclusion: Summarize and draw conclusions about your personal connection to the use of props in relation to a well-known choreographer.

Part IV

Exploring Ways to Refine and Form

The structure of chapters 12 and 13 is slightly different from the structure in the previous chapters of this text. Style and form are ways to look at the overall effect of a complete work. Creating these effects requires conscious thought and planning, rather than improvisation. These chapters provide you with definitions and discussions of particular styles and forms that you will look for as you view the works of others. Your exploration will begin by viewing complete works of well-known choreographers, identifying the styles and forms you see, and reflecting on the results. You will apply your discoveries of how complete works are refined and formed in movement studies that are assessed, and you will draw conclusions through exercises in rebellion and formal critical thinking essays.

Chapter 12

Dance Style

Initial Inquiries

What do we mean by "I like his style"?

Is it the clothes he wears? • Is it his mannerisms? • Is it the way he acts and reacts to others? • Perhaps it's the way he walks, or even talks. • Is it the way he gets the job done?

Depending on who it is, it's probably all of these things.

*S*tyle is a composite of all the distinct characteristics of a person. It's what makes each person unique. Style in dance is simply a way to categorize it, to describe it, and to label how it is distinct. Labeling a style of dance places boundaries on it. You may or may not decide that you want to begin labeling your work according to style. Eugene Loring's students used to ask, "What style of choreography are you going to do this year?" Of course they wanted to know if he was going to create a ballet or a modern dance or a jazz dance for the faculty concert. These are really **dance techniques** but are also definitely distinctive styles in their own right, because they originated from very specific cultures and for a specific purpose. Loring would respond to those students, "I tell you what. I will choreograph it, and you decide what style it is." He was not trying to teach his students to detect style on their own. He was making a statement. He did not want to be limited by the boundaries of style. He used whatever worked for the intent he had chosen for his work. He wanted to be eclectic, and he wanted to combine styles if necessary to create new work. That, of course, was a style in itself and was similar to others in the late 20th century.

The ability to define style can be important, regardless of the boundaries it sets up. For example, if you identify whether a work is supposed to be abstract, you will understand what to look for and what not to look for. As a young adult, I became very frustrated when I viewed a dance performance in which the work was completely abstract. *What's the point?* I thought. I have since learned to appreciate the beauty of abstract work and enjoy movement for its own sake, especially when it is well choreographed. Just as important is an understanding of a cultural dance form, if you are going to truly appreciate it for its style and beauty. Native American dance may seem simplistic and primitive—until you speak with a Native American about his dance and learn of the symbolism, ritual, and complexities of costuming that are all imperative to that cultural style.

In this chapter you will discover three ways to determine the style of a dance. The first defines style according to what you want to communicate anywhere on the continuum between abstract and expressive. The second defines style by the culture from which it stems and often includes formalized techniques, ritual, and social dance styles. And finally, you will discover what is meant by personal style, which is something every well-known choreographer has and something you will want to develop in your own work.

Again, because refining and forming your choreography into a complete work requires conscious thought and planning rather than improvisation, your discoveries for each of the three methods of determining style begin with a discussion to help you understand the definitions of style presented to you. After the discussion, you will be asked to explore and reflect outside the classroom by searching for examples of these styles and commenting on your discoveries. Finally, you will be given movement studies in order to apply your discoveries, which you will want to document and add to your portfolio as before, along with your evaluations and assessment. At the end of the chapter, in a critical thinking essay, you will summarize your thoughts on style as it applies to you and your work.

Essential Question

How does dance communicate?

Discussion of Key Concept

What do we mean by **abstract**? As a verb, this word means to remove something from the original while still maintaining some essence of the original. You abstract movement when you engage in the practice of motif and development. However, if we use the word *abstract* to describe or define a style of dance, we are referring to the movement as being removed from any meaning. So **abstract dance** refers to movement or dance that is created simply for the sake of the movement itself, without any intent to express emotion or narrative content. On the other side of the continuum is **expressive dance**, which communicates ideas, emotions, and narrative content (see figure 12.1). Dance exists on a continuum somewhere between abstract and expressive, often including both characteristics. For example, story ballets from the 19th century attempt to tell stories but focus on the beauty and virtuosity of the dancers and the movement itself. Although there is literal meaning and the dancers must act their parts, the story is more of an excuse to show off the dancers and to create beautiful kinetic visual images. You may think of these works as literal, but the majority of the choreography within them is abstract. Often Martha Graham used Greek tragedies as the basis of her work. She used them as a tool in focusing on the psyche of human experience. Yet, her technique was visually and kinetically breathtaking, certainly worthy of existing as movement for its own sake. So whether or not you can truly separate these styles remains to be discovered by you, but certainly it is possible to discover the intent of the choreographer and to place a piece of choreography somewhere on this continuum according to that intent.

Ever since dance became formalized in Western culture, there have been arguments about the best way to use dance to communicate. Should it be beautiful for the sake of the movement itself? Or should it have some depth of meaning? People seem to be passionate in their response to this question. They will usually lean very heavily toward one side of this continuum. The Paris Opera Ballet took advantage of this passion in creating rivalries between ballerinas to get people to come to the theater. Marie-Anne Cupis de Camargo (1710-1770) was famous for her ability to execute lovely entrechats ("The first to dance like a man," exclaimed Voltaire, which meant that she was the first to exhibit the strength and technical capabilities usually reserved for the male dancers of her time). She was considered a brilliant technician, admired for the abstract movement she was able to accomplish. Camargo's rival, Marie Sallé (1707-1756), was more interested in the dramatic approach and won people's hearts through her expressive dance. Fans were encouraged to come and cheer for their favorite ballerina. Similar rivalries existed in the Romantic era between Marie Taglioni (1804-1884) and Fanny Elssler (1810-1884). And even as late as the early 1900s, Ballets Russes dancers Anna Pavlova (1881-1931) and Tamara

Figure 12.1 These dancers use expressive style to project a playful spirit.

Karsavina (1885-1978) were pitted against each other as the technical dancer versus the expressive one. But no one would dare say Pavlova was without expression in her dancing.

In the 20th century, different camps of dancers emerged. Martha Graham spoke about dance as a "graph of the heart." George Balanchine and Merce Cunningham divorced movement completely from meaning and concentrated on movement alone. Antony Tudor, like Martha Graham, approached his contemporary ballets through a lens focused on the inner landscape of the psyche, allowing a modern style to enter his work. At that time, ballet dancers were not to be caught dead at a modern dance performance, and certainly modern dancers should never take a ballet class. The early 20th century saw the rise of a modern dance revolution filled with personalities that believed that dance should have something to say, and classical ballet did not include the vocabulary necessary to say it. But some modern dancers, tired of all the emoting and drama, returned in the 1950s and '60s to movement for the sake of movement, and untrained movement at that. Natural movement was considered beautiful in and of itself. From the 1970s our global awareness seems to have affected our dance in a way that has brought about more tolerance to new and mixed styles. Once again, being trained as a dancer is a good thing, but training in every style is almost a must. It is no longer enough to know only Graham technique or classical ballet technique from the 1900s. You must know how to be expressive and how to be abstract. Many choreographers employ both styles in their work. It seems, however, that no matter how eclectic a choreographer wants to be, there will always be a preference toward working with movement for its beauty and intricacies or toward movement for its ability to be expressive. You may already know which direction you are leaning as a choreographer.

Exploration

Search for video documentation of works by well-known choreographers. You need to watch only a three- to five-minute segment of each so that you will have time to see quite a few. Select a diverse group of choreographers from various time periods, techniques, and cultures. If it is readily available (try a search on the Internet), take a few notes on the biography of each choreographer you view. Watch each selection, recording in your journal the name of the choreographer, the name and date of the work, and a simple description of the intent of the work. Place this work somewhere on the continuum between abstract and expressive, and support this placement with the evidence you used to make this decision.

Bring your journal with you as you meet with the rest of your group, and conduct a session of reflection concerning the works that you found. Use the following reflective questions to guide your discussion. Record the reflections of your group in your journal.

> **REFLECTIVE QUESTIONS** What evidence did you use to help you decide if the work was abstract or expressive? • How do you know what to look for in a piece of choreography to help you determine the intent of the choreographer? • How important is it to know when a piece was choreographed and who the choreographer was in order to understand its intent? • Were any common works explored in your group that were placed in different spots on the continuum by each of you? Why do you think this happens, or why might it happen? • What were your favorite works, and why? • Ask yourself what kind of movie you enjoy most. Do you enjoy comedy and action films, or do you like drama, especially if there is a great deal of depth to the story, which leaves you questioning? What does this tell you about your preferences for dance styles? Is there a correlation?

Movement Studies

1. Create a movement study that is completely abstract with no focus on expressing an idea, emotion, or narrative content. The intent of your work must be focused on the elements of movement to create interesting kinetic and visual effects.

2. Create a movement study that focuses on expressive content; use an idea, emotion, or narrative content. Make sure that every movement in your work is focused on this intent. Be ready to defend your movement choices.

Assessment

Use these assessment tools in evaluating your progress toward understanding abstract and expressive style.

Class Critique

- Without being told by the choreographer, identify each work as abstract or expressive. Were your peers able to interpret the style you were working in? Why or why not?
- Identify the strengths of your peers. Do you think they are better at creating in an abstract way, or are they really good at creating expressive movement, or is anyone really good at doing both? What is the evidence you see to support your conclusions?

Rubric

Following is a sample rubric that you may use in evaluating both movement studies on abstract and expressive style. You may complete this rubric for your peers and have them complete one for you. If you wish, you may change the criteria to be more in line with what you believe to be important content for these movement studies.

Rubric for Abstract to Expressive

Criteria	Strong evidence (4 points)	Some evidence (3 points)	Little evidence (2 points)	No evidence (1 point)
Clear focus on either abstract dance or expressive dance				
Interesting movement vocabulary				
Facility of working in this style				
Strong transitions				
Beginning, middle, and end				
Total points: (maximum 20 points)				

Documentation

Record your work on video, adding it to your portfolio with a label of "Abstract" or "Expressive." Include copies of your journal entries, comments from class critique, and rubrics.

Drawing Conclusions

Breaking the Rules

Create a movement study that focuses equally on both abstract and expressive styles.

REFLECTIVE QUESTIONS Is it possible to place a work exactly in the middle of the continuum so that it leans neither to the abstract nor to the expressive side? If so, does it work? Why or why not?

 Essential Question

How is culture reflected in dance and choreography?

Discussion of Key Concept

When you hear the term *cultural dance*, you might immediately assume that we are talking about dance from *another* culture—something other than your own. But if the definition of cultural dance is dance that comes from a specific culture, then all dance may be labeled as a cultural dance, and North American and Western European cultural dances are no exception. Many cultural dance forms exist in these areas. So as we look for a style based on the culture of a dance, we simply have to look for its origins, or the origin of the specific movements within the dance. What culture did it come from?

What is your strongest technique? Is it ballet, or is it modern? Jazz or tap? These are all dance techniques that stemmed from a specific culture. Classical ballet was created out of a European royal society. Tap can be traced to its Irish roots. Modern dance was built on a fearful and angry societal culture from the late 1800s to early 1900s as a rebellion against tradition, both in Europe and the United States. Butoh stemmed from a Japanese postwar culture, with influences from American modern dance, but first and foremost as a reaction to the effects of the atom bomb. Jazz dance is the only exclusively American dance style derived from a mixture of African and American culture. There are many cultural dance styles, each distinct in its movement vocabulary. Flamenco, which stemmed from the Spanish gypsy culture, is popular in the bars in Spain. Bharatanatyam is another dance form that began in the royal courts, only this time in India. Capoeira began in Brazil as a way to practice martial arts as a defense mechanism against the ruling classes. These are all specialized techniques that take years to learn and perfect and that reflect a distinct culture through subtle and not-so-subtle movement distinctions. They are also styles that have been used extensively across cultures in the world of dance. They are familiar to those who watch them regularly within their cultures, and particularly to those trained to perform their intricacies. Using these techniques in your choreography and allowing them to be performed incorrectly may be offensive, particularly if you are not of the culture in which the style developed. Your dancers could be injured because they have not had numerous years to practice the technique safely and you will be recognized as unknowledgeable by those who know the technique well. Does this mean that only black dancers should perform and choreograph African jazz, and only Spanish dancers should perform and choreograph flamenco? Absolutely not! We live in a global society, where sharing culture has become the norm, and mixing cultures is commonplace everywhere from restaurants to street festivals and the theater. These techniques are taught in dance schools and dance camps everywhere.

So what are the rules for creating within a particular technique or cultural style? Or for mixing styles? Unfortunately, I have no precise rules for you to follow, only cautions for you to think about and observe as you find your own pathway in this complex world of multiculturalism. The best way to avoid offensive practice is to become educated in the style you wish to use. And the best way to use that style in your work is to know the intent of that use and to use it for that intent, not just because you think it would be interesting or fun. Becoming educated about a culture before using a dance style may be more important for some styles than for others. For example, the Native American culture contains elements to share and elements that are sacred and belong only to the people who are native born. It would be important to know which elements you might use respectfully and which elements should not be touched. Recently the powwows have brought to the forefront a competition style of Native American dance that tribes share with each other or with anyone who cares to attend and learn (see figure 12.2). However, some of the dances, even at the powwow, are sacred and should be performed only for a specific spiritual purpose by a Native American. If you were to use Native American dance to create a work, it would be important to know the culture and talk with someone who understands the significance of elements within the dance before you attempt to use any of the material in your work. Without this kind of background work, you run the risk of offending the Native American population. This may not be easy, because those who use dance as a spiritual connection may not be so willing to talk or share. If you have tried and failed, it is better to leave it alone than to use it with the excuse that no one told you not to use it. Once you have done the background work, then you must attempt to be authentic by respectfully taking time to learn the nuances of the technique. This does not mean you have to use the technique only in its basic form. But you should have a good understanding of the important elements of the technique so that you know what works for your intent. Trivializing a technique may be as offensive as using something that is sacred, because being trivial may be read either as disrespectful or satirical.

Is it okay to mix styles? Yes and no! So many works of art today are built as collages from many cultures. This is a reflection of the time in which we live. Dance should be no exception. If you are to reflect your current culture, then mixing styles may be inevitable. However, once again you must be educated in the styles you use, and you must use your styles according to your intent. Changing styles arbitrarily will jolt your audience and confuse them.

An often-used example that I consider a poor use of mixed styles is the haphazard placement of fouetté turns in every style of dance—be it jazz, tap, or musical theater. Imagine a flowing, emotionally expressive lyrical jazz routine interrupted by a series of 24 sharp, abstract fouetté turns for the sake of showing off the dancer. Because my training is classical ballet, and I know it well, it offends me to see fouetté turns used in this manner. These turns are part of a very structured formula that belongs in an imperial Russian style of ballet, and they do not translate well to other dance forms, even though they have been used repeatedly, particularly in dance competitions. Wherever they are placed, if not in their home of classical ballet, they break the intent of the work and transport you into a place that seems illogical. Also, they are often performed very badly by dancers who have not been instructed adequately in classical ballet. So not only do they not belong in choreography that is not in the classical style, but the inaccuracy of the performance for me is like listening to a screeching violin. For me, it isn't enough that a dancer manages to turn around 24 times without falling over. But the line of the leg must be in a precise à la seconde, the foot must be sharply pointed, the plié must be exquisitely executed and turned out, the head must snap, and the dancer must not travel all over the stage.

This might be a personal bias, but you must be aware that there will always be someone like me in your audience who knows the style you are stealing from and will expect you to treat it with reverence. So consider your intent. If you want to make a statement and those styles are important to you for your work, then use them well, and make sure you have a reason for employing that mix. And the reason should be more than just

Figure 12.2 Native American dance.
Photo courtesy of Aimée L. Schmidt.

showing off the dancer. It is always possible to show off your dancer within the cultural style of your choreography. If you do choose to change styles within your work, and you are clear about your intent, you will still need to be extremely focused on your use of transitions to help your audience through what might be a startling jolt from one style to the next.

Exploration

Search for examples of diverse cultural dance forms and techniques to view. Look for details within the techniques used in these dances, and describe them in your journal. Use some that you are familiar with and some that are new to you, but look for details in everything. You are trying to identify the distinctive elements within the movement in order to define the work as coming from a particular cultural style of technique.

For example, as you look at a jazz dance, you will notice an articulated torso, which does not exist in classical ballet. If you view Eastern dance, you will notice small, intricate movements of the hands, fingers, and eyes that do not exist in Western dance forms. Look for some works that have mixed styles as well. Describe the works in your journal, focusing on their distinctive elements. Record the origin or choreographer of each work, the time it was choreographed or performed, where it is from, and any other details you can find to help you understand the cultural significance of the work.

Bring your journal with you as you meet with the rest of your group. Conduct a session of reflection concerning the works that you found. Use the following reflective questions to guide your discussion. Record the reflections of your group in your journal.

> **REFLECTIVE QUESTIONS**   How were you able to discover distinctive elements in these technique or cultural styles? What were they and how did they compare with the discoveries made by others? • Are you able to add to your own list of distinctive elements after listening to things other people noticed in the works they explored? • Are there any commonalities that you discovered about particular styles that many of you viewed? If so, what are they? • Can you make any conjectures about some of these distinctive elements based on intent? For example, why do you think classical ballet uses turnout and a lifted, extroverted torso?

Movement Studies

1. Create a movement study in a formalized dance technique that stemmed from a specific culture. Make sure it is a technique that you know well and are familiar with. Remember to employ all the rules you have learned previously concerning the elements of dance. Just because you are using a particular technique does not mean that the elements of dance no longer apply. You will have to pay attention to the requirements of the technique, but you may find ways to bend the rules a little in order to create more interest in your work. Remember that you are not in a dance class. You are creating a unique work for the stage.

2. Select two or three cultural styles that you know well or that you have researched and practiced. Use all of those cultural styles in one movement study. Find ways to make them work together. Think about intent. You must create a reason for using all these styles in the same work. (Hint: Your reason does not have to be literal or expressive; it may be abstract.) Is it possible to play with similarities and differences within several techniques? Or take a particular quality from one technique and use it in another?

Assessment

Use these assessment tools in evaluating your progress toward understanding cultural styles and dance techniques.

Class Critique

Identify the cultural styles and dance techniques used in the work, including the distinctive elements that helped you decide how to define this style. Reflect on the intent of the work to determine if the style was appropriate for the intent. Do you think the style worked for the piece? Why or why not? Do you have any suggestions that would clarify the style or intent of the work? Are there any moments that you think are inappropriate for the established style of the work? Why? How could you fix it?

Rubric

Following is a sample rubric that you may use in evaluating the second movement study on cultural styles and dance techniques. You may complete this rubric for your peers and have them complete one for you. If you wish, you may change the criteria to be more in line with what you believe to be important content for these movement studies.

Rubric for Cultural Styles and Dance Techniques

Criteria	Strong evidence (4 points)	Some evidence (3 points)	Little evidence (2 points)	No evidence (1 point)
Clear use of multiple styles by including distinctive elements within each				
Appropriate use of style, making them work together				
Good transitions between styles				
Strong use of intent to mix styles				
Beginning, middle, and end				
Total points: (maximum 20 points)				

Documentation

Record your work on video, adding it to your portfolio with a label of styles and dance techniques used. Include copies of your journal entries, comments from class critique, and rubrics.

Drawing Conclusions

Breaking the Rules

Create a work that mixes cultural styles without thought to appropriateness or intent. Mix the elements of styles haphazardly, but consider the elements of dance to help you craft the work.

REFLECTIVE QUESTIONS What was the effect created by mixed styles that are haphazardly combined without thought to intent? • Did some movement studies work better than others? Why? What can you do to make this work? • Is this something you want to be able to do as a choreographer?

 Essential Question

What is personal style and how might it be developed?

Discussion of Key Concept

Every choreographer, whether just beginning or extremely experienced, has distinctive, recognizable elements of his or her work (see figure 12.3). The longer you choreograph and the more work you produce, the easier it will be to identify those marks that belong only to you. You may choose to create abstract and expressive dance, and you may choose to create using many diverse cultural styles, but within that work you will always exhibit something in your work that can be identified as your work and no one else's. This is not something to shy away from but to embrace.

As you develop your style and as you try to broaden the scope of your work, you will find many moments when you identify weaknesses in your work that you want to go beyond. So how do you know if some distinctive attribute about your work is a weakness that should be fixed or an element of style that should be embraced and enhanced? There is no right or wrong answer here. But the best way to discover your own style is to listen to others describe your work. And you should listen to all kinds of people. Listen to experienced choreographers and teachers. Listen to your peers who are exploring their own work alongside you. Listen to family and audience members. You will get various ideas and various opinions from each person you talk to, but if you listen to everything, you will eventually be able to piece together your own opinion of your work, with your own ideas of where your strengths lie and what weaknesses need to be strengthened.

But always ask yourself this question: "Is my weakness something that can be turned into a strength?" Weaknesses that repeat themselves in your work may be nagging elements of style trying to find their way into permanence. This is not an encouragement to be self-indulgent, because if you continue to work without intent and without movement development, then you are simply ignoring opportunities to develop as a choreographer. But if all of your work is comical, and you struggle with developing a serious piece, by all means continue to strive to create serious work. But also realize that comedy is your strength, and you should revel in that gift and explore more ways to move forward in that style.

One of my students, who is now choreographing in New York, has a very distinctive style that she exhibited from the first time she began choreographing in my classes. She has an incredible ability to take subtle gesture and make it the most important part of her work. This ability is her strength, but it is also a distinctive element of her personal style of movement. I have another student who revels in the ability to create interwoven shapes with her dancers. She explores shaping in front of the mirror and enjoys the discovery of new and sometimes amazing positions for her dancers. And she keeps the audience

Figure 12.3 Personal style is unique to the choreographer.

entranced with beautiful line and design. This is her strength and her distinctive signature. Of course there are many more elements to the personal styles of these two choreographers. Someone else might choose other elements to identify these two. But there is no question that they have developed a style that is recognized.

Personal style is what makes it possible to identify a choreographer's work without having seen a particular piece before and without having any program to identify the work. Once you are familiar with the work of a choreographer who has developed his or her style, it is usually not difficult to identify that work in a dance concert without the program notes. It is like listening to a composition by Tchaikovsky or Beethoven. Anyone familiar with these classical composers can identify their work as theirs, even if they do not know the actual composition. Likewise, you cannot mistake a Balanchine ballet; and if you do, it is because someone else is copying his style.

Exploration

Watch any master work on video. Describe the work and label any distinctive features in the work. Write those features down. Do this for several choreographers and diverse works. Try looking at more than one work from the same choreographer. Try to find repetitious elements for each that you might use to define a choreographer's style. Select choreographers from various time periods, cultures, and backgrounds. After you have watched a few excerpts from each choreographer, record in your journal what is distinctive about that choreographer. Look for any commonalities in the use of choreographic elements. How would you describe a certain choreographer's work in comparison to that of another choreographer? If you wish, you may also want to discuss other choreographers you are familiar with but unable to view at this time.

Bring your journal with you as you meet with the rest of your group and conduct a session of reflection concerning the works that you found. Use the following reflective questions to guide your discussion. Record the reflections of your group in your journal.

> **REFLECTIVE QUESTIONS** What are the distinctive elements you noticed about particular choreographers? • How do they choreograph? • Are their works abstract or expressive, or are they a mixture of both? • What dance technique do they use most? • Do they use formulas in their work, or does it seem to be without form? • How do they use energy and time and space? • How many dancers do they use in their works? • Do the choreographers dance in their own works? • Where do you think they find their movement? • What is their greatest strength? • Do you see any weaknesses in their work? • If you wanted to identify a work by a choreographer, what would you look for?

Movement Studies

Preparation: Begin by creating a short movement study for yourself. Pick any structure you like, but try to allow yourself the freedom to work with movement that is comfortable to you and that you enjoy doing. This is not a time to branch out. Keep to what you think is your natural way of moving. Perform your solo for your partner. After observing your solo a few times, your partner is to identify everything about your work that is distinctively *you*. You must do the same for your partner so that you both have an opportunity to observe and identify distinctive characteristics about your partner's choreography. I recommend you write down these distinctive characteristics.

1. Create a solo for your partner that focuses on the distinctive characteristics you identified in your partner's solo. Your work will be a caricature of your partner, meaning that you should exaggerate and enhance the characteristics you identified. Perform your solos for each other and discuss how they felt to perform and what you learned in the process about your own distinctive characteristics as a choreographer and dancer. End with each of you writing a glowing description of your partner's personal style as a choreographer. Emphasize what you perceive to be the unique and positive elements of your partner's work. Give this description to your partner to keep. This is something you may wish to continually refer to as you branch out in new directions. You may wish to remember to hold on to your strengths as you work toward being eclectic.

2. Now that you have a better understanding of your own style, create a short movement study on other dancers that focuses on your distinctive style. Allow yourself to take it further than you thought you could. Be ready to discuss the elements of style that are the focus of your work and how you attempted to enhance those elements.

Assessment

Use these assessment tools in evaluating your progress toward understanding personal style, especially as it relates to developing your own personal style.

Class Critique

- Identify the distinctive moments for you and your partner. Discuss the strengths in each of these distinctive movements and speculate how you might capitalize and develop those strengths. Discuss any observed weaknesses and reflect on how those weaknesses might be developed into strengths.
- Evaluate the work created for you by your partner. Did this work feel comfortable and natural to you? Why or why not?
- Did you find out anything that you did not know about yourself? Explain.
- What were the challenges of creating a piece on other dancers in your own identified style? What adjustments did you have to make, if any?

Rubric

Following is a sample rubric that you may use in evaluating the last movement study on personal style. You may complete this rubric for your peers and have them complete one for you. If you wish, you may change the criteria to be more in line with what you believe to be important content for these movement studies.

Rubric for Personal Style

Criteria	Strong evidence (4 points)	Some evidence (3 points)	Little evidence (2 points)	No evidence (1 point)
Style of movement study consistent with personal style as identified by peers				
Personal style enhanced by this movement study: goes further				
Focus on a few distinctive elements of personal style				
Beginning, middle, and end				

Total points: (maximum 16 points)

Documentation

Record your work on video. Include all three works that were created in your personal style—the first one you created for yourself, the one your partner created for you, and the one you created for a group. Label them so that it is clear which is which. Also include comments in your journal from class critique and your rubrics.

After completing this assignment, review all your work in your portfolio. Look for the distinctive elements that your peers identified, particularly those identified as strengths. Also notice any new distinctive elements that your peers might not have noticed. Write these down and preserve them in your portfolio. Recognizing your strengths, select the best works in your portfolio and copy them to a new folder. Make sure you keep copies of everything in your original portfolio in the correct order with your evaluation documents because this is your assessment portfolio. The best works you have just selected will be the beginning of your promotional portfolio. Share your choices with your peers and faculty. Get comments and advice from them on which to select to promote your work and which to leave for assessment only. But remember that the ultimate decision is yours, because you are the only one who knows your own unique intent as a choreographer and artist.

Drawing Conclusions

Breaking the Rules

1. Try to create a work that is in the style of someone else—either another student or a famous choreographer.

2. Try to create a work that has no style at all—nothing distinctive about it. It must be ordinary and common, something anyone might create.

REFLECTIVE QUESTIONS   What were your challenges in creating a work using someone else's style? • Is this something you might want to do with your work? • When might it be appropriate? When is it not? • How is it possible to create a work with no style at all? • Is this an appropriate way to work? Why or why not?

Drawing Conclusions

Critical Thinking Essay

Write an essay that describes your own personal style and how you have discovered it. You may want to use journal notes and work that you have developed throughout your progress rather than focus only on this particular study of style. Make sure you include a discussion of abstract dance, expressive dance, cultural style, and dance techniques as they relate to your personal style. Also discuss what your hopes are for developing your style in the future. An outline using the critical thinking model is provided to get you started, but you may use any organization for your essay, as long as you include all four parts of the model: analysis, reflection, integration, and evaluation.

I. Introduction: Brief description of identified personal style.

II. Discussion

    A. Analysis: Detailed description of specific elements of your personal style.

    B. Reflection: A discussion of your thoughts on why these elements exist in your work.

    C. Integration: A discussion of how your style has been developing in relation to your work and your peers and the work of well-known choreographers that you have viewed recently.

III. Conclusion: An evaluation of your personal style, identifying strengths and weaknesses with a plan for developing that style in the future.

Chapter 13

Overall Form

Initial Inquiries

What is form? • How is form different from formula? • Do we need form in order to acquire meaning? Or is meaning required in order to produce form? • Must all dance have form, or is it possible to create dance without form? • If form is the basis for all art, including dance, then when should we consider form as we create? • What comes first—the dance or the form? • Does form create itself, or does the artist create form?

Form is the contour or structure of something as distinguished from its substance. So far in this text, you have been exploring ways to create substance for your choreography. You have explored, discovered, practiced, and tested the elements of dance as the substance of your dance. Now you are ready to give it contour and structure in order to distinguish it as a work of art.

To recognize and understand the information we receive, our brains must categorize and then organize the information. This organization helps us to create meaning and to make sense of our surroundings. And if we can create meaning, then our memories may take hold. As artists and choreographers, we strive to offer our audiences something that will make an impact, something that will take hold in the memories of those who view our work. If we offer our audiences a structure for organizing the movement they see, then the chances of making a work to be remembered will be increased. Yet some people believe that it is not up to us to manipulate the thoughts of our audiences, but we should allow our audiences to create their own meaning from our work. After all, in real life there is no form, no map to guide us to create meaning. Or is there?

Whether or not you decide to create a structure for your audience to follow, your audience will attempt to create meaning by organizing your movement according to their own experience. They will attempt to create form, even when form does not exist. If they are successful and they are able to come to some understanding, you will be in luck. And regardless of whether they enjoyed your work, at least you will feel that you have been understood. If they cannot make sense of your work and leave confused and frustrated, then the chances of their returning to your performances have just decreased. The exception, of course, is those who love to be confused and frustrated. And there are indeed a few of those.

The crux of the matter is that none of us likes to be hit over the head with an idea or message. We are intrigued when we have to work at figuring things out. Road maps that tell you precisely how to get from A to B are very useful when you want to get somewhere, but specific directions on interpreting works of art are not very popular. Some freedom to explore the side roads and alleyways and even to take a different route to a new destination is what art is all about. So although you very rightfully may wish to help your audiences through your work with a form of your choosing, be careful to nurture that form as a natural contour of the work and coax it into place by the intent of the piece itself. Do not allow the form to become a map that controls the one and only way your audience will view your work.

I have mentioned often that a work must have a beginning, a middle, and an end. This is the very skeleton of form. It requires you to define the beginning, the middle, and the ending of your work so that the sequence becomes intentional. Formal or informal structures may be layered on this skeleton to support the intent of your work.

Form requires content that makes a statement, questions that statement, and resolves itself. Sometimes the resolution is a lack of resolution, but that lack of resolution is made evident so that the audience is left with a clear understanding that they have seen a complete work, even though it may leave us questioning. Statements may be expressive or abstract, but they must make sense. There are no rules for what makes sense in dance and what does not. This must be left to you as the choreographer. But you may consider some instances in your life to help you relate to the idea of statements. For example, choose any sentence from this text and read it out loud. Listen to the sound of the sentence and ask yourself to identify the beginning, the middle, and the end. Then ask yourself how it starts, what happens in the middle, and what happens in the end. And how do you know it is the end of the statement if you are listening to the words rather than reading them? Even if it is a question, it has an ending. Now ask yourself what the strongest part of the sentence is. What are the most important words? Which are the least important words? Would the sentence have made any sense without those words? How would the meaning change? A statement in movement is the same. It is made up of individual movements that make sense together. Some are stronger than others. Some are bigger than others. Some are less important. But without all of them, the statement cannot be made in exactly the same way. The organization of these movements makes a statement.

The rest of this chapter offers you methods of organizing your work into form through conscious thought and planning rather than improvisation. After you have read about these methods you will be asked to find examples of them in works from well-known choreographers. After reflecting on the techniques and effects these forms provide, you will be asked to plan movement studies that will be assessed as before with class critique, rubrics, and documentation. You will also be asked to draw conclusions by trying to break the rules of form and writing a critical thinking essay.

 Essential Question

How does the placement of a climax in your work affect its intent?

Discussion of Key Concept

Just as it is boring to listen to someone speak in a monotone voice, it is uninteresting to watch a dance that is formed without variation. You have learned a great deal about variation in the elements of movement in previous chapters. As you think about form, you must think of these variations in a larger picture, looking at changes in energy, space, and time in relation to your entire work. Graphing your work, similar to the process of graphing music as discussed in chapter 7 (Graphing a Sound Score), may help you see the form of your work. Consider graphing the energy of your work. The strongest energy in your work will usually be considered its climax, although it may not be the energy expended by the dancers. It may be a tension that you have built up in your audience. You might want to consider it as the impact you create. Most works include one point that is stronger than any other moment in the work. This moment is called the climax. In a story, this might be the moment of greatest conflict or the moment of resolution. Sometimes the climax is at the beginning. Sometimes it is at the end, and often it is somewhere in the middle. Some stories and choreographic works may have one very strong moment with a few moments that are not as strong. Others may have two or three equally strong moments. The peaks and valleys of each moment in your choreography become the contours of your form. Because we are natural storytellers, the placement of a climax is not an absolute must in your planning. When you focus on intent, this should happen to your work automatically. But if you find your work is lacking something and you are looking for solutions, you may wish to look for a climax to see if it exists and ask yourself whether you need to consider manipulating it.

Exploration

View a few complete pieces of choreography by well-known choreographers. Identify the moment in each piece that you consider to be the climax, the strongest moment of the work. If you do not see one moment, look for two or three. If there is no part of the piece that you determine to be stronger than the rest, then note that as well.

In your journal, describe these moments that you have identified in the choreography. What do you see in the work that leads you to believe that these are the strongest moments? What techniques has the choreographer used to draw your focus to these moments?

Now graph each of these works. Begin at the left side of your page and draw a line that indicates the energy or strength of impact of the work. Your line will be low on the page for very little energy or impact, and very high on the page for strong moments of impact. When you are finished with the graph, it should look like a mountain range with some peaks higher than others. The highest peak should coordinate with the climax of the work. Do this with at least three choreographic works.

Make sure you are viewing complete works. You may select short works. It is true that longer works may be combinations of many shorter pieces, each with its own form. However, the entire work with all of its parts will also have its own form. Make sure you identify each work in your journal by the name of the piece and the choreographer who created it. Bring your journal with you as you meet with the rest of your group and conduct a session of reflection concerning the works that you found. Use the following reflective questions to guide your discussion. Record the reflections of your group in your journal.

REFLECTIVE QUESTIONS   How were you able to identify the strongest moments in the works you viewed? • How did the choreographer craft these moments to create form? • Which forms seemed most effective to you, and why? • How did the choreographer use intent to create these strong moments? Or do you think that the form itself created the intent? • Were the moments of climax appropriate to the work? Why or why not? • What was your favorite work? Why? Did the form have anything to do with your preference?

Movement Study

On a sheet of paper, map out a form for a dance by graphing stronger and lighter moments of impact. Decide on when the strongest moment will occur, and place the highest peak at that moment. Now create a work that corresponds to your peaks and valleys created in your graph. You may decide on any intent, style, or technique to create your work. Even though you have created your graph for the form first, make sure the intent of the movement fits your graph. If you have to tweak it slightly as you are working, feel free to alter your graph. Pay attention to transitions to clarify changes in intent. The most important requirement for your work is to create an intent that fits your form. Bring your graph with you as you share your work in your group. Be ready to support your process.

Assessment

Use these assessment tools in evaluating your progress toward understanding form that is created by selecting a moment for your climax and mapping out the stronger and lighter moments of impact in your work.

Class Critique

* Before looking at the choreographer's graph, identify the stronger moments and lighter moments of impact in the work. Where is the strongest moment, or climax, in the work? How did the choreographer create these moments for you? Were they tied to the intent of the work? How do you know? Compare your observations with the choreographer's graph.

* Have the choreographer explain intent. Identify successes and make suggestions for change to strengthen the work.

Rubric

Following is a sample rubric that you may use in evaluating the movement study on form that is created by selecting a moment for your climax. You may complete this rubric for your peers and have them complete one for you. If you wish, you may change the criteria to be more in line with what you believe to be important content for these movement studies.

Rubric for Creating Form by Using Climax

Criteria	Strong evidence (4 points)	Some evidence (3 points)	Little evidence (2 points)	No evidence (1 point)
Strong obvious climax				
Intent tied to form				
Graph is good match to actual impact of movement				
Interesting movement choices				
Strong transitions				
Total points: (maximum 20 points)				

Documentation

Record your work on video, adding it to your portfolio. Label the work "Graphed Form With Climax." Include copies of your journal entries, comments from class critique, and rubrics.

Drawing Conclusions

Breaking the Rules

Create a movement study that is completely flat in its impact. If you create a graph of the work, your line would be completely flat. It might be at any level of impact—very light all the time, strong all the time, or in between all the time. You must create a work that has no change in the impact it makes with the audience.

REFLECTIVE QUESTIONS What happens to the overall effect of a work that has no particular climax but stays at the same level of impact throughout? • Is there ever a time you might want to use this in your choreography?

Essential Question

What is the overall effect created by organic form?

Discussion of Key Concept

Organic form is, as the term suggests, the most natural form and the least planned. It is a form that begins with a seed, or an idea, and develops without a particular plan about where it will end up. The seed is allowed to grow. You have already practiced developing movement organically in chapter 8 (improvisation 1). Organic form is simply an extension of movement development in that the entire work, however long it may be, uses the process of developing movement from the previous movement, without thought to where it will end up. Organic form must be created through improvisation, either by the choreographer or by the dancers, because it is based on the kinesthetic feel of the movement and where it needs to go next. It is possible to watch your dancers move and direct them the way you feel the movement will naturally go, but even that is a sort of improvisation—a directed improvisation. A choreographer may create the movement as he or she improvises, paying attention to detail and making sure that every movement and every transition is born from the previous idea. Once set, this choreography may be set on the dancers. However, if the choreographer experiments with setting this movement on the dancers in different ways, without thought to how all the dancers relate to the initial idea, the piece slips into another form, something more planned. If the choreographer sets the original idea or statement and asks the dancers to move from there in the most natural way possible, watching for awkward moments and asking them to try again, until the choreographer is happy with smooth and logical movement development, then the organic form will remain intact.

To create organic form, the dancers must take ownership of the movement, and they must feel completely natural in the movement choices (see figure 13.1). When I viewed the work of Sue Schroeder (founding artistic director of Several Dancers Core and Core Performance Company; www.severaldancerscore.org), I was amazed that the work looked crafted and organic at the same time. How could this be? To use craft is to plan. Crafting requires shaping and the use of formulas, which were distinctly evident, but at the same time the work looked so beautifully natural on the dancers that it seemed impossible that the movement had not been created

Figure 13.1 Organic form is created when each movement and shape grows out of the previous movement or shape.

organically. After employing Sue Schroeder to set a work on my dancers, I discovered the process that created this incredible juxtaposition. She allowed the dancers to create what was natural to them first, chose from those creations, and crafted the movement for them after they had created their own movement. So the dancers felt completely natural in their own movement, and Sue crafted the movement to offer form. So this was a mixture of organic and formulated work. In order for this to work, there must be an expert eye for transitions to ensure that the organic movement fits together in a natural way, even though it is planned.

Exploration

Search recorded dance works in the library and on the Internet. Look for choreography that you believe to have been created organically. Most organic work will have been created by contemporary choreographers, so you should search through recent works. You may find some if you use the word "organic" in your Internet search, but be careful, because not everything labeled organic is truly organic. In organic work, you will never have a transition that does not grow out of the movement previous. This does not mean that there can never be a sudden movement that surprises you. But it must look natural and it must come from an internal impetus.

After you have found a few pieces that you deem to be organic, make sure you indicate the sources for each work so that you may get to them again if you need to. Then describe the works in your journal, including the reason you believe the work was created organically. Then take a few movements from the choreography and try to duplicate them yourself. Find a few favorite movements, learn them well, and be ready to share them by performing them for your group.

Bring your journal with you as you meet with the rest of your group and conduct a session of reflection concerning the works that you found and the movement you share. Use the following reflective questions to guide your discussion. Record the reflections of your group in your journal.

> **REFLECTIVE QUESTIONS** How were you able to identify organic form? • What specific qualities did you notice about the work? • How did you rule out some of the work you found? • What is the quality of a work created and arranged by sequence and formulas rather than organically? • Are some techniques and styles more likely than others to be organic? Why or why not? • How did it feel to perform movement that you believed to be organic? • Were you able to re-create the feeling from the original? How were you able to do that? What did you have to think about to make it work? If you did not feel successful, what happened? • What suggestions do you have for others to help them create organically?

Movement Studies

1. Create a single and simple movement. Make it important. Study everything about it, how it feels, what energy and shape it has, where the tension exists, and where it is free. Begin your study with this simple movement. Then, using improvisation 1 in chapter 8 as a guide, create a complete dance where every part of the work has grown from the previous movement. Take your time and make sure every transition you create is based on what happened previously. Be ready to defend each transition you create, explaining how it grew from the previous movement.

2. Create a duet, a trio, or a group work. Think of a seed idea to begin. Your idea might be as simple as falling, or as literal as trudging through snow, or as complex as relationships between diverse personalities. Make sure your idea may be expressed easily through movement. Once you have settled on an idea you wish to use, ask your dancers to begin improvising movement that makes some kind of statement within or about your seed idea. Allow them to work alone or together. Watch the improvisations, looking for movement that you think might be a good beginning for your work. When you

see something, stop them immediately and ask them to repeat what you saw. You may have to help them through it, because they may not remember what they have done. So you must be a diligent observer and describe what you saw. If you lose something because it cannot be remembered, don't worry about it. Simply return to the improvisation and select something else. Have your dancers repeat this initial movement until it feels very comfortable and you are happy with your beginning. They do not all have to be doing the same movement. But if you select different movement for different dancers, make sure the movement works naturally together. You may make any changes to this movement as you observe, but your changes should work to make the movement more natural. You may see something that could grow out of the original idea that will enhance the natural feel to the movement. Then ask your dancers to do what they think would be most natural to do next. Take the movement in small pieces like this, refining it as you go until you have come to a point where you feel like a statement has been made and it is time to come to an ending. Or you may stop at a place that has come to an ending by itself. As you are working this way, it is all right to give directions to your dancers because you think the piece needs something that is not materializing from their improvisations. For example, you might say, "How would you move from there with lots of energy? Where would the energy come from? Use it and go." Or you might say, "I need you to separate from each other. Can you think of a reason to isolate yourself from everyone else? Once you've established that reason, do it." Be ready to say to your dancers, "No, that doesn't work. Let's do it again." Or "Let's try it another way." You may even suggest a point of impulse from which to originate a new movement. Your job as the choreographer is to watch everything to make sure that each new movement grows out of the previous movement. If there is ever a moment when you do not see a logical connection, you must go back and redo it. Do not progress ahead and think you will come back later, because this transition could change the entire piece. Also listen to your dancers. If they cannot understand the logic of going from one point to the next, then it is not organic for them, and you must work with it until it is. It can be a slow process, but you will find, once the work is finished, that it needs practically no rehearsal to get it ready for the stage because your dancers will feel the movement naturally. And you will have rehearsed it almost to perfection as you created the work.

Assessment

Use these assessment tools in evaluating your progress toward understanding organic form.

Class Critique

- Identify the moments in the choreography that look the most organic to you. Explain why you believe this to be true. Make conjectures about how these moments were created and discuss it with the choreographer to discover the process used. Make suggestions to fix moments in the choreography that do not look organic. Perhaps you need to fix a transition or help a dancer through a transition. Be ready to explain why these moments do not look organic.

- Which pieces look the most organic? Why? Evaluate the success of working organically, including the ability to make a work interesting this way. Think about what makes the organic process work.

Rubric

On page 266 is a sample rubric that you may use in evaluating the movement studies on organic form. You may complete this rubric for your peers and have them complete one for you. If you wish, you may change the criteria to be more in line with what you believe to be important content for these movement studies.

Rubric for Organic Form

Criteria	Strong evidence (4 points)	Some evidence (3 points)	Little evidence (2 points)	No evidence (1 point)
All movement related to previous movement				
Strong intent in individual movements				
Natural transitions				
Dancers comfortable and able to move naturally				
Movement allowed to come to a natural conclusion				
Total points: (maximum 20 points)				

Documentation

Record your work on video, adding it to your portfolio. Label the work "Organic Form." Include copies of your journal entries, comments from class critique, and rubrics.

Drawing Conclusions

Breaking the Rules

Create a movement study beginning the same way you did for the first movement study on organic form. But this time, after studying what would be a natural movement to follow your original movement, think of the most unnatural movement to follow and perform it that way. Keep doing this for each movement so that no movement naturally flows from the one before it.

REFLECTIVE QUESTIONS What is the overall effect of a work that is created with the intent of not being natural when moving from one movement to the next? Can you imagine a time when creating this way might be useful to you?

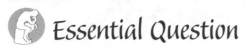 Essential Question

How does cyclic form affect the interpretation of a piece of choreography?

Discussion of Key Concept

You have already explored canons in movement as a formula, which are small cycles of movement that repeat over and over. Canons can give the effect of waves or anything in life that changes but continually returns to the beginning and starts again. Cyclic form is created when an entire piece returns to its beginning before it ends. Suppose you create a first section to your work and call it A. Then you go on to complete a second section quite different from the first. Call that section B. Then you go back to repeat your first section, A. Now you have created **cyclic form** (sometimes called rondo form). You might also do ABCBA or ABCDA. Anything that returns to the beginning creates a cyclic form.

There are some definite advantages to choosing this form. First, it is the easiest way to establish a beginning, a middle, and an end. There is no question about sequence. Everyone recognizes your first section when it is repeated and automatically knows you are coming to a close. The work is balanced and familiar. It may be quite pleasing to your audience, because it provides comfort and is easy to read. The audience does not have to work hard to figure out your conclusion. But what is the effect of this form on the intent of the overall work? What does a cycle mean?

There are many cycles: the cycle of life, the water cycle, cycles in history. If you want to reflect any of these ideas from life, then cyclic form can be effective. If you want to make a statement that no matter how hard you try, you never get anywhere and always return to your original state, a cyclic form will help you make that statement. When you use this form, you are communicating something that says, "This happens repeatedly and never changes." Or you might add some slight differences in the repeat of section A to show that there are some differences, but basically most things remain the same. Kurt Jooss used this form in *The Green Table*. He made the statement that for humanity, regardless of who we are or what side we are on, war will always return. The piece begins and ends with a group of masked politicians negotiating terms before the next round of war. During the work, the audience is shown many horrific scenes that would convince anyone of the need to dispense with the human practice of fighting each other for noble causes. But the work ends at the same table of negotiations and you know that the war will continue. There is no better ending for this work, even though it is predictable. It leaves the audience with an inevitable sense of despair. The statement is made that there is no escape from this human practice.

However, if you are intending to reflect a change that never returns to a preexisting condition, then you should not choose a cyclic form for your work. If you want to focus on how something starts small and grows to something new, then organic form will meet your needs in a way that cyclic form could not. If you want to show a sequence of events that take your dancers on a journey to a new destination physically or psychologically, then cyclic form will not work. For any statement you want to make, where the dancers are not the same in the end as in the beginning, it will be important not to choose to end your piece the way it begins, even if it helps your audience recognize an ending.

You may decide that you do not want to make a statement and that you want to create movement purely for its beauty. Cyclic form may be attractive to you for this purpose. But you must be careful. Whereas the form itself is pleasing in general and offers balance, it can also be predictable and tedious. Once you begin that section A again, the audience knows what to expect; if they are not interested in seeing it again, you could lose them. So, if you are going to repeat A in its entirety, you'd better make sure the movement is interesting enough or dynamic enough to bear that repetition (see figure 13.2 on page 268).

I have watched the works of many choreographers who have decided to use the idea of ending a piece the way it starts as a device to let the audience know it is the ending. Sometimes the transition to that ending is completely illogical, because the choreographer has simply run

Figure 13.2 Strong pictures may be used to start and end a dance, creating cyclic form.

out of ideas and decides to quit and returns to a starting pose to let the audience know that it is the end. Sometimes the transitions to the last pose are worked so that they take a great deal of time, but you know at the beginning of this manipulation that the same ending will be realized, and you get tired just waiting for something that you already know is going to happen. Neither of these effects is desirable, unless . . .

You can use this negative effect to your advantage if you want to set your audience up for a surprise ending. Suppose you begin this long and arduous task of returning to the beginning, and you set your audience up to believe they know what is going to happen, and then when you finally get to that last moment, when the audience is anticipating the final movement, you actually go somewhere quite different. This may be a technique for adding that surprise element to your work. Hopefully you will not have lost your audience before you get to the surprise. Timing is everything.

Many pieces of music are created this way, without reason for making any statement and simply organizing material in a pleasing way. Anything that returns to the beginning will indicate a cycle and infer to the audience that whatever has happened will happen again. In an abstract way, it may be a return to stasis. You are taken on a journey and are returned to where you began.

Exploration

Search for choreographic works that have similar beginnings and endings. You may need to fast-forward through several works first to find some with similarities. After you have found a few, go back and watch the works in their entirety. Notice the intent of each work and decide for yourself whether you believe the cyclic form is appropriate for the intent. In your journal, describe the beginning and ending of each work and explain why it seems to work or not, according to your opinion.

Bring your journal with you as you meet with the rest of your group and conduct a session of reflection concerning the works that you found. Use the following reflective questions to guide your discussion. Record the reflections of your group in your journal.

REFLECTIVE QUESTIONS   What is the intent of the work you viewed? Is it meant to be abstract or expressive? • If it is expressive, is the cyclic form appropriate for the intent of the piece? What message or statement is being made? • If the work is abstract, does the movement lend itself well to being repeated at the end? • Why do you think the choreographer chose to end the piece this way? • What is the overall effect?

Movement Studies

1. Create an abstract work in cyclic form. Make sure the movement is interesting enough to bear repetition. Find ways to keep the movement from being too predictable. Make sure your transitions into the ending are logical. Use the form to create a pleasing effect.

2. Create an expressive work in cyclic form. Use the form to make a statement about something important. Make sure your idea is clear enough for your audience to understand your intent. Although it will not be necessary for the audience to understand literal content, the return to the beginning will need to make sense. Help your audience by making your transitions clear as you develop your statement.

Assessment

Use these assessment tools in evaluating your progress toward understanding cyclic form.

Class Critique

- Did you find the cyclic form appropriate for the intent of the choreography? Is the cyclic form the best choice of form for the intent of the work? Why or why not?

- Discuss the strengths of the work as it relates to the use of cyclic form. If you think it would strengthen the work, make suggestions to create more surprises and less predictability.

- For the expressive work, discuss why the cyclic form is appropriate for this particular message. Would it work with any other ending? Why or why not?

- Is the movement at the beginning and the end of the work strong enough to be repeated? Why or why not?

Rubric

Following is a sample rubric that you may use in evaluating the expressive movement study on cyclic form. You may complete this rubric for your peers and have them complete one for you. If you wish, you may change the criteria to be more in line with what you believe to be important content for these movement studies.

Rubric for Cyclic Form

Criteria	Strong evidence (4 points)	Some evidence (3 points)	Little evidence (2 points)	No evidence (1 point)
Beginning and ending are the same				
Movement is strong enough to bear repetition				
Cyclic form is appropriate for intent of the work				
Intent is clear				
Transitions are logical				
Total points: (maximum 20 points)				

Documentation

Record your work on video, adding it to your portfolio. Label the work "Cyclic Form Abstract" or "Cyclic Form Expressive." Include copies of your journal entries, comments from class critique, and rubrics.

Drawing Conclusions

Breaking the Rules

1. Create an abstract work in cyclic form without worrying about interesting movement choices or transitions. Try to make the work predictable so that the audience knows what will happen next.

2. Create an expressive work using an intent that has nothing to do with a cycle or stasis. Make sure the work is about something that is dynamic and changing. Then force the work into a cyclic form to see if you can make it work. Good luck.

REFLECTIVE QUESTIONS   What is the overall effect of a piece of choreography that is predictable? • Is there ever a time when you think you would be able to use this in your choreography? • What happens to an expressive work that is trying to communicate change and ends up being forced back into the beginning state? • What is the overall effect? • Why would you use it? Or would you?

Essential Question

Why does linear form challenge us as choreographers?

Discussion of Key Concept

Linear form, like organic form, starts with a beginning and never returns to that beginning. However, linear form is not necessarily organic. It is a sequence that follows from one section to the next, or one idea to the next, but that sequence does not necessarily have to be a logical sequence built on what happened before. It is possible to put sections together that are completely unrelated in a sequence, leaving the relationships between sections for the audience to figure out. If letters are used to denote sections, linear form is represented in this way: ABCDEF. . . . This is a story, or narrative, format as well (see figure 13.3). In a story you have a beginning, a sequence of events, and an ending. Examples of stories often used in dance are *Romeo and Juliet*, *Sleeping Beauty*, *Cinderella*, and *Firebird*. They all use narrative, or linear, form to tell their stories. The trick to using linear form is finding a way to hold the work together. In a story, the plot holds the work together. In an expressive work, the threads of related emotion take a logical sequence. In an abstract work, you must find other ways to create material that holds the work together.

One way to connect sections that are sequenced arbitrarily is to use similar material in each but develop them in different ways in each section. That way, the original material holds the work together and the development provides the variation in each section. This is a type of theme and variations, which is discussed next, but it may not be structured as formally as the typical theme and variations. For example, you might have a first section built completely on canons. The second section might take the original material and develop it as you would in motif and development. The next section might be an adagio with the same material you used as allegro in the first movement. Each section might be a choice of how to play with the original material.

Figure 13.3 Narrative form is used to tell the story of *Cinderella*.

You may use a progression to hold the work together. A simple example of a progression is building the number of your dancers. Begin with a solo and progress to a duet, then a trio, then four dancers, five dancers, and finally a large group. This kind of progression helps you build momentum to the end of your piece. You might also progress from a simple movement to very complex movements. Or you might start from a simple idea and allow it to become very complex.

However you decide to create related material, you need to know that creating material that seems to go together is considered a must in choreography. If you do not follow this rule, you might be criticized. Allowing your movements to stack up one after another with no thought to how they fit together logically or how they carry your intent is a typical error made by many choreographers. Yet, choreographers have used unrelated material intentionally and have been well accepted—mostly because when they decided to do it, it was a revolutionary thing to do. It is no longer revolutionary. In the history of the development of dance, choreographers have already rebelled against form. Creating without form is now accepted *if* it works for the intent of the piece. So that must become your rule. If it works, then you may rebel; if it doesn't, then you may want to think about returning to tradition. Only you can decide what is best for you as an artist.

Exploration

Search for some examples of choreography created in linear form. Try to find some stories, some abstract work, and some expressive work. As you review these works, look for connecting material that seems to hold the works together. Notice how the choreographer crafts the sequence to create interest and dynamics, and record this information in your journal. Pay attention to the transitions and evaluate the work, deciding whether the sequencing is appropriate and effective for the intent of the piece.

Bring your journal with you as you meet with the rest of your group and conduct a session of reflection concerning the works that you found. Use the following reflective questions to guide your discussion. Record the reflections of your group in your journal.

> **REFLECTIVE QUESTIONS** How does the linear form support the intent of the work? • What are some techniques used by the choreographer to hold the sequence of movement together? • How is related material used, and is it effective without becoming too predictable? • What key choreographic concepts are used to create interest in the sequence? • Do you think that linear form was the best choice for this particular work, or do you think another form would have worked as well or better? Why?

Movement Studies

1. Create an abstract work in linear form. Find a way to create your sequences so that they belong together and would not work in any other order. Pay particular attention to transitions.

2. Decide on a dramatic narrative that occurs in sequence like a story. Make sure the narrative lends itself to movement. Create your dance using the narrative structure. Do not try to be literal. Allow the inner drama to surface. Pick something that is supported well by linear form.

Assessment

Use these assessment tools in evaluating your progress toward understanding linear form.

Class Critique

- Identify the methods used in creating a sequence that fits together logically and works for the intent of the choreography. Evaluate those methods for success by identifying particularly strong moments. Describe those moments and explain why you see them as successful. Make any suggestions for choreography that you think might benefit from change. Try the changes and see if they work.

- Were you able to follow the plot in the expressive dance? Why or why not? If there were times when you were confused about the progression of the plot, ask the choreographer to explain the intent and then make suggestions that might clarify the sequence.

Rubric

Following is a sample rubric that you may use in evaluating the movement studies on linear form. You may complete this rubric for your peers and have them complete one for you. If you wish, you may change the criteria to be more in line with what you believe to be important content for these movement studies.

Rubric for Linear or Narrative Form

Criteria	Strong evidence (4 points)	Some evidence (3 points)	Little evidence (2 points)	No evidence (1 point)
Continuous sequence without any repeated sections				
Sequence belongs together and needs to be in the order presented				
Linear form is appropriate for intent of the work				
Intent is clear				
Transitions are logical				
Total points: (maximum 20 points)				

Documentation

Record your work on video, adding it to your portfolio. Label the work "Abstract Linear Form" or "Expressive Linear Form." Include copies of your journal entries, comments from class critique, and rubrics.

Drawing Conclusions

Breaking the Rules

Create a dance in linear form that presents a sequence of movement without related material or any plot or thread to hold it together. Try to find ways that would actually keep it from looking as if it belongs in the sequence you present. You might want to start at the end of a narrative and work backward, or place it completely out of order. You might want to try mixing styles and techniques without thought to logical transitions. Try to do a bad job of linear form and notice the overall effect you have created.

REFLECTIVE QUESTIONS What is the overall effect of a work created this way? • What happens when you break the rule of using related material to hold a work together? • When, if ever, might you want to use this effect?

 **Essential Question**

What is the overall effect created by thematic form?

Discussion of Key Concept

Thematic form occurs when there is one idea, or theme, that is used in developing the entire work. You might argue that this should always be the case in any choreographic work, and you would be right. There should always be an underlying idea or theme that holds a work together. But when the focus is on one particular idea and the rest of the work is built around that idea, then the form is thematic. For this form, sequence may not be dictated. It need not be organic or cyclic or linear. Sections may be placed in any order depending on the whim of the choreographer because the theme exists in each section unifying the work. A Broadway show such as *Cats* has an automatic theme for a choreographer to follow. All the movement must be created to look like cats. However, not every Broadway show will require thematic form. *The King and I* will require a Western polka, a Siamese march, and the story of *Uncle Tom's Cabin*, each employing separate forms for their intent.

An expressive example of thematic form might be a choreographic work based on grief. The theme is grief, and the work might explore the many stages of grief. If you choose to use this theme, you might research the stages of grief (i.e., shock, denial, anger, and so on) and present those stages in a sequence. Or you might relate grief to a life experience and sequence your work in a narrative that tells the story of a particular experience. Or you might decide to put the sections together arbitrarily, and the piece would still work, because the general theme would hold it together.

An abstract example of thematic form is to take an abstract idea, such as movement in 3/4 time against movement in 4/4 time. Each section might be a different tempo, or a different number of dancers, or a different amount of energy. But keeping the theme of playing 3/4 movement against 4/4 movement might hold the work together. You might choose any number of themes to hold an abstract work together: movement that falls and recovers, movement that intertwines, movement that focuses on a symbolic space, movement that is stiff and sharp.

Another way to work with thematic material involves the formal theme and variations, taken from the musical form of the same name. This is an abstract form based completely on formulas; the material is altered during repetition. It involves a main theme, which is made up of movement phrases that work together to make a complete statement. In music, the theme may be a sequence of notes and musical phrases that fit together as a whole. The theme has its own form, such as ABA form or organic form. It can be anywhere from one to five minutes long. It is a work that can stand by itself without its variations. It has a beginning, a middle, an end, a climax, and interesting but simple contrasting elements of time, space, and energy.

This theme is the original material of the work and is usually performed first in sequence. The rest of the work is a sequence of variations on the original theme. As you create the first variation, you decide on a means for manipuating the theme. Perhaps you decide to change the tempo. Your original theme may have been adagio; then the first variation would be the same material performed allegro. Your allegro variation maintains the same sequence and form that was established in the theme. For the next variation, choose some other method to manipulate the entire theme. You should be able to label each variation according to the method you use to manipulate it. For example, you might label your first three variations as "Variation I—Tempo," "Variation II—Dynamics," and "Variation III—Embellishment."

Theme and variations is similar to the formula called motif and development in that you are taking material and developing it from its original source. However, motif and development is a tool used to develop a single movement, whereas theme and variations is a form used to create a complete dance work. A variation is much longer than a developed motif because it involves manipulating the combination of movement phrases that were established in the original theme. It is a very structured and confining way to construct a dance. Of course, there is nothing that says you must adhere strictly to this structure. You may wish to use this idea only at the beginning of your work or place variations throughout, interrupted by different material entirely. The wonderful thing about choreography is that you get to choose what to do and you really do not have to follow any rules. You may borrow any tools and forms as long as they work for your intent.

One of the challenges of working with theme and variations in dance is that you might have difficulty finding music that will complement the formality of your structure. You may be able to use some background music or sound score that will allow the movement variations without competing with them. Or you may find a piece of music that is in the form of theme and variations and construct your dance to fit the music form. The problem with that is that you probably do not want to mirror the music exactly; yet if you go against it, you might be committing a musical sin. Some music forms such a theme and variations and fugue scream to be acknowledged. You might consider working with a composer, but again you have the reverse challenge. How does your composer compete against the formal structure of your theme and variations without committing the same sin against your work? You may think it is probably not worth the challenge to even try this form; yet when you realize how much fun it is to play with the movement in creating your variations, you won't want to forgo it altogether. My recommendation is to use either music or sound that does not compete at all, or find subtle ways to enhance the mirroring of the music so your movement is not an exact duplicate but does not go against it, so the structure is recognized and respected.

Exploration

This exploration is a little different. This time, search for one or more pieces of recorded music that has the words "theme and variation" in the title. You will find a few listed in the Music Resources of this text. Sit quietly and listen to the music, analyzing it for its structure. Identify the original theme and look at the label to see if each variation has a name. As you listen to the variations, listen for the manipulations in the music. Imagine how you might translate those manipulations to movement. Take notes about the things you notice, relating the music to what you know about the elements of movement. For example, if you notice that the melody in the music has been turned upside down, with the high pitches becoming low pitches, ask yourself how you might manipulate movement in the same way. Would you change the level of the movement? Or might you change the dynamics or weight of the movement? Keep listening until you have many ideas recorded in your journal of how you might manipulate a theme of movement in order to create a variation.

Bring your journal with you as you meet with the rest of your group and conduct a session of reflection concerning the music that you studied. Use the following reflective questions to guide your discussion. Record the reflections of your group in your journal.

> **REFLECTIVE QUESTIONS**   During the theme, what did you notice about the structure of the music you listened to? • How was the melody created? • Which instruments were used? • What quality was created? • What parts were more important than others? • What details can you hear? • How might you use all this as ideas for creating your own theme? • What manipulations did you hear in the variations of the music? • How might you translate those variations into movement? • What music elements were employed in the work to create interest? • How might you use those ideas to create interest in your work?

Movement Studies

1. Create a movement study based on a single idea or theme. You decide whether you want it to be abstract or expressive. Create the work in a way that will allow it to be performed in any order. Use the theme to unify the work, but create sections that might be sequenced in many ways and still work. Be careful not to be so focused on the theme

that you forget to create with interesting movement choices and strong intent. Share the work with your group, changing the order each time you perform it.

2. Using one of the pieces of music you analyzed, create a theme and variations in movement that mirrors the music you selected during the exploration. You will probably not have time to do the entire work, so you may select a part or parts of the music to use. This is not for a performance, so if you need to use only part of the music for this exercise, that will be okay. Try to create at least one theme with two variations of movement. If the theme is too long, just do a small segment of it. Do the same for the variations. Perform your theme and variations without the music as you share it. After performing it in silence, find some music or a sound score that does not have a steady beat that will compete with the rhythms in your work, and play it as background to your work. Try it one last time accompanied by the original music.

Assessment

Use these assessment tools in evaluating your progress toward understanding thematic form.

Class Critique

- For the work based on a single idea or theme: Identify the theme used in the work. Reflect on how the theme works to unify the piece. Evaluate the work according to the appropriateness of the form for the intent. Does it work? Is the intent clear? How does changing the order of the sequence affect the overall work? Is there one sequence that you prefer over the others? Why?

- For the theme and variations: Which performance did you like best? The one in silence? The one with background music? Or the one performed with the music that inspired it? Does the movement stand well on its own without any music? Can you see the rhythms and structure of the music without having the music to accompany the movement? What is the overall effect created by the theme and variation structure? Obviously this is an abstract structure. Expression might be layered into the form, but the focus is on the abstract structure of the work. Does this work for you as a structure for creating movement? Why or why not?

Rubric

Following is a sample rubric that you may use in evaluating the first movement study on thematic form. You may complete this rubric for your peers and have them complete one for you. If you wish, you may change the criteria to be more in line with what you believe to be important content for these movement studies.

Rubric for Thematic Form

Criteria	Strong evidence (4 points)	Some evidence (3 points)	Little evidence (2 points)	No evidence (1 point)
Recognizable theme				
Theme unifies work				
Form is appropriate for intent				
Interesting movement choices				
Intent is strong				
Total points: (maximum 20 points)				

Documentation

Record your work on video, adding it to your portfolio. Label the work "Theme" or "Theme and Variations." Include copies of your journal entries, comments from class critique, and rubrics.

Drawing Conclusions

Breaking the Rules

Thematic form is a way to create using related material. The theme in all cases establishes the material which remains consistent throughout the work. Try creating a work without a theme. This will be similar to your attempts to break the rules for linear form. You must create a work without a particular idea or emotion, and without manipulating material in an abstract way. You will not have anything to help you relate the material within your work.

REFLECTIVE QUESTIONS What happens from the audience's perspective when a work is created without meaning or intended relationships between dancers and movement? • How is it possible to create a successful work without relating the material within a work? • Have you seen any professional choreography that seems to be created this way? If so, do you think it was successful? Why or why not?

Drawing Conclusions

Critical Thinking Essay

Write an essay on form particularly as it applies to your work. Reflect on the work you completed before this chapter to identify any forms that may have materialized on their own from your intent. Reflect on the work you completed specifically on the use of form in this chapter. Compare the two and draw a conclusion about how you should deal with form in your work, including a discussion about when or even if you should consider forming your work. An outline is provided to help you get started, but remember to use your own judgment on the organization of the essay. Use the critical thinking model as you write.

I. Introduction: Include a definition of *form* and hint at the relationship you currently have with the process of developing form in your work.

II. Discussion

   A. Analysis: Describe your experiences with the specific forms presented in this chapter.

   B. Reflection: Reflect on your experiences and discuss why these forms work or do not work for you.

   C. Integration: Describe the work you have done in the past and how it relates to the work you have done on form in this chapter. Relate any forms that you came upon naturally in your work.

III. Conclusion: Evaluate your use of form and make a statement about your plans for using form in the future. Include your preference for when, if ever, form should be considered in the choreographic process. Make sure you defend your final statement in the body of your essay.

Considerations When Arranging Production Content

Dealing with a full-length production is outside the purview of this text, and there are many things to consider that require further study, including costuming and lighting. Each of the additional considerations requires its own course of study. However, it is rare that anyone considers the structure of an evening-length concert. I have some comments and advice on the subject. But before I begin, ask yourself these questions:

- How do you want to leave your audience?

- What is the best way to grab your audience's attention and keep it?

- How is it possible to get your audience to pay attention to that deep and serious work, which may not be entertaining but which has an important statement to make?

- How do you create a sequence of works without large blocks of downtime in which the audience waits for costume or scenery changes?

- What do you do during downtimes to hold your audience?

So often, companies, both professional and amateur, forget to consider the audience in the all-important task of creating the production order and the scheduling of breaks and intermissions. For example, a small company that employs every dancer in every work presented may use long intermissions between every choreographic work to allow the dancers rest and time for costume changes. I have been to dance concerts where individual performances are between 5 and 15 minutes long, intermissions are interspersed between each choreographic work, and the length of the intermissions are sometimes as long as 20 minutes—longer than the performances themselves. It reminds me of the commercials during a great movie presented on television. And perhaps our society has grown accustomed to this structure. However, the development of technology that allows us to rid ourselves of these commercials and view the movie commercial-free at an alternative time is evidence to the contrary. I believe today's audiences are even more impatient than audiences in the past. There is immediacy about our expectations. Our time is so critically packed with activities that even a little downtime becomes irritating because we wonder where else we could be and what else we should be doing. And I have often seen audiences slip out of the theater at these opportune times. The greatest enemy to an enjoyable performance is time that is spent not watching the performance.

To alleviate long intermissions, plan your program so that you alternate dancers, and think carefully about costume changes and how long they will take. Use fewer dancers in each work if necessary. If you must have one or two breaks that require costume changes, then train your dancers to do them quickly by rehearsing them as much as you rehearse their time on stage. It is great to think of caring for your dancers by allowing them to rest, but if you don't take care of your audience first, there will be no one left who will watch the dance. Don't forget that pointe shoes take a lot of time to get on and off, and unitards do not go on sweaty bodies easily. So you will need to consider what kinds of costume changes are required. You may need to place all the pointe pieces at the beginning of a concert or after an intermission. You may even need to alter your costume choices to speed up the process backstage. If the hair has to be up in some pieces and down in others, remember it is easier to take hair down than it is to put it up so that it will not fall down while dancers are onstage. Design scenery changes to go quickly and smoothly, and consider doing them as part of the choreography or behind a center-stage curtain while the dance continues in front. It is possible to make it part of the performance. Are you thinking about intermissions as a necessary break for the audience? This is also important, but audiences do not need intermissions as often as you might think. You can easily do an hour-long concert without an intermission. An hour and a half is pushing it, but it can be done. You might want to consider turning some intermissions into pauses that allow your audience to read their programs as you bring the house lights to half during a quick costume or scenery change. And finally, you should consider where the audience goes during downtime. When I created my first full-length ballet *Cinderella*, the piece lasted 90 minutes and required two intermissions. The guild for which I worked complained about having to deal with the audience during two intermissions. Since our audiences were primarily children, the guild used the intermission to sell homemade souvenirs of the production (ballerina dolls, finger puppets, pipe-cleaner coaches) as a fund-raiser for the company. Although the guild was concerned that the children in the audience might leave during the second intermission given the chance, they discovered that twice as many souvenirs were sold, and the children would not leave until Cinderella had returned to her prince. After that it was requested that I place two intermissions in each of our productions. That happened, however, only when appropriate for the intent of the work. Adults enjoy souvenirs as well. You might have an art sale in the lobby to support your company or at the very least refreshments if the theater allows. Thinking about intermissions creatively may contribute to the enjoyment of a night out for your audience and leave them wanting to return soon.

When considering how long a dance concert should be and how many intermissions are reasonable within that time, consider this: It's been a long time since the birth of ballet and the six-hour production of *Ballet Comique de la Reine* produced by Catherine de Medici in Paris in 1581. Remember that during the six-hour extravaganza the audience was offered a huge banquet and opportunities to participate in the production. Three hours in a theater, with no food and no audience participa-

tion in a production, should be considered the absolute maximum time you should hold your audience. One or two intermissions are usually plenty. A dance concert of less than two hours is much better. You must have a riveting program to hold the audience's interest for three hours.

As an aside, please do not think of school recitals as an exception to this rule. It is not okay to do a five-hour performance so that every child may perform and every parent may see every child. No parent should be put through that ordeal, nor should the children. They will come to hate dance eventually, or decide it is something to be tolerated for the sake of the child. It would be much better to split up your age groups and do two performances rather than present one marathon performance.

Once you settle on a length for your production and get your costume changes down to as fast as possible, you also need to think about the works you are presenting in the same way you think about the form and individual elements of movement in a single work. For example, you do not want to present only slow lyrical pieces. You will put your audience to sleep. Nor do you want all the work to be high energy and fast, although I have seen a few companies do this successfully, leaving me exhausted but satisfied. If you are doing a dance concert, you should present a variety of material. If you are doing a complete work that lasts the entire concert, then hopefully you will have already tackled the ideal form and sequence with variety for your audience in that work. Your only dilemma may be where to place the intermissions, if you need them.

There are some simple rules to follow. Your first piece is considered the "throw-away" piece. I cannot tell you how many times I placed my favorite choreography first on the program only to find that the people whom I asked about it had arrived late and missed it entirely. But don't dare put your weakest piece there, either. If you have been lucky enough to secure a reviewer to write about your concert, you may lose that reviewer after the first work if it is not strong enough to hold the serious dance aficionado. You want your first piece to be strong enough to grab the attention of your audience, but not so important that if it is missed, you and the dancers will be disappointed. A strong, dynamic, and entertaining piece would be a good choice for the beginning of your concert.

The last piece of the performance has always been considered the place of honor. Besides being a tradition, it makes sense. The last thing the audience sees is what they will remember. This is important to think about not only in an individual work but also in an evening-length performance. If you save the best for last, your audience should leave wanting more, and that is your goal. Most audiences love a good finale, and finale means strong, dynamic, amazing choreography. It's the kind of work that receives encores if done well. However, there are times when a finale is not appropriate and you may wish to end on a dramatic note. If you have a piece that is thought provoking and complex, and you want to give your audience time to think, you must place this type of work either at the end or right before an intermission. You do not want to throw your audience back into an entertaining and fun piece right after you have stunned them with a passionate and riveting drama. You have to leave some space for your audience to digest a piece with great depth. Even though the audience may leave rather quietly, I like to leave a thought-provoking and complex piece for the end. If the audience does not clap right away, it is usually a good sign. They are too stunned to react. If you have stunned your audience, you need to let them go home to think about the impact you have made. They will be back for more. You cannot always measure your success by the sound of the applause.

Within the sequence, you should think of building to the end. Each piece need not be stronger in dynamics than the previous one, but there should be a build-up of energy overall right until the end. That energy need not be energy of movement, but it could be energy in the impact you make with your audience. It might be a dramatic tension or exuberant celebration, but it should be something you are willing to leave with your audience.

If you are mixing styles in your concert, there is something to be said for keeping styles together, such as all the classical pieces first, then the modern pieces, and then the jazz pieces at the end. Alternating styles with every piece can be disconcerting and jolting to an audience who is just beginning to get used to a particular style as you throw them into a new one. On the other hand, changing styles frequently might offer the variety you need. Again, there is no hard and fast rule. Be aware of how your audience will feel after seeing the performance in the order you have selected. And ask yourself if that is how you want them to feel, or if there is a way to manipulate the order to improve the reaction you are trying to get.

If you are designing an entire concert season for a dance company, you also want to think about the order of your offerings. If you have a dance company that always offers the same kind of performance, then this may not relate to you. But if you have a company that sometimes does short works in concert form and sometimes does full-length pieces, you may wish to think about which type of performance is most popular to your audience, and save the most esoteric for the end of the season after you have educated your audience slowly and gradually shown them the value of attending your performances. If you always do serious, difficult-to-understand pieces, and you expect your audience to come along with you, you may end up with no audience at all, even if you are a genius choreographer. Most communities have to be educated, and most audiences must be nurtured. Just as it takes a dance student a long time to practice and be a good performer, it takes a while for an audience member to become a sophisticated dance enthusiast. So you must always think about giving your audience some things that are just plain fun to watch. Coax them with more complex work slowly, and eventually they will be ready for as much sophistication as you can throw at them.

Finally, because communities need to be educated and audiences need to be nurtured, you need to know your community and what the audience will bear. Are you in a community that is accustomed to classical ballet and you are trying to introduce them to the most innovative modern dance available? That will not happen overnight. You must analyze what will bring them to the performance. Do you need to begin by offering stories that are costumed exquisitely, and can you do this and still stay true to your style? Sometimes, if you give yourself this kind of challenge, you will find yourself in a new and exciting direction. And you will be able to wean your audiences away from the stories and the costumes once you have gained their trust. Are you in a conservative area, where suggestions of sexual content will offend 90 percent of your audience? You may decide you don't care and that the audience needs to hear what you have to say. Unfortunately, in most cases, if you shock them in that way, they will not listen and simply go away telling everyone how horrible your work is. With a little care, you might have been able to elicit the effect you desired with a gentler and more subtle approach and kept your box office receipts coming in.

As artists, we never want to think that we will cater to our audiences. We want to believe that our personal statements come first. If the audience likes it, fine. If not, it is their loss. This take-it-or-leave-it attitude might work for a visual artist who has been able to solicit a patron who believes in his work and will support it. But to fill an auditorium, it takes many patrons. Your audience, as possible long-term patrons to your work, must be cajoled to a certain extent. That does not mean that you must think only about what the audience wants to see and not what you want to create. On the contrary, you must be creative enough to be true to yourself as you create in the environment that surrounds you. Dance is a performing art. It belongs to the choreographers, the dancers, and the people who will come to watch. If every piece to this puzzle is not present, the dance cannot exist.

Suggested Activity

You are already well equipped to practice putting works together for a full-length concert. You may use the works in your digital portfolio to create a virtual dance concert. I recommend that you try a few configurations, indicating your sequence, places for pauses, and intermissions. Describe a virtual audience to go with each configuration. After you have a few configurations worked out, share them with your peers. Comment on each other's choices and make suggestions. Hopefully, you will have an opportunity to present an actual dance concert that includes your original work.

An Evening with the Alvin Ailey American Dance Theatre, presented by RM Arts, The Classis Performance Collection, 1986.

Atkinson, Brooks. *The Selected Writings of Ralph Waldo Emerson.* New York: Modern Library, 1992.

Blackwood, Michael. *Butoh: Body on the Edge of Crisis.* (VHS). New York: Michael Blackwood Productions, 1990.

Blom, L., and Chaplin, L.T. *The Intimate Act of Choreography.* Pittsburg: University of Pittsburg Press, 1982.

Chujoy, Anatol. *The Dance Encyclopedia.* New York: Simon and Shuster, 1967.

Dell, Cecily. *A Primer for Movement Description using effort shape and supplementary concepts.* Hightstown, NJ: Dance Notation Bureau Press, 1977.

Disney, Walt. *Walt Disney's Masterpiece Fantasia.* Burbank, CA: Walt Disney Company, 1990 restoration (VHS).

Einstein, A. *The World as I See It.* Citadel Press, 2006.

Frost, Robert. *Mountain Interval.* New York: Holt, 1920.

Humphrey, Doris. *The Art of Making Dances.* Princeton, NJ: Dance Horizons, 1987.

Jason, Philip K. *Anaïs Nin Reader.* New York: Avon Books, 1974.

Joffrey Ballet. *The Green Table,* choreographed by Kurt Jooss (1932). WNET Great Performances Series, circa 1970.

Kaplan, Robert. *Rhythmic Training for Dancers.* Champaign, IL: Human Kinetics, 2002.

Langer, Susanne K. *Feeling and Form.* New York: Charles Scribner's Sons, 1953.

Migel, Parmenia. *The Ballerinas.* New York: Macmillan, 1972.

Noverre, Jean Georges. *Letters on Dancing and Ballets.* Translated by Cyril Beaumont. New York: Dance Horizons, 1975.

Here are some guidelines on using this list of music resources: Each section is organized according to genre of music or specific music element to be studied. The majority of entries begin with the title of an album. Italics are used for album titles. Quotation marks are used for song titles or shorter works of music. Track numbers are listed when no song title is given.

Variations in Dynamics

Bloch: America; Concerto Grosso No. 1. Seattle Schwarz. Delos, 1994.

Beethoven: Symphonie No. 9, etc. Karajan, Berlin PO, Herbert von Karajan, Berlin Philharmonic Orchestra, Vienna Singverein and Gundula Janowitz, "Finale." Deutsche Grammophon, 1996.

Grieg: Peer Gynt Suites 1 and 2. Sibelius, Karajan, "In the Hall of the Mountain King." Deutsche Grammophon.

Mussorgsky: Pictures at an Exhibition, Night on Bald Mountain. Paavo Järvi and Cincinnati Symphony Orchestra. Telarc, 2008.

Stravinsky: Concerto in D for Violin and Orchestra. Deutsche Grammophon, 2002.

Soft Dynamics

Narada Decade: The Anniversary Collection. Narada Productions, 1993.

Satie: Gnossiennes, Gymnopédies, etc. Reinbert De Leeuw. Phillips, 1996.

Windham Hill: The First Ten Years. Various artists. Windham Hill Records, 1990.

Strong Dynamics

Copland: Fanfare for the Common Man; Appalachian Spring. Dennis Russell Davies, Eduardo Mata, Enrique Bátiz, and Leonard Slatkin. American Classics, 2008.

Fanfares for the Uncommon Woman. Joan Tower. Koch International Classics, 1999.

Joan Tower. Lynn Harrell, Peter Bowman. "Island Rhythms." First Edition, 2005.

Emotional Content

Barber: Violin Concerto; Cello Concerto. Steven Isserlis. RCA, 2005.

Devil's Dance. Gil Shaham and Jonathan Feldman. Deutsche Grammophon, 2000.

The Music of Elliott Carter Vol 4. William Purvis, Speculum Musicae members, Allen Blustine and Chris Finckel. Bridge, 2001.

Shoenberg: Chamber Symphonies Nos 1 & 2; 5 Orchestral Pieces. Jeffrey Tate. Simon, Sir Rattle, Artemis String Quartet and City of Birmingham Symphony Orchestra, 20th Century Classics, 2008.

Shostakovich: Sonata for Violin, etc. Kremer, Bashmet. Gidon Kremer, Kremerata Baltica, Gidon Kremer and Yuri Bashmet Deutsche Grammophon, 2006.

Strong Pulse

Bolero, Daphnis et Chloe, Suite; Debussy. Herbert von Karajan and Berlin Philharmonic Orchestra). DGGalleria, 1989.

Glassworks, Expanded Edition. Philip Glass. Michael Riesman, Philip Glass Ensemble, Jack Kripl, and Michael Riesman. Sony Classical Masterworks, 2003.

Hands On Semble. Hands On Semble company, 2000.

At the Edge. Mickey Hart. Rykodisk, 1990.

Planet Drum. Mickey Hart. Shout! Factory, 2008

Drumming Inside Mother Earth. Allen Hayes. Allnight Productions, 2003.

Percussion Maddness. Luisito Quintero. Rapster Records, 2007.

Moderato

The Chairman Dances. John Adams. Nonesuch, 1995.

In C. Hillier, Ars Nova Copenhagen, et al. Terry Riley. Dacapo, 2007.

Light and Fast

Suite For Flute No. 2. "Irelandaise." Claude Bolling and Jean Pierre Rampal. Fremeaux, 2007.

Still: Afro American Symphony. "Animato." Jindong Cai, Cincinnati Philharmonia Orchestra and Richard Fields. Centaur Records, 1997.

Stravinsky: Pulcinella, Le baiser de la fée. Robert Craft, London Symphony Orchestra, Mark Beesley, Diana Montague, Robin Leggate. Track 5. Naxos, 2006.

Strong and Fast

Devil's Dance. Gil Shaham and Jonathan Feldman. Track 1. Deutsche Grammophon, 2000.

The Dharma at Big Sur. Track 2. John Adams, BBC Symphony Orchestra, Tracy Silverman, and William Houghton. Nonesuch Records, USA, 2006.

Light and Slow

Chopin: Nocturnes. Maurizio Pollini. Deutsche Grammophon, 2006.

Ravel: Piano Concertos. "Piano Concerto in G, Adagio." Deutsche Grammophon, 1999.

Satie: Gnossiennes, Gymnopedie. Jacques Loussier Trio. Telar, 1998.

Strong and Slow

Nixon in China. "I am the Wife of Chairman Mao." John Adams, Edo De Waart, Orchestra of St. Luke's, Carolann Page, James Maddalena, and John Duykers. Nonesuch Records, 1990.

Still: Afro American Symphony. "Moderato assai, first movement." Jindong Cai, Cincinnati Philharmonia Orchestra, and Richard Fields. Centaur Records, 1997.

Stravinsky: The Firebird. "Apotheosis." Pierre Boulez and Chicago Symphony Orchestra, Deutsche Grammophon, 1993.

Andante

Fauré: Requiem; Cantique de Jean Racine. Laurence Equilbey, Accentus. Naive, 2008.

Adagio

Adagio. Herbert von Karajan, Berlin Philharmonic Orchestra, David Bell, and Frank Maus. Deutsche. Grammophon USA, 1995.

The Best of Barber. "Adagio for Strings." Samuel Barber, Leonard Slatkin, Robert Shaw, Yoel Levi, and Atlanta Symphony Orchestra. , Telarc, 2003.

Cello Adagios. Antal Dorati, James Judd, Neville, Sir Neville Marriner, and Nicholas Cleobury. Decca, 2004.

Tobias Picker. Sergiu Comissiona, Houston Symphony Orchestra, Mendelssohn String Quartet, and Leona Mitchell. Track 11. First Edition, 2005.

Satie: 3 Sarabandes. Jan Kaspersen. Classico, 1996.

Allegro

Gulf Coast Blues and Impressions: A Hurricane Relief Benefit. George Winston. Windham Hill Jazz, 2006.

The Strauss Family: Waltzes, Polkas and Overtures. Disc 1, "Seufzer-Galopp, Op. 9." EMI Records, 2004.

Natasha's Waltz. Nancy Blake and Norman Blake. Rounder Select, 1991.

Tempo Variations

Best of Hungarian Gypsy Tunes: Czardas! Andras and Ensemble Farkas. Arc Music, 2005.

Chopin: 14 Waltzes, Barcarolle, etc. Dinu Lipatti. EMI Records, 1999.

Devil's Dance. Gil Shaham and Jonathan Feldman. Track 5. Deutsche Grammophon, 2000.

Scriabin: Complete Mazurkas. Eric Le Van. Music & Arts Program, 2003.

The Strauss Family: Waltzes, Polkas and Overtures. Disc 2, "Accelerationen," Op. 234. EMI Records, 2004.

Duple Meter

All-Time Piano Hits/Melody & Percussion for Two Pianos. Ronnie Aldrich. Dutton Laboratories/Vocalion, 2006.

Dance Phrases by June Olsson. Asgard Productions, 1993.

Planet Drum. Mickey Hart. Shout Factory, 2008.

Percussion Madness: Revisited. Luisito Quintero. BBE Records, 2007.

Prokofiev: Peter and the Wolf, Basic 100 Volume 43. "Finale." Arthur Fiedler, Eugene Ormandy, Boston Pops, Philadelphia Orchestra and David Bowie, RCA Victor, 1994.

Top Percussion. Tito Puente. RCA International, 1992.

Triple Meter

Spinning World: 13 Ways Of Looking at a Waltz. Gunnar Madsen. GSpot (Ladyslipper), 1998.

20/21—Reich: Variations, Six Pianos. "Music for Mallet Instruments, Voices and Electric Organ." Edo De Waart, San Francisco Symphony Orchestra, Bob Becker, Glen Velez and James Preiss. Deutsche Grammophon, 2002.

Five Beats

Spinning World: 13 Ways Of Looking at a Waltz. "Five Lakes." Gunnar Madsen. GSpot (Ladyslipper), 1998.

Time Out. "Take Five." Dave Brubeck Quartet. Legacy Recordings, 2006.

Mixed Meter

Copland: (El) Salon Mexico. Minnesota Orchestra, Marri. EMI Red Line Classics.

Dance Phrases by June Olsson. Asgard Productions, 1993.

Kodály, Bartok. Sir Charles Mackerras and Scottish Chamber Orchestra. Linn Records, 2006.

Solo Instrument

Masters of the Oboe. Deutsche Grammophon, 2006.

Itzhak Perlman: A La Carte. Foster, Abbey Road Ensemble. EMI Classics, 1996.

Original Masters: Julian Bream Plays Dowland & Bach. Margaret Field-Hyde, Golden Age Singers, Beatrice Reichert, and Edith Steinbauer. Deutsche Grammophon, 2008.

Perspectives. Gidon Kremer, Leonard Bernstein, Nikolaus Harnoncourt, and Seiji Ozawa. Deutsche Grammophon, 2006.

Trio: The 20th-Century Cello. Matt Haimovitz and Philippe Cassard. Deutsche Grammophon, 2005.

Narciso Yepes: Guitarra Espanola. Garcia Navarro, Odon Alonso, R. Frühbeck de Burgos, and London Symphony Orchestra. Deutsche Grammophon, 2004.

Chamber Music (Distinct Instrumental Voices)

Alban Berg Collection. Claudio Abbado, James Levine, Pierre Boulez, and Boston Symphony Chamber Players. Deutsche Grammophon, 2004.

Dawson: Negro Folk Symphony; Brahms: Serenade No 1. Dimitri Mitropoulos, Leopold Stokowski, and New York Philharmonic Scholarship Winners 1949-50. Deutsche Grammophon, 2007.

Dvorak, Janacek, Hummel, et al.: Wind Music. COE Records, 2006.

Janacek: Chamber Music. Starker, Korcia, Firkusny. Red Seal, 2.

Samples for Mapping the Counts

Prokofiev: Romeo and Juliet Suites; Respighi. Riccardo Muti and Philadelphia Orchestra. EMI Classics Encore, 2005.

Dvorak: Slavonic Dances. Szell, Cleveland Orchestra. Centennial Classics, 2002.

Elgar: Enigma Variations. Gardiner, Vienna PO. Deutsche Grammophon, 2002.

Samples for Graphing the Sound Score

Echo 20/21 Maderna: Quadrivium. Giuseppe Sinopoli and North German Radio Symphony Orchestra. Deutsche Grammophon, 2005.

Music for Airports. Brian Eno, Bang on a Can. Point Music, 1998.

Thursday Afternoon. Brian Eno. EG Music (BMI), 1985.

Yoshimatsu: Cello Concerto, Age of Birds. "Concerto for Cello, Op. 91." Sachio Fujioka, BBC Philharmonic Orchestra and Peter Dixon. Chandos Records, 2004.

Motif and Development

Beethoven: Symphonies No. 5 & 7. Carlos Kleiber and Vienna Philharmonic Orchestra. Deutsche Grammophon, 1996.

Britten: 4 Sea Interludes. Vernon Handley and Ulster Orchestra. Chandos Records.

Desplat, Alexandre. *The Painted Veil* (Original Soundtrack). Deutsche Grammophon, 2007.

Theme and Variations

Britten: Variations on a Theme of Frank Bridge. Laurent Quenelle, European Camerata, and Jean-Paul Minali-Bella. Fuga Libera, 2008.

Herzogenberg: Variations on a Theme of Brahms. Anthony Goldstone and Caroline Clemmow. Toccata Classics, 2006.

Kodaly: Psalmus Hungaricus, Peacock Variations. Kodaly. Dorati Antalo. Hungaroton, 1994.

La Folia: Variations on a Theme. Purcell Band, Purcell Quartet, Elizabeth Wallfisch, Richard Boothby, and Robert Woolley. Hyperion, 1998.

Canon and Fugue

Albinoni: Adagio; Pachelbel: Canon. Herbert von Karajan and Berlin Philharmonic Orchestra. Deutsche Grammophon, 1991.

Rochberg: String Quartets Nos. 3-6. "String Quartet No. 4: Fuga." Concord String Quartet. New World Records, 1999.

Scarlatti: The Cat's Fugue, Sonatas. Track 9. Elaine Comparone. Lyrichord, 2000.

Bach: Fugues. Emerson String Quartet, Da-Hong Seetoo, David Finckel, Eugene Drucker, and Lawrence Dutton. Deutsche Grammophon, 2008.

Suggestions for Movement Studies and Choreography

Busoni: Complete Works for Cello and Piano. Duo Pepicelli. Naxos, 2004.

A Day Without Rain. Enya. Warner Brothers, 2000.

Watermark. Enya. Reprise, 1989.

Fiesta. Gustavo Dudamel and Venezuela Simon Bolivar Youth Orchestra. Deutsche Grammophon (USA), 2008.

Golijov: Oceana. Robert Spano, Atlanta Symphony Orchestra, Gwinnettt Young Singers, and Kronos Quartet. Deutsche Grammophon, 2007.

Gottschalk: Piano Music, American Classics. Cecile Licad. Naxos, 1993.

Gurdjieff, Tsabropoulos: Chants, Hymns and Dances. Anja Lechner and Vassilis Tsabropoulos ECM New Series, 2004.

Chakra Suite. Steven Halpern. Halpern Sounds, 2007.

Indigo. Sugo Music and Design, 1996.

Jakajan: Music From New Siam. Fong Naam, Boonrut Sirirattanapan, Bruce Gaston, Dusadee Sawangwibulphong, and Hugh Webb. Nimbus, 1996.

Joplin: Piano Rags. Roy Eaton. Sony Classical Essential Classics, 2002.

The Mystery of Santo Domingo de Silos. Deutsche Grammophon, 1994.

Orff: Carmina Burana; Stravinsky: Fireworks, Circus Polka. R. Frühbeck de Burgos, New Philharmonia Chorus, and New Philharmonia Orchestra. EMI Classics Encore, 2003.

Tobias Picker. Sergiu Comissiona, Houston Symphony Orchestra, Mendelssohn String Quartet, and Leona Mitchell. First Edition, 2005.

Music from the Penguin Café. Penguin Café Orchestra. EG Records, 1976.

Sarasate: Spanish Dances. Naxos, 2006.

Tibetan Tantric Choir. Gyuto Monks. Windham Hill Records, 1990.

Tippett: The Rose Lake, Ritual Dances. Richard Hickox and BBC National Orchestra of Wales. Chandos Records, 2005.

Tolle, Eckhart: Music to Quiet the Mind. Gemini Sun Records, 2008.

Joan Tower: Black Topaz. Isbin, Wincenc, Emelianof. New World Records, 1995.

The Ultimate Jesse Cook. Narada, 2005.

Kryptos. Andreas Vollenweider. Sony Music Entertainment, 1997.

Out of Silence. Yanni. RCA Records, 1987.

Music With Text

Alive 2007. Daft Punk. Virgin Records, 2007.

MCMXC A.D. Enigma. Charisma, 1991.

Electronic Sounds

Digital Bass. Bass 305. DM Records, 1992.

Rediscovering Lost Scores Vol. 1. Wendy Carlos. East Side Digital, 2005.

Oxygene. Jean-Michel Jarre. Dreyfus Records, 1993.

Silk Road Volume 2. Kitaro. New World Music, 2004.

Official U.S.A.C. Bass Competition. Various Artists. Pan-disc Records, 1997.

Tangram. Tangerine Dream. Blue Plate, 2005.

Multicultural

Congotronics 2: Buzz 'n' Rumble From the Urb 'n' Jungle. Various artists. Crammed Discs, 2006.

Didgeralia. David Hudson. Indigenous Australia, 2007.

Paradise Lost. Steve Kindler. Mesa/Bluemoon, 1993.

La Mer Jolie : Chants d'Acadie. Suzie LeBlanc. ATMA, 2007.

Music of Indonesia 3: Music From the Outskirts of Jakarta—Gambang Kromong. Various artists. Smithsonian Folkways Music, 1992.

Putomayo Presents the Best of World Music, Volumes 1 and 2. Various artsts. Rhino Records (USA), 1993.

Steelbands of Trinidad. Various artists. Delos, 1989.

Traditional Music From East Siberia. National Dance Theatre of the Republic Of Sakha. Arc Music Productions International, 2007.

Wind River. Andrew Vasquez. Makoché Music/BMI, 1997.

World Dance: Caribbean Tropical Dance. Various artists. ARC, 2008.

abstract (verb)—To remove or change from the original while retaining some essence of that original.

abstract dance—Dance without literal meaning or expressive content; movement created for the sake of movement.

accelerando—Music term that indicates the movement gradually speeds up.

accent—Point in music, sound, or movement that is strong. Traditionally the first beat in a measure is accented, but many variations exist.

acute angle—Shape formed by two lines at less than 90 degrees from each other.

adagietto—Music term used to indicate a tempo not quite as slow as adagio.

adagio—Music term that indicates a slow tempo.

allegro—Music term that indicates a fast tempo.

analyze—Breaking down and describing the parts of a whole; the practice of identifying the elements of the dance.

andante—Music term that indicates a normal walking tempo.

arrange—Act of placing dance steps or movement in order without thought to choreographic elements or form. Dance classes often use steps that have been arranged in order to teach the technique rather than to offer a choreographic work for the stage.

artist's statement—Document that explains the intent of a choreographer's work and the process used in creating it.

arts integration—Process of learning that combines equal and significant instruction simultaneously in arts and non-arts subjects.

assessment—Determination of whether a goal has been met.

asymmetry—Anything that is not symmetrical is considered asymmetrical, or without symmetry. Stage balance is achieved through asymmetry when the size and number of dancers on one side of the stage seem to balance visually with those on the other side of the stage.

body sounds—Sounds and rhythms created by using parts of the body to slap, clap, brush, and pat other parts of the body.

breath rhythm—Rhythm created to coordinate with the timing and energy of a dancer's breathing.

canon—Form that is created when two or more dancers perform the same movement phrase or phrases at the same time but at different places in the time continuum. The space in time that takes place between the dancers remains constant. For example, dancer 1 begins, and dancer 2 begins 4 counts later as dancer 1 performs the fifth count. The dancers remain 4 counts apart.

centrifugal force—Pulling away from the center of a spinning object.

choreography—Movement created with an intent to be showcased in a theatrical performance.

commitment—Complete and uninterrupted focus on the intent of a dance.

complementary lines—Lines that look like they belong together, creating a unified effect.

concept—Idea created by the use of dance elements.

contact improvisation—Technique of exploring opportunities for weight sharing through improvisation. Its invention is credited to Steve Paxton, who presented it during the early 1970s.

craft—Mechanics used to create a work of art.

critique—Complex process for making judgments about a work of art, including analysis and evaluation.

cyclic form (sometimes called rondo form)—A composition in which an entire piece returns to its beginning before it ends. Can be denoted as ABCBA or ABCDA.

dance technique—Style or code of movement that has been established as belonging to a particular genre, such as classical ballet, tap, or flamenco.

developed material—Movement that comes out of an original idea, movement, phrase, or theme. The material may be developed through an organic approach or by manipulating the original material into variations.

direct focus—Effect that is created when a dancer's eye, shape, or movement is drawn in a straight line toward a single point.

director—Person who is responsible for the quality of a performance or a dance company. A director is not necessarily the choreographer but may be. The director is responsible for the accuracy and quality of a performance.

documentation—Recorded examples of learning and artwork for the purpose of measuring and evaluating.

duple meter—Two beats or a multiple of two beats per measure.

dynamics—Range of visible energy used in performing a dance. High dynamics is perceived as a lot of energy or strong. Low dynamics is perceived as very little energy or light. In music, dynamics refers to the amplitude of sound and ranges between loud and soft.

effort actions—Eight specific movement actions created by combining the extremes within the three movement elements of time, weight, and focus.

effort shape—System of movement analysis devised by Rudolf von Laban and colleagues.

elements—Components of movement and choreography as defined within energy, space, and time.

embedded assessment—Continuous measuring of knowledge and understanding within a learning process.

energy—Force involved in the creation of dance.

evaluation—Value judgment based on particular criteria.

expressive dance—Dance that has emotional or narrative content.

flip symmetry—Similar forms that mirror each other.

flow—Range of effort between bound and free. Bound movement takes a lot of effort, whereas free movement takes very little effort.

focus—One or more points where the audience's eyes are drawn because of the shape, direction, and intent of a dancer.

form—Overall shape of a work of art. The structure that unifies the work and allows us to see it as its own entity.

general space—All of the space that exists in the performance space. A dancer who is traveling through the performance space is said to be performing in general space.

gesture—Movement of a body part to express or emphasize ideas or emotions.

grave—Music term used to indicate an extremely slow tempo; slower than largo.

improvisation—Extemporaneous exploration of movement; creating without planning.

indirect focus—Effect that is created when a dancer's eyes, shape, or movement are drawn to many points in the performance space at once, causing the dancer to meander through space or settle in a shape with curved lines.

inquiry-based approach—Process for learning through questioning and exploration.

integration—Process of finding relationships between choreographic material and all other experience.

intent—Visible reason or purpose for being in a position or moving in dance.

internal focus—Concentration on one's kinesthetic sense, excluding external stimuli. The feel of the body, joints, and muscles becomes prominent. Removing the visual sense helps in achieving this state of mind, but it can be achieved with the eyes open.

kinesthetic—Sensation of body position and movement.

kinesthetic response—Muscle reaction to music, sound, or visual stimuli.

larghetto—Music term indicating a tempo not quite as slow as largo.

largo—Music term indicating a very slow tempo; slower than adagio.

level—Space occupied by the dancer in relationship to the supporting surface of the dancer or the performance space. High is as far above the supporting surface as possible. Low is as close as possible to the supporting surface. Middle is the space halfway between high and low. Levels may be enhanced with set pieces and partnering by increasing the distance between high and low.

lifts—Feats in which one dancer takes all the weight of another dancer and raises that dancer off the floor and often overhead.

liturgical dance—Movement created for public worship.

logical (as in transitions or movement choice)—Choreographic choice that makes sense to the viewer.

march—Music and dance form in 2/4 or 6/8 time with strong, even accents occurring at a walking tempo.

meter—Arrangement of beats in music that forms groupings called measures or bars.

minimalism—A form used a great deal during the postmodern period of dance, where a very small and insignificant movement is repeated many times to obtain a powerful effect.

mixed meter—Variations of meter within a music or dance phrase, such as duple, triple, duple, duple.

moderato—Music term used to indicate a moderate or medium tempo.

motif—Small distinctive movement repeated or developed in a piece of choreography.

movement auralization—The act of taking movement and making it aural, or translating it to sound.

movement problem—Requirement for creating dance within given parameters.

movement quality—Effect created by the combination of choreographic elements within energy, space, and time.

movement study—Short dance work created in order to test the understanding of choreographic elements. Movement studies usually involve the solving of a movement problem.

movement vocabulary—Movement within a particular style, or movement that has been mastered by an individual.

music visualization—Act of taking music and making it visible through dance movement.

musicality—When a dance is accompanied by music, this refers to the intentional and logical connection between the dance and the music. When the dance is not accompanied by music, this refers to the visible rhythmic quality projected by the dance. A dance that projects this rhythmic quality with or without music is said to have musicality.

narrative—Story line or sequence of events that follow each other logically.

negative space—Empty space surrounded and defined by lines and shapes created by dancers' bodies, scenery, and props.

observation—Process of viewing a dance in order to gather meaning and evaluate its intent.

organic—Process of creating movement from one idea, allowing it to grow naturally so that each addition to the work comes directly from the previous position or movement and relates back to the initial idea.

personal space—Space that exists around the dancer that is within reach. Personal space stays with the dancer as the dancer moves through the performance space.

phrase—Short statement that has an apparent beginning, middle, and end. In music, a beginning of an idea is heard and the idea comes to a conclusion before the next phrase begins. In dance, the movement idea is perceived as beginning something new and completed before a new idea begins. Some phrases are obvious and some depend on the interpreter to perceive them.

pitch—Music term that distinguishes how high or low a note sounds.

portfolio—Collection of personally created artwork, specifically for dance: video and photographs.

positive space—Space filled by solid figures such as dancers' bodies, scenery, and props. Positive space defines the negative space around it and within it.

prestissimo—Music term that indicates an extremely fast tempo; faster than presto.

presto—Music term that indicates a very fast tempo; faster than allegro.

proscenium theater—A theater that is built with the structure of the baroque theater, including a proscenium arch, wings, and backdrop. A proscenium theater has an obvious front. The audience looks through the arch as if it were a window into the lives of the performers.

quality—Effect created by the combination of elements within energy, space, and time.

reflection—Practice of looking back to discover meaning.

reflective questioning—Act of forming questions to encourage reflection.

rhythm—Duration of movement, accented beats, and nonaccented beats arranged in a way that creates an animating effect. Rhythm exists within meter.

ripples—Wavelike effect created by multiple dancers performing the same movement one after the other, with only a slight difference in the time the movement is begun. In order for this effect to work, dancers need to be close together and the movement needs to be precise.

ritardando—Music term that indicates the movement gradually slows down.

rotational symmetry—Three or more similar forms arranged equidistant around a common point.

rubric—Tool for evaluating success by listing criteria and describing what will be included in order to obtain a particular score or grade.

scene d'action—Scene in a piece of narrative choreography that moves the plot or story line forward.

sculpture—In dance, a still, unified shape created by two or more dancers working closely together.

self-space—Space that exists around a dancer who is not traveling through the performance space but is anchored to one spot.

slide symmetry—Similar forms that are parallel to each other.

somatic approach—Using a focus on the relaxation of unneeded muscle groups to acquire the most efficient way to perform a particular movement. Some examples of somatic approaches to dance are Alexander Technique, Feldenkrais, and Pilates.

space—Visual relationships created by dancers and their environment.

split focus—Two focal points in the performance space that cannot be seen from the audience at the same time. An example is a dancer performing on stage right while another dancer is performing on stage left. The audience must choose which dancer to watch..

symbolic space—Empty space that is given meaning through the intent of the dance.

symmetry—Similarity of form on two sides of a dividing line or similarity of multiple forms around a point.

syncopation—Rhythm that is created with accents occurring in places that are not typically accented

synthesize—Practice of combining elements to create a choreographic effect.

tempo—Music term used also in dance to indicate the overall speed of a dance or movement within a dance.

theme—Idea that unifies a piece of choreography, or a phrase of movement to be developed, as in theme and variations.

time—Duration of movement.

tour de force—Term in classical ballet used to indicate a specific feat to show off the virtuosity of a dancer. Usually found in a solo.

transition—Place where a dancer changes from one idea, phrase, position, or place in the performance space to another idea, phrase, position, or place.

triple meter—Three beats or a multiple of three beats per measure.

turn symmetry—Similar forms that are upside down in relation to each other.

vivace—Music term used to indicate a tempo that is lively.

waltz—Music and dance form in 3/4 time. Usually lyrical in quality.

weight sharing—Two or more dancers working together in such a way that each is either supporting or leaning on others to the extent that there is complete dependence. Unlike traditional partnering where one dancer is usually responsible for all the support, weight sharing implies equal responsibility between all dancers involved.

Note: Page numbers followed by an italicized *f* or *t* refer to the figure or table on that page, respectively.

Diana F. Green, MFA, is celebrating her third career in the arts as the arts in education program manager for the Alabama State Council on the Arts in Montgomery. Having founded the first P-12 certification program in dance in the state of Alabama, she stays informed of the latest research on teaching and uses dance as an integration tool for learning.

Preparing for her first career, Green studied under Eugene Loring and Antony Tudor, learning diverse styles and concentrating on choreography and pedagogy. She taught at a preprofessional ballet school and youth company in Silver Spring, Maryland, for 15 years. Her students have gone on to dance with nationally recognized companies performing on Broadway and throughout the world. During her tenure in Maryland, she was selected to choreograph and direct a performing arts tribute for Maryland's 350th birthday.

Moving from private studio to higher education, Green designed and directed the dance program at Huntingdon College in Montgomery, Alabama, for 12 years. Her program was among the first to receive the National College Choreography Initiative Grant funded by the National Endowment for the Arts and Dance USA, and her dancers were selected to showcase at the Kennedy Center and have won awards as choreographers and performers.

Green has choreographed eight full-length ballets and numerous concert works in varied styles. She has received grants for her work in both Maryland and Alabama. She continues as guest choreographer and master teacher for schools and companies in Alabama and has received an invitation to teach choreography in Pietresanta, Italy.

You'll find other outstanding
dance resources at
www.HumanKinetics.com